# TO BE A JEWISH WOMAN

Lisa Aiken

This book is dedicated to my parents,
Janet and Sidney a"h Aiken,
and in memory of their parents,
Rose and Phillip Segall
and Anna and Louis Aiken—
Peace be upon them

# Contents

## PART II  RELATING TO PRAYER

# Foreword

Strangely enough I was introduced to Dr. Aiken by the student applications I received in the last few decades. One of the questions I asked in the form is: Which books have had a profound influence on you? Time and time again, potential students have listed Dr. Aiken's works as having a major impact on their lives.

Dr. Aiken uses her writing skills as well as her experience as a psychologist and her extensive research to weave together Halacha (Jewish law) and Hashkafa (Jewish values) in a way that resonates with the challenges of the modern woman in Judaism. Chapter after chapter, Dr. Aiken clearly elucidates Torah values and our Sages' wisdom, presenting them in a way that gives us a picture of what a balanced and healthy Jewish woman looks like.

In the present book, Dr. Aiken has rewritten her original monumental work to make sure it continues to be relevant to the 21st century woman who lives in a world which changes constantly and quickly. My hope is that Dr. Aiken's work will be valued by both laymen and Jewish educators as it gives real answers to many of the difficult questions that today's woman struggles with—without apologetics and confusion.

Rabbi Yitzchak Shurin
Rosh Midrasha
Midreshet Rachel v'Chaya

# Preface

This book developed from a series of lectures that I gave in North America in the late 1980s. At that time, almost all Torah-observant Jews who spoke about women's issues were rabbis or rebbetzins (rabbis' wives). As a rare lay person who discussed these issues from the vantage point of someone who was not raised as an observant Jew, I became a sought-out speaker for audiences who were not (yet) observant.

Although I did not grow up in an observant home, my background was not bereft of any Jewish education. My parents thought that there was great value in being Jewish, and that it was important for Jewish children to understand what it meant to be a Jew. To that end, they sent me to a Conservadox Jewish day school for six years where Rivka Shapiro, of blessed memory, was my fourth grade teacher. She inspired me to become observant.

By the time I entered college in the 1970s, the Women's Movement was in full swing. The more I studied, the more distressed I was by the way women were treated in various religions and by secular societies. As I struggled to find a niche for myself as a Jewish woman, I tried out many unorthodox Jewish practices, such as leading women's *minyans*, performing traditional men's rituals in group settings, and trying to encourage observant Jews to become more open to feminist ideas.

Eventually, I discovered that observant Judaism was a complete and satisfying system in its own right. However, it required years of investigation, introspection, and honesty to appreciate how fulfilling it could be intellectually, emotionally, and spiritually. My search involved looking for, and finding, role models who lived and practiced authentic Judaism. In the process, I learned that the fulfillment, status, prestige, and power that Jews often seek from the world at large are paralleled by or exceeded by what observant Jewish women enjoy. These women derive their self-esteem from having been created in the image of God and knowing that they have a vital role to fulfill in this world.

During my years of searching, there were few books written by knowledgeable, observant Jewish women about women's issues. What little there was often focused on how a modern Jewish woman could find a place for herself in traditional Judaism as a wife and mother. Most of the other books that addressed Jewish women's issues were written by women with axes to grind about what they assumed were anti-feminine biases in a male-dominated religion. Such authors rarely researched primary sources, and they tended to spurn the belief in a God-given Torah, its inviolability, and the integrity of traditional textual and legal interpretation. Their books tended to be emotional diatribes against traditional Judaism, with insistence on reform.

Over my two-decade-long quest for an authentic expression of Jewish femininity, I have been privileged to have met a number of remarkable women who excel in every aspect of Jewish womanhood. They combine scholarship, continual growth, true femininity, charity, and excellence in raising children; they are true "women of valor." They have inspired women like me to learn more about Judaism and to live it in an authentic way.

It is impossible to appreciate traditional Judaism by merely studying it intellectually. It must be experienced from within and appreciated as a total way of life in order for it to feel gratifying. It is difficult to experience the self-esteem that observant women have when one only reads about Judaism in books or views Judaism from a distance.

Over the years, this book has inspired tens of thousands of Jews to better appreciate the richness and wholesomeness of traditional Judaism and the role of women within its system. As a result, many have decided to experience the treasures of traditional Judaism first-hand. I hope that this revision of my original book will inspire new readers to also find value in Torah Judaism as well.

*Shwat, 5776*

# Acknowledgements

I am indebted to Rebbetzins Tzippora Heller, Feigy Twerski, and Leah Kohn and to Rabbi Yitzchok Kirzner z"tl for sharing with me some of the ideas that appear in this book. Rebbetzin Twerski, Rabbi Yehoshua Leiman, and Shelly Fish all gave generously of their time as outside readers. Rabbi Mordecai Tendler spent countless hours reviewing and improving the original manuscript, locating obscure sources, clarifying and correcting ideas.

I also thank Dr. Henry Azrikan and Rabbis Pinchas Stolper and Yitzchok Rosenberg who enabled me to give the talks that formed the basis for this book.

# Introduction

We live in a world of instant gratification, where hard work and waiting often seem anachronistic. Today's technology reinforces the mentality that if anything is worth having, we should get it immediately. We can now communicate in seconds that which once took weeks or months to convey, and travel easily in hours to places that were once inaccessible.

Most Anglos live in places where people believe that the goal of life is to find ease, comfort and fun. When life feels painful or distressing, people do things like drinking alcohol, taking a drug, or paying the right people to remove the discomfort instead of working hard to develop coping skills. Too often, people take the painless track in life at the expense of their personal development.

As well, secular societies believe in the importance of rights, including every person's right to pursue instant happiness however each wishes, as long as no one gets terribly hurt in the process.

These are two of many reasons why it is hard for Torah-observant Judaism to compete with the secular world on the secular world's terms. Traditional Judaism is based on the belief that some 3,300 years ago, God revealed His will to more than two million Jews at Mt. Sinai when He gave the Torah. No other religion has ever dared to claim that God revealed Himself to a large number of people all at once. Ironically, both Christians and Moslems believe that God revealed Himself to the Jewish people, they just claim that the One Above changed His mind and came up with a new plan 1,300 and 2,000 years later, respectively. All other religions except for Judaism say that God revealed Himself to one or a very select few founders, who then spread the new truth to others. Until the 1800s, when Reform Judaism was created, there was never a large group of Jews who dared claim that Revelation at Sinai never happened. Jews have an unbroken transmission of Torah going back to the time of

Moses.

When the Almighty revealed Himself to the Israelites, they promised that they and their descendants forever would faithfully observe the structured and restrictive life-style that God commanded them to keep. This divine system was designed to help people become holy and spiritualize the material world. It teaches how to channel our animalist and egotistical drives in ways that will serve our Creator's goals instead of being slaves to our instincts and to the whims of one's society. Torah teaches us how to elevate every part of our lives to a higher purpose.

Observant Judaism promises no instant gratification, no easy highs, no guaranteed emotional or financial outcomes. Nor does it teach that we are entitled to rights simply by virtue of being alive. We have rights because we were created in the image of God, who wants us to live by His code of morality. His laws dignify us and teach us how to treat others with dignity.

Authentic Judaism challenges us to direct our material, psychological, and sensual drives in ways that allow us to grow spiritually. This involves limiting or channeling our desires in ways that we would not ordinarily choose. Because we are supposed to grow spiritually throughout our lives, integrating Judaism into our lives at one point in time does not stay fulfilling forever. As we change, our Creator will send us circumstances that will challenge us to see Him in ever more mature and valid ways, and to have faith in Him through increasingly complex experiences.

We often have to work hard to observe Jewish laws because they require us to give up what comes naturally to us, and to be very disciplined in all areas of our lives. We also have to change our views and attitudes about many things that we formerly accepted as correct simply because that is what we grew up with in our culture. Therefore, in order for us to appreciate what Judaism offers, we can't gauge it by how it makes us feel in the short run. We can expect that being observant will often feel uncomfortable, especially as we make initial behavioral and attitudinal changes. As we are more comfortable with observance, the Almighty will be sure to challenge us continually to commit to ever higher levels of moral and spiritual refinement.

## WHAT IS TORAH-OBSERVANT JUDAISM?

Torah-observant Judaism is predicated on the belief that God created the world in order to give of His goodness to people. He wanted us to get maximal pleasure from the world, but without our feeling like freeloaders who only take what is provided for us. He created a spiritually imperfect world where our lives have meaning and a purpose—to make the world a better place. As we do our job, He gives us many opportunities to feel good that we are living up to our purpose. Ultimately, He will reward us in a spiritual afterlife for the efforts that we make in this world to live up to His plans for us.

God gave us a Torah (which means "teaching") so that we will know what His plan for living is. It would be pointless to put us in a world where we had to guess how we should best live. The Torah tells us how to act in order to fulfill the divine will for us. By following the Creator's plan, we can bring the world to fruition, while we earn our keep and feel good about ourselves in the process.

If we were naturally attuned to wanting to do exactly what God asks of us, He would not have needed to command us to do various things— we would automatically fulfill His desires. His telling us what to do or refrain from doing initially feels disturbing to us. Such observances create a tension until we get used to seeing the world with new eyes, and living in it with a new GPS. As we go through life, we can continually grow by overcoming challenges that will entail falls and failures, discomforts and frustrations. Yet in the end, we hopefully evolve as spiritually refined people who live fulfilled lives with a close relationship with our Creator. It takes time and ongoing work to have a real relationship with God that grows and matures as we do, just as happens in our human relationships.

Jews must be suspicious of any quick spiritual fixes. We must also be wary of trading in the difficult process of spiritual growth for the ease of comfort and familiarity. People typically resist change. We automatically seek comfort in what is familiar and emotionally reassuring. Unfortunately, if we value feeling comfortable above all else, we can undermine our ability to realize our tremendous spiritual potentials.

If we are willing to accept the challenges of growing, instead of letting discomforts thwart us, we can become amazing people who reach great spiritual heights along the journey.

Many Jews want to express their Judaism only in ways that feel good, are comfortable, or are politically correct. By equating religious with what feels good, we mold God in our image and reduce His will to what we subjectively define as the way things should be. For one person, watching a beautiful sunset is a religious experience. For another, being under the influence of mind-altering drugs is religious. For yet a third person, believing in liberal ideas is being "religious."

For Jews, a truly religious experience is connecting to the Almighty however He wants us to relate to Him. A truly spiritual experience for us can only be in the context of doing His will as He revealed it to us in the Torah.

Modern Jewish women are challenged to feel good about ourselves when we are surrounded by secular influences and values that are at odds with Jewish ones. The secular world primarily values us according to how visible we are, how much money or possessions we have, how much observable power we wield, and how many educational degrees we possess. None of these really gives us value.

This challenge was highlighted to me when I lived in Manhattan's Upper West Side. I frequently hosted Sabbath dinner guests whom I first met when they appeared at my door. After sitting down to eat, the guests typically asked me about my various endeavors, which included being the Chief Psychologist of a hospital, doing therapy in my private practice, writing books, and giving scholar-in-residence lectures at synagogues around North America. Once they found out about my professional life, we often had lively discussions about a wide range of topics.

One week, I was exhausted and had no energy to be a talkative hostess. In addition to my usual activities, I had spent many hours cooking for my fourteen Sabbath guests. When my dinner guests asked what kind of work I did, I replied that I was a housewife. Not surprisingly, no one spoke to me for the rest of the meal, except to ask me for a recipe for the dessert that I had made. At subsequent Sabbath meals I would tell my guests that I was a housewife whenever I was too tired to verbally entertain them. The results were uniformly the same. The guests invariably directed their attention to others at the table and assumed that I had nothing worthwhile to say.

Another example of how secular people often relate to others according to their profession or formal education: When venues publicize my upcoming lectures about topics of Jewish interest, they invariably note my professional accomplishments, even though they are largely irrelevant to my lectures. Were they to emphasize my personal endeavors to advance my spiritual growth, it is doubtful that more than a handful of people would come to hear me.

Many secular values are at odds with Jewish ones. Judaism values humility, which in secular terms is akin to being a "wimp." Judaism values modesty and privacy, which is often erroneously viewed as lacking self-esteem. Our religion values imbuing a family with a strong moral and spiritual compass. Judaism does not view all choices and cultural ideas as having equal value. It prefers that we nurture religious growth over material and socioeconomic success. It prizes self-control and introspection rather than ostentation and publicity.

It can be difficult to find Jewish values appealing when we are raised on American dreams. Some Jewish women feel that being encouraged to find great fulfillment in being a wife and mother is demeaning, and denigrates her identity and self-worth. It is ironic that they rarely think about how they have sacrificed their femininity by defining success according to the values and goals of a male-dominated professional and business world.

Once women assume that equality means that they must achieve what men have, and gauge their value using male benchmarks, authentic Jewish perspectives about the uniqueness and value of women seem anachronistic. Torah-observant Judaism does not believe that men and women should be equally visible in public, identically educated, nor should they have identical roles. Women who value having male "rights" often feel that traditional Judaism strips them of their validity, recognition, self-esteem, and power.

Some women believe that they can only get spiritual fulfillment from experiences that are in public view and publicly demonstrate that they are on par with men. When women observe a law here and a ritual there, rather than immersing themselves in a totally observant way of life, certain Jewish laws and practices seem to disenfranchise them. Women must realize that their roles and obligations were never meant to be observed in a piecemeal way, and they cannot be appreciated in bits and pieces. Doing so is akin to taking a small patch from a huge mosaic and questioning why those specific pieces were included.

Judaism is, and was always meant to be, a total way of life. It can only be truly appreciated when it is experienced within the totality of its system. Reacting emotionally to individual commandments or to women's exclusion from certain commandments is not a useful way of appraising the validity of observant Judaism. People should not identify "problematic" parts of Judaism in a vacuum, question their relevance for women, and dismiss them because they are not emotionally appealing.

We can assume that women who limit their religious involvement mostly to synagogue worship will feel like second-class Jews unless they participate in those services' rituals. On the other hand, traditional Judaism informs every aspect of life, only a small part of which pertains to the synagogue. As an all-encompassing system, Torah Judaism recognizes women's importance and has means built into it that develop their self-worth. One of the main ways that it does this is by emphasizing the essential and unique contributions that women make, and by highlighting their input which the world requires in order to achieve perfection.

People often expect observant Judaism to provide the emotional nurturing to make up for deprivations in other parts of their lives. Judaism can help people to feel self-worth and happiness, but not necessarily by providing what secular society values. It takes patience and study to discover how Judaism validates women's identities, feelings and self-worth. We must also be willing to abandon our need for Judaism to validate us on our terms; rather, we must find validation in Judaism's terms.

To be intellectually honest, we must pursue the truth, even when continuing along familiar paths feels more comfortable. We should ask if traditional Judaism can help us to develop our spiritual potentials and not concern ourselves with whether it feels easy.

No one would expect to appreciate the genius of people like Beethoven, Michelangelo, or Einstein without intensively studying their works. Similarly, it take years of studying, performing Jewish rituals, being part of an observant community, and asking questions to people who can give satisfying answers in order to appreciate how authentic Judaism provides women with a vehicle for true spiritual development and expression.

## THE JEWISH CONCEPT OF FREEDOM

How can a modern woman find a place for herself within the framework of observant Judaism? A main component of secular freedom is the ability to make personal, social, political, and financial choices. These choices are determined by one's emotions and intellect, social norms, and cultural factors. Frequently, this means that fulfilling one's personal desires becomes a primary goal in life.

Judaism views freedom differently. Our first experience as a nation with freedom was when God liberated the Israelites from the slavery of Egyptian overlords. As slaves, we were not masters of our bodies, possessions, or time.

When we were freed at the time of the Exodus, God brought us through four stages of redemption: our physically leaving the land of Egypt; our salvation from Egyptian oppression outside of the land of Egypt; our redemption from the physical deprivation and material poverty of slavery, which also allowed us to make free choices; and God's taking us as His special nation when He gave us, and we accepted, the Torah.[1]

Our Sages tell us that if God had only liberated us from the prison conditions of Egypt, allowing us to have physical well-being, that would have been valuable in its own right. Had we only been rescued from the mental and emotional persecution by the Egyptians, that would have been worthwhile by itself. By contrast, the third stage of redemption gave us the ability to make free choices, but this was not valuable in its own right.

Freedom of choice is only worthwhile when it is followed by the fourth stage—our willingness to act according to God's will, as it is expressed in the Torah. Exercising free will for its own sake may feel good, but it has no intrinsic value to the Jew.

Freedom from subjugation by mortals is only important if it is replaced by something greater. That "something greater" is gaining freedom in order to live a life that is God-centered. There is no point to being free only in order to serve ourselves, have greater worldly pleasures, and be slaves to sensual, material and egotistical drives. Such freedom is simply exchanging the limitations set by others for those dictated by our inner drives.

There is no true freedom from worldly masters unless we accept the Torah. It teaches us how to take our physical, intellectual, spiritual and emotional drives, and channel them in a way that we can uplift ourselves beyond the confines of our physical beings. We are only liberated when we exchange the servitude of mortal limitations to a connection with an infinite God.

All physical endeavors will be relegated to oblivion when we die or during the course of history. The only way that we can transcend the finitude of the physical and mortal world is by attaching ourselves to God, who is immortal. When we infuse our actions and possessions with holiness, we invest them with infinite meaning and immortality. We do that by bringing the One Above into our daily thoughts and actions.

A totally free world is chaotic and full of confusion and illusions. A world that is free of constraints does not necessarily pave the way for us to discover our true selves or find true meaning in life. By limiting some of our freedoms, Judaism gives us the benefits of structure, clarity, and goal direction.

For a Jew, freedom is not the ultimate goal in life. A person whose life is unbound by the structure and constraints of Torah can be analogized to a violin. When the strings of the violin are not yet bound, they are free. However, it is only after the strings are bound that they can make beautiful music. Similarly, it is only when we bind ourselves to Torah that our souls are free to sing their songs.

When we accept the structure and constraints of a Torah way of life, we have a framework within which we can make meaningful choices on a daily basis. Our lives can then have more focus and direction. Judaism also gives us a better understanding of why we encounter various challenges and adversity and how to respond when they happen.

## THE MODERN JEWISH WOMAN

Can a modern woman find satisfaction in observant Judaism? If her goal is to make unencumbered choices about her body, her material wants, and how she spends her time and energy, then she won't be happy with a Torah way of life. Observant Jews live with the belief that our bodies and possessions are gifts loaned to us by our Creator. We are supposed to use them according to the owner's manual that He gave us as a divine gift.

On the other hand, if a woman lives a life that is governed by Torah, she will be able to actualize herself. She can develop the physical, emotional, intellectual, and spiritual wherewithal to transcend the material and physical world. She can find ultimate meaning in every facet of life, along with an inner sense of satisfaction, dynamism, and self-esteem.

# 1

# *Traditional Biblical Interpretation*

We can only understand traditional Jewish perspectives about women by first understanding relevant biblical sources. Jewish belief and practice is largely based on the Five Books of Moses (also known as the *Chumash*, or the Written Law), and their elucidation through homiletical explanations (*Midrash*) and the Oral Law (known as the Talmud). The ideas in the Midrash and the Oral Law were conveyed by God to Moses when He explained the Torah (used to refer to both the *Chumash* as well as the entire body of Oral and Written Laws) to Moses on Mount Sinai some 3,300 years ago.

God gave the *Chumash* as an instruction manual to the Jewish people for how He wants us to live. It was written in Hebrew and cannot be understood without the Oral Law and the *Midrash*. This is because the Almighty wanted the *Chumash* to be a "shorthand" expression of His will that would require us to interact with a spiritual mentor in order to understand it. Our Torah teachers throughout history learned the Talmud and *Midrash* from their teachers, whose connections go back to Moses himself. In this way, the oral traditions were faithfully transmitted from one generation to the next from the time the Torah was given until the present.

The Torah was never intended to be a mere history or legal textbook but rather a guidebook for getting the most out of life. What better way to

1

insure that than by writing it in a manner that requires people to explain it who live what they have learned? Our Torah teachers not only give us factual information, they also model how to live a moral and spiritually-informed life-style.

The stories and laws of the *Chumash* require explanation by the Talmud and *Midrash*, as well as the very meanings of the Hebrew words and verses. Biblical Hebrew is a very precise language, with every letter and word in the *Chumash* deliberately chosen by God to convey certain meanings. No letter or word is superfluous or written by mistake. Therefore, when a given word appears in the text instead of its synonym, or when a phrase uses more words than are absolutely necessary to convey an idea, their significance requires explanation.

Since biblical Hebrew is so precise, appellations of people and things are neither accidental nor haphazard. When the *Chumash* gives something or someone a name, it is not simply supplying us with a conventional way of referring to it. A name denotes the essence of that thing or person. Not only do Hebrew words give us information about the person or object in question, but the very structures of every Hebrew letter do as well.

In part due to this precision, certain Hebrew terms have no English equivalents. This means that any translations will necessarily be inaccurate. For this reason, a proper understanding of biblical texts requires reading them in the original Hebrew with attention to their nuances.

Every word in the Torah is subject to analysis in order to understand its deeper meanings. However, we are not allowed to interpret these meanings willy-nilly. Rather, we have traditions and exegetical principles that were given along with the Torah that guide us in understanding it. We also have commentators who have elaborated on many of these verses according to our traditions. Their ideas will frequently appear in this book.

This book will present both facts and theories about men and women. Many of the theories are interpretations of Jewish laws or Torah verses that have been suggested to help us understand the meanings of some concepts or reasons for God's laws. Readers who find these theories disagreeable should feel free to reject them. When this happens, it should not deter them from appreciating the value of the factual presentations of Judaism, which are the major thrust of this book.

# 2

# *All about Eve–What Really Happened in the Garden of Eden*

**M**ost feminist literature views the biblical accounts of Creation as showing Judaism's sexist views about women. In order to lay to rest the distorted ideas that have appeared in such books, this chapter will examine the biblical accounts of the creation of First Man and First Woman, how they came to sin in the Garden of Eden, and what ramifications these events have for us. By presenting the original text with traditional commentaries, this chapter will illustrate how Judaism believes that women have great importance, while recognizing that both men and women can misdirect their potential greatness.

The traditional Jewish views of men and women are derived from the Creation narrative in the Book of Genesis.[2] Interpretations of this narrative were transmitted to us through oral traditions by our sages. The creation of Adam and Eve is detailed in the Torah as follows:

> God created the man in His image, in the image of God He created him, male and female He created them. And God blessed them.[3]

The Almighty created the world in order to give of His goodness to humanity. He wanted people to be partners with Him in creating and spiritually perfecting the world. There are various interpretations to the idea that man was created "in the image on God." One interpretation is that Adam was endowed with the Godly potential to give. One of the Creator's distinctive qualities is that He is a total giver. Being perfect, He gives, but never takes. Another divine quality is the ability to exercise free will, which was also imparted to Adam. If Adam would choose to act in ways that fulfilled God's will, he would thereby express the divine image within himself.

Adam was the progenitor of all humans who possessed a Godly soul. He had within him all of the qualities and souls of every person who would ever exist. As such, the Almighty's plan for Adam was also His plan for all people who would ever live.

When the Torah refers to Adam in the above verse as "them," instead of as "him," our sages explain this to mean that Adam was a singular being who was dual-faceted.[4] In other words, he was a man and a woman joined together like a Siamese twin.[5]

Apart from his physical duality, he also had a passive side and an active side. In this state, Adam was totally self-sufficient and wanted to be the source of everything that he needed. (In keeping with this interpretation that the first person was originally created with both male and female characteristics, we will refer to Adam in the neuter form.)

> The Lord God formed the person (from) the dust of the ground, and He breathed into its nose a soul of life, and the person was a living creature.[6]
>
> And the Lord God took the person, and He placed it in the Garden of Eden, in order to work it and to guard it. And the Lord God commanded the person saying, "From every tree in the garden you may surely eat. And from the tree of knowledge of good and evil you should not eat from it, for in the day you eat of it you shall surely die."[7]

At this point, the first person is referred to by the Hebrew term *adam*. This is why, after it was divided into its male and female parts the first man is called Adam in English. Adam derives from the Hebrew word *adamah*, which means earth.[8]

## THE NATURE OF THE FIRST PERSON

The earth and everything in it were created to fit into a plan that the One Above had for all of creation.[9] He wanted to give of His goodness to humans because His nature is to give. But He did not want people to feel like freeloaders by having them take without doing anything to earn what they received.

This is one reason why God gave the first person a commandment to observe. By doing the Creator's will, s/he would have earned the many gifts that the Almighty had already bestowed on him/her. S/he would also have a feeling of self-esteem resulting from having made an effort that fulfilled the Almighty's desire for him/her.

### The Name "Adam"

It has been suggested that Adam's body was created from the earth to teach us that just as earth is passive, the earth in each of us should encourage us to be passive in accepting the Almighty's plan for creation.

A second interpretation as to why Adam was created from earth is because s/he was supposed to strive to fit into the plan which the Creator had for earth overall. That plan required people to observe His commandments.

The Hebrew name *Adam* can also be broken down into two parts—the letter *alef* and the word *dom*. This can be translated to mean, "the one (*alef*) who is silent (*dom*)." This also alludes to the fact that Adam was created to accept God's plan for how the world was supposed to operate and for how people were supposed to act within it. In order to accept God's will people would need to be somewhat passive.[10] The name Adam alludes to the fact that the first person had a side that was passive, receptive, and silent. This facet was necessary so that human beings would subjugate their egos enough to accept the Master of the World's plan for how they should live.

God created Adam as a person whose every physical need was provided. In this state, s/he wanted not to depend on anyone else for what s/he needed. However, no one can realize his or her divine image if he or she supplies all of his or her daily needs themselves.[11]

## MAN'S SELF-SUFFICIENCY

Although Adam was physically self-sufficient, s/he had a deep emotional void. Since s/he was so unique, there was no one else in the world with whom s/he could have a relationship of equals. The Almighty made Adam this way so that s/he would feel an existential loneliness. In this state of physical self-sufficiency, with no one to whom s/he could give, the Torah says:

> The Lord God said, "It is not good, a person's being alone. I will make for the person a helper against itself."[12]

This verse has been interpreted to mean that as long as Adam was physically self-sufficient without having to work, the Almighty viewed him/her as "not good." This was because as long as Adam had everything provided, s/he was essentially a taker. In order to imitate God, which is our greatest calling, Adam would have to be a giver. In a state of self-sufficiency, s/he had no one to whom s/he could give. The One Above did not want people to take from the world without contributing to its upkeep.[13]

> And the Lord God had formed from the earth all of the animals of the field, and every fowl in the heavens. And He brought them to the person to see what s/he would call each (one). And whatever the person called each living being, that is its name. And the person gave names to every animal, and to every bird of the heavens, and to every animal of the field. And the person found no helper against itself.[14]

The Creator showed Adam all of the animals so that s/he would see that all of the animals primarily related to their mates only out of sexual need.[15] S/he had to see that no animal could be a physical, intellectual or spiritual partner.[16] At this point, s/he realized that the kinds of relationships that animals had with their mates were not what s/he was seeking. S/he wanted a relationship of intimacy and caring. At this point, Adam felt terribly lonely because s/he lacked a soul-mate. It was only after s/he realized what was missi ng, and expressed this need to the Almighty, that He made Adam sleep and created an appropriate partner for him.[17] This mate was designed to be an equal partner—someone to whom he could subsequently give and from whom he could receive.

At this point, the reader might be wondering how God could have made the first person in a way that seemed to be flawed. Adam seemingly needed to be improved upon later by being divided into male and female halves.

A possible explanation for this is that the Master of the World deliberately made Adam as He did so that s/he would later recognize his/her shortcomings. Before having a partner, s/he felt very lonely and couldn't relate to or give to another person. S/he was unable to imitate the Creator in this state.

The Almighty did not put people in the world so that He could abandon them and leave them to their own devices. He wanted people to yearn for a relationship with Him since connection with God—the Source of all goodness, wisdom and love—is the greatest pleasure possible. Since the human soul once experienced familiarity with its Source before it came into the physical world, it always yearns to reconnect with Him. However, we may not be aware of this yearning until we discover that we need things that only the Master of the World can provide. When Adam recognized that s/he was not truly self-sufficient, s/he was more motivated to seek out God as s/he strove to develop and grow.

God wanted the first person to realize that the presence of another human being should not distract one from the mission of serving Him; rather, a man and woman should combine forces in a total union of body and soul in the emulation of the Creator.

This helps explain why God created humanity as sexual beings, not merely as emotional, social, or spiritual ones. He wanted humans to combine together in a physical union as a poignant reminder that a total combination of physical and spiritual forces is necessary to truly serve the Creator.

## THE CREATION OF WOMAN

Once the Torah explains why it was necessary for woman to be created, it tells us how this was done:

> And the Lord God caused a deep sleep to fall on the person, and s/he slept. And God took one of the ribs and closed the flesh underneath.[18]

The Almighty made the woman by separating the first person into two people—one female and one male. This gave man the opportunity to contribute to the woman what she lacked and vice versa. In this way, God made man a "helper against him." This means that the woman was created to be of equal value to the man being helped.[19]

> And God built the rib which He had taken from the man into a woman. And He brought her to the man.[20]

The Torah says that God made the woman by "building" (*vayiven*) her from Adam's rib. Some interpret this unusual wording to mean that

He gave woman greater understanding and comprehension (*binah*) of emotions and human relationships than He gave man.[21] Both *binah* and *vayiven* come from the same root, meaning "within." Building is the act of taking something from within and expanding upon it. Comprehension is gaining an understanding of something from within.

The fact that woman was "built" from the inside of man predisposes her to understanding entire situations from the "inside." That is, women can generally see a forest without first having to see all of the trees.

> And the man said, "This time it is bone of my bones, and flesh of my flesh. This one shall be called woman (*ishah*) because she was taken from man (*ish*)." Therefore shall a man leave his father and his mother and cleave unto his wife, and they shall be one flesh.[22]

When a man and his wife join sexually with each other in a holy way, they can re-create the original state of the first person as a dual-faceted being. Moreover, as separate beings, the first man and woman could join in an act where each was a giver instead of a taker.

This story teaches us that God intended men and women to be different from each other. It follows that erasing these differences is not good. He made woman because there was something unique and essential about her without which the world wouldn't be complete. The *Midrash* underscores this by saying that a man who has no wife lives without good, without help, without joy, without blessing, without atonement, without peace, without life, and is incomplete.[23]

Since women and men each need to contribute something essential to the world, a world where men and women act the same or don't need each other reinstates the very same self-sufficiency and taking that was originally termed "not good."

Once the first woman was separated from her mate, they could form a complete human being only in partnership with each other.[24] Yet, as separate entities who can unite, men and women can create something that is greater than the sum of their parts, including the creation of a child.[25]

Women's presence in the world also allows men to mature. Until a man marries, he directs his love to his parents.[26] This means that when he leaves his role as a child, he must also leave behind the kind of relationship a child has with his parents.

Children are primarily takers, but this hopefully changes as they grow up. They must therefore leave behind their unique relationship with their parents to be in a mature relationship that will develop their emotional and spiritual potentials. The ultimate relationship is when a man joins with his wife as a giver, not as a taker. When that happens, a man and woman can form a unit that is truly divine.

## The Critical Importance of Women

Since the first person was put here to perfect the world by giving, the Creator needed to separate its male and female parts so that Adam would have an equal partner to whom he could give. Until woman was created as a separate entity, Adam was not good.

Woman was also necessary so that Adam would not think he was a demigod. After all, he was created qualitatively superior to all other creatures and was the sole creature who had no mate. Man realizes his limitations when he sees that a woman can provide him with the love, companionship, and nurturing that he can't give himself. This is not the case with God, who is perfect. The Almighty doesn't need anyone to take care of His emotional needs since He has none.

## FIRST WOMAN AS A HELPER

Woman was put here to be man's equal partner.[27] Women have their own intrinsic godliness. They use this in many ways, including helping men to recognize their strengths, overcome their limitations in spirituality and self-discipline, and be less egocentric, controlling, and honor-seeking.

The fact that the first woman was designed as a "helper against" man has various interpretations. One interpretation is that the Creator will cause the following to occur: A husband and wife will work harmoniously when they strive to reach spiritual goals. They will be in an antagonistic relationship when they try to accomplish goals that don't foster spiritual growth.[28] The fact that women were designed to help men overcome their spiritual limitations implies that women can sometimes see shortcomings in their mates and can help them overcome them. (Men sometimes also act as spiritual advisors to their wives.)

The One Above did not want man or any creatures to think that man was the ruler on earth the way that He is the ruler in Heaven.[29] This partly implies that a woman will want to help her mate conquer his arrogance. She will try to motivate him to channel his greatness toward divine service, rather than serving his ego and personal desires. By making the woman a "helper against him," the Master of the World enabled her to evaluate the correctness of her husband's actions and advise him spiritually. As long as he was alone, he couldn't objectively evaluate himself. His wife could, by being removed enough to criticize him in a loving and constructive way.

When the Torah says that women were created to be helpers, one might think that this is an unimportant role. Yet, just the opposite is true. This role is critically important and is one means by which women imitate the Almighty.

Helping relationships are often between two people who are of unequal status. For instance, a homemaker and her domestic workers, a king and his servants, and a boss and his workers are all in relationships where the helpers are of lesser status than the one being helped. When God helps us, when a mother helps her child, and when a doctor helps a patient, the helper has greater status than the one being helped.

In general, how much power a helper has in a relationship determines whether the helper has more or less status than the one being helped. When a woman helps her husband, her role often has greater status than his.

Non-Jewish English books refer to the first woman as "Eve," but the Torah refers to her by different names at different times. When she is created as a helper to Adam, she is referred to simply as *ha-ishah*—literally, "the woman" *par excellence*.

Biblical Hebrew has many words for "female." To name a few: *almah* (a female between the ages of 12 and 12½), *nikeivah* (female), *yaldah* (girl), *aishet ish* (a married woman), and so on. The term *ishah* denotes a woman who has achieved spiritual greatness. *Ha-ishah*, the term used to refer to the first female, tells us that the first woman was extraordinary. Such a woman was an appropriate partner for Adam, who was also created with enormous spiritual potentials. He is described in the *Tanach* (Jewish Bible) as being "just a little lower than the angels"[30] when he was created. Presumably, his wife was of equal spiritual stature.

The Torah's description of the first woman as a helper has little in common with current ideas about helping. It uses the term "helper" to refer to someone who acts like God. Both He and the first woman are referred to as helpers.[31]

The Almighty helps human beings by assisting us as we play a role in our own accomplishments. We are not supposed to passively receive His help. We are supposed to actively contribute to the upkeep of the world. The ultimate way that He acts as a helper, or asks us to do the same, is by assisting others in their growth. We can't expect others or the Almighty to do that work for us.

Since God created the first woman to be like Him, she was also termed a helper (*ezer*). This is interpreted to mean than an integral desire for a married woman is to want to help her husband. Part of his nature is that he will want to be helped.

This relationship becomes oppositional (*kenegdo*) when men don't want to be helped, or when women don't want to help. Normally, part of a woman's nature is to want to help her husband. When he rejects her desire to do so, or she refuses to do so, it can create tension and opposition.

### Theories about Men's and Women's Natures

Once God formed woman as an entity separate from man, the male part was termed *ish* (man) and the female part was termed *ishah* (woman). In Hebrew, both of these words share the two letters *alef* and *shin*. Together, these letters form the word *aish*, which means "fire." In addition, the man's name contains the letter *yud*, whereas the woman's name contains the letter *heh*.

Our bodies were created from earth, share many of the earth's properties, and return to it when we die. The fact that the words for man and woman contain the word "fire" teaches us that once the first person was separated into a female and a male, they and their descendants got the ability to be like fire. Fire is extremely active. It always rises, and it can alter things quickly. The soul is analogized to fire, insofar as it always strives to rise to its Source (i.e., God), and can change a person's physical nature.

Adam had a soul that enabled him to be as intense and powerful as fire in elevating his physical being, and the world, to great spiritual heights. However, as long as he was physically self-sufficient, he had no motivation to channel this "fire" to perfect the world. Such is what often happens to people who feel totally comfortable. The Almighty often sends us circumstances that force us out of our complacency and get us to do more with our lives.

Once Adam was separated into *ish* and *ishah*, he and his wife were able to perfect themselves by acting on the world and giving of themselves. This was because as discrete beings, fire was now a dominant force in each of them. They could use such passion (fire) to actively do God's will.

## DIFFERENCES BETWEEN MEN AND WOMEN

It has been suggested that men's natures are generally more predisposed than are women's to expressing their spirituality in terms of strength. Men's natures predispose them to ridding the world of negativity, such as fighting wars to remove evil people, uprooting injustice, and so on. Women, on the other hand, are more predisposed to nurturing and creating a home. Women help men develop their connections and rootedness with the world around them. Whereas men may want to rid the world of what is negative, women's main desire is to nurture and contribute that which is positive.

God is characterized by attributes of power, as well as nurturing. He wanted men and women to develop their respective attributes of power/ control and nurturing and to give to each other what the other lacks. In this way, a couple who are harmoniously married can bring the Holy Presence (*Shechinah*) into their lives. Too often, spouses have separate and conflicting desires instead of channeling their desires to form a Godly partnership.[32]

## HOW PARADISE WAS LOST

Once the Torah discusses how and why man and woman were created, it explains how they sinned and damaged their spiritual greatness.

When God created Adam, He commanded him not to eat of the fruit of the tree of knowledge of good and evil. It has been theorized that the Almighty wanted Adam to limit himself in certain ways for his own benefit. Had Adam followed his Creator's command, he would have showed that he had subjugated his need to know and be in control of everything to the divine will.

Instead, the Torah says that Adam allowed his personal desires to supersede God's will, thanks to the encouragement of a serpent.[33] The serpent in the Garden of Eden represented evil and took it upon himself to try to get the first couple to disobey their Creator. He succeeded in getting the woman to question why the Almighty wanted her not to eat the forbidden fruit. After all, if her Creator really loved her, why should He make anything that appeared good off-limits to her?

The woman should have refuted the serpent's questioning of God's command and accepted that the benefits of disobeying Him were mere illusions. In other words, she should have shown that our Heavenly Parent limits us for our own good.

God made the temptations and sensual pleasures of this world so that we will enjoy them in a state of spiritual elevation, or reject them when that is impossible. Each time that we reject illusory benefits, we show that following our Creator's will is more important than anything else. The long-term spiritual benefits of observing His will outweigh any short-term benefits that often take center stage in our minds.

Had they done what they should have, Adam and his wife would have reinforced God's role as the ultimate Master and Director of the Universe. The serpent was in the Garden only so that the first couple would reject its arguments, thereby showing that everything in the world—the illusions and temptations included—comes from the same divine source. He puts things in this world that feel good but are supposed to be off-limits to us so that He can reward us for rejecting them.

With this in mind, we can now understand the story of the serpent and woman in the Garden of Eden, using some interpretations by our sages of the events that took place.

## THE FIRST SIN

Shortly after the woman was formed, the serpent approached her in the Garden of Eden. He asked, "Didn't God tell you not to eat from every tree of the garden?"[34]

In fact, the Almighty had only told Adam that he couldn't eat the fruit of one tree. The serpent used this provocative remark as a pretext to get her to talk to him.[35]

From time immemorial, bad or misguided people use the serpent's approach and engage us in conversation that will lead to our getting harmed. At the risk of seeming impolite, we have to recognize that talking to them isn't good for us and walk away.

Unfortunately, the woman fell into the serpent's trap and responded to his ploy. She explained to him that she was allowed to eat from every tree in the Garden with the exception of the one in the middle. She told him that were she to eat from or touch that tree, she would die.

Although the woman said that touching the tree was forbidden, God had only forbidden eating its fruit, not touching it.

All too often, people exaggerate the Torah's restrictions and view them as far more extensive and unrealistic than they are. Some people go the other way. They add stringencies to the commandments, thinking that doing so makes the person more pious. They end up not serving God properly because they have made Judaism so burdensome and illogical. Either situation can lead to our going astray by convincing us that following divine commandments is too restrictive.

After the woman embellished the Almighty's directive, the serpent told her, "You shall not surely die."[36] It then pushed her into the tree, and she saw that nothing happened to her.[37] Through a variety of personal reasonings that are too complicated to detail here, the woman began to doubt God's word. She began to convince herself that sinning would have no negative consequences.

This is paradigmatic of how temptation operates. It tells us that if we do something wrong, nothing bad will happen to us.[38] When nothing observably bad follows immediately, we convince ourselves that what we did was really okay.

The serpent continued enticing the woman by telling her that God's real reason for prohibiting her from eating the forbidden fruit was because "on the day you eat of it, your eyes will be opened, and you will be like God, knowing good and evil."[39] It suggested to her that her Creator had eaten of that fruit, which then gave Him the ability to create the world. She could do the same if she would only eat it as well.[40]

The serpent used this argument to convince the woman that the One Above was unreasonably limiting her ability to become wise, powerful, creative, and independent of Him.[41] These are the same rationales that people have used throughout history to justify not living by God's rules.

The Torah says that the woman now viewed the forbidden fruit as "a desire for the eyes" (*taavah l'eynayim*).[42] She believed that the fruit would make her Godlike in knowing everything.[43] How our imagination and desire can convince us to believe what our logic knows is impossible!

The woman's thirst for knowledge, creativity, and physical pleasure, which no fruit could possibly provide, led to her initial downfall. Once she ate the fruit, it internalized within her an impulse to go against the divine will, as well as feelings of jealousy, lust, and a desire for honor.[44]

As well, she now realized that sinning would cause her to die, while Adam would remain alive and remarry. Her fear that Adam would love a second wife who would supplant her in his affection made her decide to bring him down as well. She also felt that misery loves company. She decided to give her husband the fruit thinking, "If we die, we will both die. If we live, we will both live."[45]

Adam listened to his wife because he wanted more to stay connected to her than to obey God's command not to eat the forbidden fruit.

(A different interpretation suggests that he sinned because he imagined that by eating the fruit we would internalize a desire to go against

God's will. Then, he would become even greater spiritually by eventually overcoming that negative inclination. He didn't feel that obeying God was much of a spiritual accomplishment as long as the drive not to listen to Him was not a part of him.[46])

According to either explanation, Adam substituted his judgment and made emotionally-based decisions instead of listening to the divine will.

Our sages suggest several fruits that could have been the forbidden fruit (none of which is an apple)[47] because of the quality that each symbolizes. For example, some say that the "fruit" was wheat. It symbolizes knowledge. Just as people are nourished by knowledge, wheat in ancient times was eaten for its nourishment. Wheat suggests that Adam and his wife mostly wanted to have knowledge by eating the fruit.[48]

Figs are also suggested. They are only eaten for their sweet taste. Thus, they symbolize that the man and woman sinned by misdirecting their desire for physical pleasure.[49]

## FIRST WOMAN AFTER HER SIN

The warning that God gave the first couple—that they would die if they ate the forbidden fruit—seems draconian. However, a deeper reading of the text reveals that the Creator was teaching the man and woman about the consequences that our actions have. They could then use their free will to decide which choices to make.

The reality of life is that the consequences of some of our actions are readily visible, while others are not. God told Adam something that he could not see—that he would live forever if his spiritual soul totally guided his physical self. On the other hand, were Adam to disengage his body from his soul by disobeying his Creator, he would subject his body to the normal limits of everything material. Indulging in the physical world as an end in itself would inevitably cause death. Death was not an external punishment for disobeying the One Above by eating the forbidden fruit. It was an inevitable consequence of disobeying, and detaching from, the Creator's immortality.

When the first woman ate the forbidden fruit, she let her physical desire rule her spiritual, immortal side, thereby making it inevitable that she would die. Had people used their physical desires only to serve God, they would have remained immortal.[50] Once they used their physical drives to achieve ends that were at odds with serving their immortal souls, they became subject to their bodies' limitations. This meant that they would die, as does everything that is physical.

The woman recognized that her husband's weak point was his desire to stay attached to her.[51] After she sinned, instead of helping Adam to spiritually perfect the world, she convinced him to share her fate. She told him, "I will die. You won't get a new mate, nor will you remain single (i.e., you will eventually die, too). Let us stay together and share a common fate."[52]

Adam very much wanted to stay attached to his wife, and could not imagine living forever without her. There were no other women for him to marry, and he could not fathom how the One Above would create another mate for him. Therefore, he agreed to eat the fruit that his wife offered him.

It should be noted that Christian ideas about sex and original sin have little in common with the Jewish view of what happened in the Garden of Eden. The Torah says that Adam and his wife had sexual relations before they sinned by eating the fruit.[53] Sex between them was considered desirable and good. It was only after eating the forbidden fruit that sex could be misused for lust and sinning, and only under such circumstances was it negative.

Before she sinned, the woman did not have nine months of pregnancy. Every time that she had sexual relations with Adam, she gave birth to a child afterward. Her sons Cain and Abel were both born this way, before the couple sinned.[54] It was only after sinning that childbirth and childrearing took their present form.

## GOD'S REACTION

After the man and women sinned and blamed their misbehavior on others, the Almighty punished them, as well as the serpent, with ten curses each. These ten curses were not expressions of divine vengeance. Although people sometimes punish out of revenge, this is not how our Heavenly Father operates. Whenever He punishes, His goal is to educate the recipient, as well as provide a means by which the person can rectify what he or she did wrong.

This was the case with the first woman as well. When the Torah says that she was "cursed," it really means that her physical existence was changed. These ten changes were intended to help her rectify what she had damaged by sinning. Given her state after sinning, these changes were the best way to help her live productively and repair the damage that she had caused.

Since the woman was originally created to be Adam's partner in perfecting the world and she didn't do this, she had to learn to correct this part of herself. Her punishments were considered curses because they felt bad and she could mischannel or neglect her spirituality if she did not use them properly.

All of her changes interfered with her attachment to her husband, since it was her inappropriate manipulation of this attachment that led her to encourage him to sin.

The first woman's changes affect all of her female descendants because it is up to them to fulfill the mission that she did not. All people are expected to spiritually perfect the world because the first couple failed to do this.

Just as women have taken over the first woman's role (and men Adam's), they are also subject to the limitations and changes that the first woman (and Adam) brought into the world. At the same time, Jewish women were given specific commandments whose observance enables them to bring back into the world the spirituality that was lost when the first woman sinned.

## WOMAN'S TEN CHANGES

When the Almighty changed the first woman, he altered her physical being, and pain became part of her reproductive life. He told her, "I will greatly increase your pain and your travail (of childbirth). In pain you shall bear children, and your passion shall be to your husband, and he shall dominate you."[55]

The details of the ten changes that the first woman (and her female descendants) experienced were:[56]

1. Women would have uncomfortable menstrual cycles. Prior to this time, the first woman had no such cycle.
2. The first time a virgin has intercourse, it will be painful.
3. Raising children would cause anguish, including the need to nurse, dress, clean, and carry them around until they are independent. Mothers would worry that their children would not grow up the way they would like.
4. A woman would be overly shy about her body.
5. A woman would feel discomfort during nine months of pregnancy. Initially, a child emerged after every act of intercourse.
6. Childbirth would be painful.
7. A woman would be forbidden to marry two husbands.

8. A woman would have a sense of sexual longing when her husband was away on a trip.

9. A woman would desire her husband sexually, but would find it emotionally difficult to openly request intercourse with her. Women would sexually desire their husband even though it would result in the pain of pregnancy and birth.[57]

10. A woman would desire to stay home.

These changes were not meant to be prescriptions about what women *should* seek; rather they were meant to be starting points in helping women correct and perfect their abilities to nurture properly. Thus, although a menstrual cycle, pregnancy, childbirth, and the like may be uncomfortable, it doesn't mean that women shouldn't try to alleviate their pain. Their awareness of these discomforts and pains should heighten their sensitivity to using their life-creating abilities as vehicles for spiritual growth for themselves and others.

In general, the changes heighten women's awareness of their potentials for nurturing and how they can be misused. For example, Adam's wife used her persuasive abilities to get him to sin. Since she was the embodiment of all female souls that would ever exist, her female descendants have the role of correcting the errors that she made. The changes would help ensure that women will fix the first woman's failing, and thereby bring the world back to Paradise. To this end, the changes encourage women to use their persuasive powers and creative abilities to nurture, rather than for the opposite.

*Explanation of the Changes*

Our sages elaborated what these ten changes mean. For example, they interpret the idea that parents will find it painful to raise children beyond the obvious physical and emotional challenges of child-rearing. They suggest that the pain of child-rearing painful will occur when children mimic their parents' shortcomings. Whatever contradictions and character flaws parents express, children pick up and imitate with impunity. One of the most painful things for parents is seeing their children repeating the bad deeds that the parents model, rather than doing what the parents say. This pushes parents to overcome their own negative traits in order to better their children's lives, as well as their own.

Another facet of women feeling anxious about raising children is that children do not turn out exactly as the mothers hope they will.

Mothers must recognize that they can't control their children's lives. This forces them to recognize the centrality of the Almighty's protection and intervention, without which children can't possibly thrive.

When the first woman ate the forbidden fruit, she wanted to make a life for herself and Adam without including God. The anxiety over raising children can encourage women to draw closer to their Heavenly Father, pray for His help, and include Him in everything they do.

### Women's Sexuality

Our sages interpret the woman's subservience to the man as meaning that women will sexually desire their husbands but will not be able to ask them for sexual intimacy.[58] This idea reflects the divine awareness, based on the first woman's actions, that a sexually outgoing personality would not be conducive for women's spiritual growth. Therefore, He changed the first woman so that she would be more perfect than she was initially. A woman must make her husband desire her sexually by properly directing her nurturing. Metaphysically, this corrects the first woman's mistake.

## MAN'S TEN CHANGES

Just as the first woman was changed in ten ways, so was the first man, as follows:[59]

1. He was originally taller than normal as a physical reflection of his spiritual greatness. His physical stature was reduced to reflect his spiritual decline.
2. He would feel weak whenever he would ejaculate.
3. The earth would grow thorns and brambles.
4. Man would have anguish in earning a livelihood.
5. Man was to eat the grass of the field. (When Adam heard that he and his cattle would eat the same food, he pleaded with his Creator, and the next curse was substituted for this one.)
6. Man would eat bread by the sweat of his brow.
7. Adam lost the initial extraordinary beauty that the Almighty had given him. (His original beauty was a physical manifestation of his spiritual beauty.)
8. The serpent lost his hands and feet and could no longer serve his intended role as a servant for man.
9. Adam was banished from the Garden of Eden and lost his status

as lord and master of the world.

10. Man, being dust, would return to dust. He was destined to die and be buried.

All of Adam's changes interfered with his ability to stay constantly with his wife. For example, having to work hard to make a living, as opposed to having God provide food without any human effort, takes a man away from his wife. It also physically tires him so that he can't have marital relations as frequently as she might want.[60]

When men use their changes properly, they can see God in all aspects of their lives. For instance, when they work for a living, they are supposed to recognize that their financial success depends on the Almighty granting it.

## "CHAVA"

Only after God changed the first woman did Adam name her *Chava* (Eve), derived from her being "the mother of all life."[61] Until this point, she was always referred to as "the woman at the pinnacle of her spirituality"—*ha-ishah*.

Before she brought death into the world, the woman's primary focus and nature were not to be a mother. It was to be a partner with Adam in spiritually perfecting the world. After her sin, mothering became a primary role for Chava. Instead of bringing death, she could nurture people to gain physical and spiritual life.[62] After sinning, her new role was to be a "mother of all living" because humanity's mission shifted to future generations.[63]

Chava also means "conversation." [64] Chava was created to be a helper to her husband. She misdirected her helping energies, and misused her speech, by enticing Adam to sin. Our sages tell us that women were granted greater linguistic potentials than men in order to create connections with people that can nurture and constructively connect us. Thus, it made sense that after her sin, the woman was renamed to reflect the new potentials by which she could rectify the world.

## IMPLICATIONS FOR FUTURE DESCENDANTS

The first man and woman had within them the souls of every person who would ever exist. Just as they each had a unique soul, so do each of their descendants. The nature of every soul is that it wants to do God's will.

The Creator gave us bodies as physical vehicles to perform His commandments. When we do a commandment (*mitzvah*), which represents the divine will, it draws His Holy Presence into us. Thus, we actively connect ourselves to Him each time we do a *mitzvah*. We bring spiritual values and Godliness into the world through our actions. Our thoughts alone can't do this because we need to concretize reality in the tangible world in which we live. We do this through our actions, not only via thoughts or feelings.

Once Adam and Eve sinned, each of their descendants inherited the task of rectifying the world. As generations went by and this was not done, the mission of fixing the damage caused by their sin was eventually transferred to the Jewish people when they accepted the Torah. It is the task of every Jew to draw down the divine presence into the material world as much as possible. Men behaving appropriately corrects Adam's mistake, and women exercising their free will properly does the same for Eve's errors. The Torah teaches us how to do both.

Since the nature of Adam's and Eve's sins were slightly different, men and women have somewhat different roles in bringing holiness into the world. These roles and behaviors will be explored throughout this book.

## LILLITH

Feminist literature often speaks about Lillith as Eve's more enlightened and admirable counterpart. Lillith is a woman who is described in a text known as the Book of Jubilees. She again appears in a text known as the Alphabet of Ben Sira. The latter story says that God created Adam and Lillith at the same time, from the dust of the earth. Lillith did not want to be Adam's helper, so she escaped from him. God then made Adam a second wife, Eve, who was content to be his helper.

The Lillith legend does not reflect mainstream Jewish thinking. The sources where it primarily appears reflect sectarian ideas and are almost never used to derive Jewish law. The sects who wrote these texts died out long ago, and their ideas were rejected by mainstream Judaism.

The story about Lillith is not found in the Talmud and is therefore not a theme that was prominently discussed by the rabbis. Thus, the sources of stories about Lillith are not considered to derive from traditional Jewish sources.

There is only one scriptural reference to Lillith, and it appears in Isaiah.[65] It refers to Lillith as being among the beasts of prey and spirits that will lay waste to the land on the day of vengeance, when evil will be destroyed.

On the other hand, the Talmud makes several references to a *lillith*.[66] A *lillith* is a female demon of the night who has a human face, long hair, and wings. (There are also many varieties of male and animalistic demons.) These Talmudic references do not describe the origins of the Lillith concept.

### God's Attributes–Kabbalistic Concepts

To understand what Lillith represents, we need to know a bit of Jewish mysticism (*Kabbala*). Since we are mortal and we have limited perceptions, we cannot understand God's essence. We can only understand and know Him based on how He acts in our world. His actions are categorized as seven divine emanations (*sefirot*): loving kindness, strength, beauty (truth), triumph, glory, foundation, and royalty. Just as God has these attributes, He has given people comparable (but obviously smaller) potentials which we can develop. For example, we can emulate the divine attribute of loving kindness by visiting the sick, giving charity to the poor, dowering poor brides, comforting mourners, and so forth. We can imitate His attribute of strength by exercising moral fortitude, not sinning, and by conquering our negative inclinations. We display the attribute of beauty when we integrate the physical and the spiritual worlds.

We can display foundation (*yesod*) by channeling our sexual energies constructively. This can include creating and sustaining a good marriage and by being loyal.

Just as God created positive energies that He lets flow into the world, He also created negative ones that parallel the positive attributes. *Lillith* is the negative sexual energy that parallels the positive sexual energy. For example, when someone is disloyal to a friend or unfaithful in marriage, he or she misdirects sexual energy and *lillith* results.

This is a metaphysical explanation of what *lillith* is. Here is a more philosophical explanation:

The stories that describe Lillith's creation can mean that God gave people the freedom to properly channel, or to misdirect, their sexual potentials. When Lillith refused to channel her sexuality in a way that could elevate the union of a man and a woman, she frustrated the divine plan for the world.

In this context, *lillith* is a characterization of a woman's refusal to channel her sexual energies in a way that complements those of her husband. When people misdirect those energies, a couple cannot metaphysically unify their divine attributes. Philosophically, *lillith* is the expression of a person's ego fighting God's master plan for the world.

This is why Lillith should not be viewed as a role model for Jewish women. Her rebellion was not merely her personal striving to be independent from a man or her quest to have an egalitarian relationship with him. Rather, she rejected the divine plan for how she needed to bring the world to its intended goal. She rebelled against the Creator who put her here for a critical purpose.

## The Masculine and Feminine Aspects of God

The union of a husband and wife is supposed to reflect the divine image. What does this mean?

In Kabbalistic literature, God is described as having a female and a male aspect. God's male aspect is called *Kudshah Barich Hu* (The Holy One, Blessed is He). It is an anthropomorphism that describes how we experience God as being close to us (immanent), even though His essence transcends anything that we can comprehend.

The female aspect of God is known as the *Shechinah* (Divine Presence). This is what enables us to experience God as a nurturing presence. Our life task is to make ourselves receptive to that. This entails acting in ways that let Him give to us, and allowing ourselves to experience and receive from Him. In this description, the male force of providence is the aspect of God that acts upon the world. The female force is that which allows us to be receptive to His power and giving.

We should not learn from the Lillith story that women must be helpless and powerless. Rather, a woman must be receptive to God's immanence and her husband's giving in order to create a Divine Image within her marriage. When she is prepared to emulate the Divine Presence, she can complement her husband's purpose. Only when they each appropriate their respective roles can they fulfill their purpose in having been created.

# 3

# Men and Women in Traditional Judaism

With the Creation story as background, we may better understand traditional Jewish perspectives about men and women.

## DIFFERENCES

God decided that it was necessary to create the first man and woman with different characteristics. The Torah underscores the importance of maintaining these differences through laws that apply differentially to men and women. For example, it is prohibited for a man to wear women's clothing or to engage in feminine behavior (e.g., wearing makeup), and vice versa. In general, Judaism emphasizes maintaining and appreciating the differences that God created, rather than diminishing them.

There are many other instances where the Torah makes it clear that things should be valued in their own right, and not be improved upon by erasing differences between species or kinds. It forbids us to graft plant species together, to mix dairy with meat, to use fabric with wool interwoven with linen, and so forth. If the Creator had wanted us to eradicate certain differences, He would not have deliberately created and blessed them.[67]

Judaism has a premise that every physical creation has a spiritual message to teach or a spiritual contribution to make. It cannot convey that message or do its job when its distinctiveness is undermined and obliterated.

The Creator deliberately designed the human body in a way that it teaches us how to use it. Rather than our evolving as biological accidents, our anatomy reflects our spiritual challenges and gifts. It has been suggested that we have two ears and two eyes but only one mouth so that we can observe and listen more than we speak. Our minds are higher than our hearts (which is not the case with many animals) so that our intellect (based in our heads) will rule our feelings (based in our hearts), rather than the other way around.

The Creator formed the first woman from Adam's rib. This was so that her influence on him, and her main mode of development, would be internal.[68] The fact that women's reproductive organs and genitalia are internal also suggests that the optimal way for women to function is to develop internally. Men's corresponding externality suggests that they should develop themselves more in their external functioning in the world.

With this knowledge, we can examine the Jewish roles for women and contrast them with modern secular values.

## POWER

Critics often claim that traditional Judaism renders women powerless. They assume that many of the ways that observant Jewish women function differently from men reflects women's lesser importance. This is exemplified by how many societies reward the ways that men, but not women, exercise power.

If we define power as the ability to cause change in the way people live, or in the way a society functions, we can see that Americans value external power. For example, they prize political power, positions of authority and status, military power, and money. If you had to name the three most powerful people in the world, you might think of the President of the United States, and another two political leaders (probably all men), or possibly someone who creates far-reaching economic policies. These people represent externalized power.

On the other hand, there are many other ways of changing a society without using visible or external means. For instance, one such type of power is the ability to influence people to change in ways that are neither visible nor readily apparent, such as happens by educating or personally influencing others. These effects may be hard to see immediately, but over time, they can be every bit as potent as the previously mentioned forms of power. Psychotherapy is a very powerful agent for change but it doesn't work by using external or visible forms of power.

If you think about the person who influenced you the most, chances are that it was a parent, teacher or mentor who affected your character, values, goals and behavior. Presumably, these effects were caused much more subtly than those caused by political, financial or physical power. The lack of recognition for parents or teachers who mold us does not negate their inherent power or value.

Chances are excellent that one of the people who affected you the most—for better or for worse—is your mother. Mothers' power comes through their personal influence on their children, but is not readily visible.

Judaism believes that men and women should have equal rights to influence others, but that women generally should not exercise this from positions of authority. The positions of legal and external authority are usually reserved for men, while the power that is exercised in the home and in personal domains is mostly wielded by women.

## ROLE DIVISIONS

Secular society frequently encourages its members to compete for its prized goals—externalized power, money and material things, and a visible place in society. This contrasts strongly with the Torah's perspective, which promotes a society that has multiple goals, each of which is attainable by, and designated for, different groups.

The Jewish people originally consisted of tribes and families that were assigned various roles, each of which made a unique contribution to the Jewish nation. For example, the priests served God in the Tabernacle (and later the Temples) and taught Torah. The men from the tribe of Levi (Levites) sang praises to the Almighty and played musical instruments in the Temples. Other tribes were shepherds and raised livestock. Some were farmers who grew specific crops such as olives and grapes. Still others were merchants and sailors. From the time that David was crowned king, all legitimate Jewish kings descended only from him, and so on.

In some cases, no group was allowed to usurp the mandated role of another group. For instance, a man could only be a priest or Levite if he had inherited that lineage from his father. It was strictly forbidden for outsiders to usurp their roles. While these roles had many privileges, they also had some downsides. One such "drawback" was that priests and Levites did not inherit any land when the land of Israel was divided among the tribes. They had to depend on various tithes and gifts given by the rest of the Jewish people for their support.

The importance of the above pluralism is also reflected by the fact that the Torah gives the Jewish nation 613 *mitzvot* to observe. No individual can personally observe all of them. It requires the collective input of all Jews to fulfill them.

Similarly, the multiple spiritual goals of Judaism allow women to be valued in their own right, not only when they are like men. This contrasts with modern innovations by some Jewish groups to make women "equal" to men by minimizing the importance of their femininity and unique female roles and encouraging them to be male. For example, "egalitarian *minyans*" (groups of at least 10 male Jews who form a quorum for public prayer) have women performing male rituals in public, as opposed to having men pray in more introspective ways where they put aside their egos and are less on display.

Each sex has its unique gifts and contributions to make to the Jewish people. A variety of roles allows each group of Jews to make its special contributions to the beautiful symphony that brings the Divine Presence into our world.

## IMITATING GOD

In a secular society, many people measure their importance and the value of their lives by what they acquire and how much money they have, rather than by what they give. One of a Jew's obligations is to imitate God. We were not commanded to become millionaires, professionals, or politicians. We are required to imitate the One Above. One of the main ways that we do this is by imitating His deeds of loving kindness. It is only by giving that we can fully exercise the divine image inside us.

Our Creator wants us to be interdependent and unified through giving. In addition, when we give, we expand our influence over others and our importance to them.

On the other hand, we reinforce our finitude when we take. This is because the more we take, the more we tie ourselves to the limited, finite world. Furthermore, our taking from the material world deprives someone else of what we have. Therefore, taking from the finite world creates separations and barriers between people. When we take, we necessarily exclude others. Giving includes them in our consciousness and we view them as extensions of ourselves.

Women were created with the potential of imitating God in the two greatest ways possible—by creating new life and by giving of ourselves as we help and nurture others. Much of this is done in the context of one's family. Judaism values women's ability to bear, nurture, and raise children. It also stresses how important it is for them to be stabilizing forces in their husbands' and children's development. Yet, despite Judaism's preference that women marry and have children, men are the ones who are commanded to marry and to procreate, not women.[69] The preferred role for women is to marry and have children, but the Torah does not require this of them. Should a woman not be able to, or not wish to develop her potentials as a mother, she still has many other ways of imitating her Creator and actualizing herself as a Jewess.

While the most desirable goal in secular society is for women to imitate men, the highest goal for both Jewish men and women is to imitate God. As long as a woman's goal is ultimately to serve her Creator and not herself, and develop a close relationship with Him, many paths are open to her. This is not the case for a man, for whom Judaism proposes that he can never fully actualize himself without being married and having children.

Judaism doesn't view women as "baby machines" if they choose to take on the challenges and joys of bearing and raising children. Rather, such women have the enviable opportunity to create and raise a Jewish body and soul to eventually help perfect the world in accordance with the divine will.

## SELF-ACTUALIZATION

Judaism is a totally encompassing way of life. It tells men and women how to actualize their respective strengths by taking what the Almighty has given them and using it to refine their character traits and make the world a better place. The Torah teaches that there are different paths by which men and women can best do this.

Before we can develop what is positive in us, we must first avoid doing things that harm or destroy ourselves or others.[70] Then we must do what helps us actualize ourselves and develop the world. We accomplish both of these goals by observing the Torah's commandments that delineate what we should and should not do.

Although the Torah has lots of stories and history, it teaches us how best to live by giving us 613 *mitzvot*. Of these, 365 are called negative commandments, because they tell us what not to do. There are also 248 positive commandments, which tell us what we should do. Since Judaism is a system that helps us to use every aspect of our lives to come close to God, we can analogize the *mitzvot* to the ways we create and sustain intimate human relationships.

Two people who want a close and loving relationship must do things for each other that bring them together and express their love for one another. They must also be respectful and not do things to their partner that destroys their trust, love and devotion.

There is a high divorce rate in many Western countries because many people know how to "fall in love," but they don't know how to stay in love. Marriage counselors know that people need to use tools that build a loving relationship, communicate and problem-solve effectively. There are also rules that need to be observed to prevent spouses from taking each other for granted, making sure not to say or do hurtful things, and make sure they will act respectfully no matter how stressed, angry, or upset they are.

The Torah's rules and *mitzvot* do the same for us. The more we bring all facets of ourselves into a relationship with God, the closer the connection will be. To that end, we have many *mitzvot*. Some involve our intellect, others involve our emotions, still others require us to behave in certain ways. Some *mitzvot* pertain only to men, some only to women.

Yet, the Torah refrains from legislating every conceivable behavior. No code of law could possibly do that. It leaves innumerable behaviors up to us. We deduce how to act in these situations based on how we should act in legislated ones, in light of who we are and our personal circumstances. This area of life is known as "the realm of permitted things," or *divrei reshut*.

Since the negative *mitzvot* were designed to keep us from harming ourselves or others, they apply equally to men and women (with only three exceptions).[71] This is because both sexes have similar ways of not harming ourselves. The positive *mitzvot* are specific tools that we use to actualize ourselves. These apply differentially to men and women, as we shall see.

## INTELLECTUAL DIFFERENCES

Just as women were created physically different from men, some Jewish sages say that they were also created with a primary way of thinking that is different from that of men. Women and men are presumed to have equal *chochmah*—innate knowledge. However, some other types of intellectual faculties are presumed to be different for most men than for most women.

As was mentioned earlier, some sages suggest that God created women with a primary intellect of *binah*72 and that they have more of it than do men.[73] *Binah* is typically mistranslated as "intuition." Intuition is simply an innate ability. It doesn't require any intellectual processing. *Binah* actually refers to our ability to enter another person's emotions and thoughts and draw conclusions from what we learn. It might be better translated as "inner reasoning."

Men are considered innately to have more *daat*—the ability to tie themselves into facts, figures, and details. *Daat* is a form of analytical reasoning. This does not mean that all men or all women think only in one realm to the exclusion of the other. It does mean that most women tend to have more *binah* than do most men, whereas most men tend to have more *daat* than do most women. There are nonetheless some women who have better analytical reasoning than do some men (she might be your attorney, your accountant, or your math teacher), and some men have better inner reasoning abilities than do some women (he might be your therapist or your favorite actor).

All three of these intellectual faculties are important. The Torah says that God created the world by using the faculties of *chochmah*, *binah*, and *daat*. Some 2,000 years later, He told the Israelites who left Egypt to build Him a Tabernacle (*mishkan*) in the desert. This *mishkan* represented a world in miniature where the Divine Presence could dwell among the Jewish people. He told the Jews to create this mini-world using the faculties of *chochmah*, *binah* and *daat*.[74]

If the Creator did not believe that the faculties of *binah* and *daat* were equally important and equally valid, He could have made the world using only one of them. The fact that He created the world with both, and required the Jews to use both in building the *mishkan*, reflects the fact that the world cannot flourish without both of these. Rather than argue about which is better, men and women are supposed to value their respective intellectual capabilities and use them in their daily functioning.

There are many ways by which women can develop and enjoy their *binah*. One way is by studying Torah in a manner that nurtures their intellectual strengths. They can analyze and understand the emotional and religious characteristics of our forebears, the significance of various symbols, rituals and objects discussed in the Torah, and the spiritual and emotional motivations that fueled the behavior of biblical characters. Focusing on the whys and overall pictures of biblical narratives, as opposed to the academic study of legal details, are some ways by which women nourish their *binah.*

*Binah* can also be nurtured by relating to people and doing deeds of loving kindness. Being wives and mothers, hosting guests who need a place to stay and eat in a caring environment (especially on Jewish holidays and the Sabbath), visiting the sick, and working for charitable causes allow women to use and develop their *binah.*

Jewish women have traditionally sought employment in the helping professions and in teaching. Although secular societies have their own reasons to relegate women to "helping" kinds of jobs that often pay far less than male-dominated positions, many women choose professions that require them to be sensitive to the nuances of human relationships. Their job satisfaction in such fields is often due to their use of *binah* and nurturing abilities.

Apart from the physical and intellectual differences between men and women, there are also emotional differences that should be valued. Since we process emotions through our minds, men and women perceive experiences differently, depending upon whether or not they use their filters of *binah* or *daat.* This is partly why women are often more emotionally aware than men are, and men tend to be more tied to the details of their experiences than are women.

Psychotherapists often find that women tend to be more emotional than men, and men tend to intellectualize and obsess about details more than women. It is quite interesting that male patients often focus on the details of their experiences, while women tend to more readily describe how they felt about events that happened. When these characteristics are exaggerated, a person may be respectively obsessive-compulsive or histrionic (overly emotional). Obsessive-compulsive males outnumber females, and females are more often histrionic than are males.

Keeping the above differences in mind, we can now look at how, and perhaps why, Jewish laws apply differently to each sex.

## WOMEN'S EXEMPTION FROM CERTAIN *MITZVOT*

Although it might seem otherwise to those who only view Torah-observant men and women in the synagogue, women are only exempt from keeping seven of the 613 Torah *mitzvot* that apply to all men.[75] (There are other commandments that apply only to certain individuals or groups, such as priests, first-born males, Levites, kings, married men, and so on.) These seven are referred to as "time-bound positive *mitzvot.* These require men to say the *Shema* prayer, wear *tefillin* (boxes containing parchment written with Torah selections, bound on the arm and head with attached leather straps), wear a four-cornered fringed garment (*tzitzit*), count the *Omer* (the days between the Passover and Shavuot holidays), hear the blowing of the *shofar* (ram's horn) on the Jewish New Year (*Rosh Hashana*), sit in the *succah* (a temporary hut) during the holiday of *Succot* (Tabernacles), and take a *lulav* (a palm branch bound with willow and myrtle) and *etrog* (citron) on the first day of *Succot*. With the exception of wearing *tefillin*, women may perform, and often do, five of the other six commandments (the exception is wearing fringed garments).

One suggested reason as to why men are supposed to observe more time-bound *mitzvot* than women is that men need more external reminders of the preciousness of time, and they need extra assistance to use it for spiritual ends. Certain external reminders of time are superfluous for women who generally have internal, biological clocks that run according to days, months, and years.[76]

Judaism teaches that time is potentially holy. Each moment has its unique meaning and purpose. For example, noon today has a different spiritual purpose than noon yesterday or tomorrow. The time-bound *mitzvot* keep Jews constantly aware of the potential sanctity of time, which we can bring to fruition by our actions. Since men are not tied to biological clocks, one way they can become more aware of time is by surrounding themselves with *mitzvot* that are time-dependent at the start of every day. Soon after waking, males put on a four-cornered, fringed undershirt. Later, they put *tefillin* on their head and arm, many wear a fringed prayer shawl, and they say the morning prayers.

Every month, they remind themselves of the importance of time by sanctifying the new moon, and set spiritual goals for the month ahead. Every year has an annual cycle of holidays, whose rituals help to create a reservoir of spiritual strength to draw on during the intervals between one holiday and the next.

Since men tend to be more attuned to, and distracted by, the details of the external world, they need external reminders of time's sanctity. Most women have internal biological rhythms that serve the same purpose. Jews do not consider a woman's menstrual cycle to be either a nuisance or an accident of nature. God created it to be used for spiritual purposes.

One way that Jewish women use their monthly cycle is by observing the laws of family holiness (see Chapter 11). This observance heightens women's awareness of the sanctity of time. Both men and women can imitate God and spiritualize life by doing *mitzvot* in general, as well as their respective externally- and internally-directed ones. This insures that both achieve the same goal—to make life holy—by using different means that are best suited to each sex.

## DIFFERENT PRIORITIES

It has also been suggested that women are absolved from doing certain time-bound commandments because these would create tension for them. Although Judaism does not require women to marry nor to have children, God knows that most women will choose to do so. To make this choice easier, the Torah absolves women from seven *mitzvot* that might otherwise make it difficult to properly take care of her family. A married woman's primary responsibility, especially if she has children, is to her family and to her home. It would unfairly stress women if they had even more time-dependent responsibilities hanging over their heads.[77] What women are required to do is so critically important in guaranteeing the eternity of the Jewish people, it overrides the requirement to do certain time-bound *mitzvot*.

Since men are supposed to refine themselves vis-à-vis the external world, Judaism presumes that their interactions with it are likely to draw them away from spiritual goals. Therefore, the time-bound commandments that govern men's time and behavior every morning remind them that their first priority upon awakening is to dedicate their hearts and minds to serving God for the rest of the day. This helps men to not eat, work, or focus on the material world or their desires as ends in themselves.

Since women are supposed to actualize themselves by developing their inner selves, they don't have to be legislated away from the external distractions that men have in order to focus on their relationship with their Creator. It is presumed that women are more innately focused on their internal states than are men and that women are more aware of, and responsive to, others' needs. Thus, they can fulfill their spiritual potential with somewhat fewer rituals. Torah assumes that women will use their *binah* to appropriately give of themselves to others, rather than being distracted by the goings-on in the world at large.

As an example, when a mother wakes up every morning, she must immediately make judgments about what each person needs. If she has young children, the first order of the day may be to feed the baby, make breakfast for the other children, get them dressed and off to school. If she were obligated to attend the synagogue for morning prayers and sequester herself away from the distractions of her children, it would be counterproductive to raising a family. Her first priority is to imitate her

Creator by tending to the children that He gave into her care. Once they are taken care of, if she can reasonably make time for it, she can then focus her attention on directly relating to God. Were she required to observe time-bound *mitzvot*, they would often interfere with her ability to tend to the family's needs, which are primary.[78]

Although women are not obligated to attend prayer services in the synagogue, if they don't have conflicting responsibilities to their families, they are encouraged to make time to develop their connection with the Almighty. This can include attending prayer services if they so desire, or praying at home. They should also try to give of their time, caring and resources to others. For instance, if they have an income, they can give 10 percent of it to charity. They can volunteer professional or free time to those in need. They are also encouraged to learn Torah in a way that is relevant to their spiritual growth.

## WOMEN'S TORAH STUDY

Many people erroneously believe that Jewish women are not required to study Torah. There are actually two aspects to Torah study—learning it in order to properly live as a Jew, or learning for its own sake. Women are required to learn Torah in order to properly fulfill their religious obligations. They are exempt from the *mitzvah* that men have to study Torah for its own sake.

One explanation for this exemption is that women do not need to study Torah for its own sake in order to develop themselves intellectually or spiritually. Since women have more *binah*, it is unusual for them to feel spiritually nurtured by analyzing details in the manner that Talmud is characteristically studied. Men's Torah study tends to delve into the details of events and the commandments. It includes questions like, "How much is required?" and "What are the various opinions about how one must do a specific ritual act?" Women tend to be more interested in the deeper meanings of the commandments and scriptural stories and the ethical lessons that can be gleaned from them.

Women's *binah* is as much an intellectual gift to be appreciated as is *daat* for men. Women have historically nurtured their *binah* via family and personal interactions, such as teaching their daughters about Judaism, rather than their learning it through books. Nowadays, it is rare for women to get this type of spiritual nourishment from their homes. That is why most Torah sages recommend that women nurture themselves by studying Torah, but in a different way than do men.

If a woman wishes to learn Talmud in order to understand Torah better, God will reward her for so doing. However, it is inappropriate for anyone to insist that women be spiritually and intellectually nurtured through the same means that men find most gratifying. Men are required to study Talmud and to learn it for the sake of learning. Due to men's *daat*, such learning can nurture them spiritually and intellectually.

One Jewish commentator says that men have psychological traits and aggressive tendencies that are incompatible with the peace and tranquility of the World-to-Come. Their constitutions can only be rectified through constant immersion in Torah study. Since women are innately predisposed to serenity, they do not require constant Torah study in order to merit the World-to-Come.[79]

Women are required to learn all of the things that Judaism obligates them to do or not do. They must familiarize themselves with the Five Books of Moses, the Prophets, and the Holy Writings.[80] In addition, they must study Jewish ethical works that teach how to properly relate to God and to other Jews.[81]

Women (or men) who excuse themselves from learning Torah tend to starve themselves spiritually. Without formal Torah study, it is impossible for most Jews to develop religiously. Moreover, when women neglect their spiritual growth they tend to feel disenfranchised as Jews. Whereas men may identify as Jews through daily or weekly rituals such as praying in a synagogue, getting an *aliyah* to the Torah, or putting on a *tallit* and *tefillin*, women who do not nurture themselves through Torah study will find it very hard to feel good as Jews.

## NURTURING THROUGH PRAYER

Some people mistakenly think that because women aren't commanded to pray in the same way that men do that women don't have to pray. Women should try to pray the *Shemoneh Esrai* (main daily prayer)[82] every morning and afternoon. If they can also say the *Shema* prayer, affirming our belief in one God every morning, and the preliminary morning blessings, it is advisable to do so. When they cannot do this, they should at least pray in some manner every day.

Women who neglect praying deprive themselves spiritually, since our current lifestyles don't enable us to sufficiently nurture our relationship to our Creator without prayer. Therefore, a fundamental aspect of women's self-actualization is through Torah study and prayer.

## WOMEN'S *MITZVOT*

Feminist literature has stressed how traditional Judaism excludes women from doing many rituals that men do. These articles tend to omit the specific rituals that women are required to observe. Each sex has specific commandments that are necessary to fulfill the divine goal of sanctifying daily life and the material world.

A lifelong task for Jewish men and women is to elevate the spheres of time, place/objects, and person to a higher spiritual level. To this end, women are exempt from seven time-bound commandments, but they also have three special commandments that are custom-made for them. These are the *mitzvot* of creating sexual holiness (*taharat hamishpacha*), separating a piece of dough when they bake bread (taking *challah*), and lighting Sabbath and holiday candles.[83] It has been suggested that each of these *mitzvot* gives women a unique opportunity to contribute spiritually to the world.

Women have the ability and mission to bring Godliness into their bodies and homes. They partly do this by observing their special *mitzvot* and by using their *binah* to discern how to make holy the details of what is otherwise mundane, daily life.

### Contribution of Laws of Sexual Holiness

When the first couple was created, the only function of their reproductive organs was to serve their Creator. After they sinned, they could misdirect their sex drive to fulfill their personal lusts and desires. A husband and wife can return to the sexual primeval state of the first couple in Paradise when they observe the Jewish laws of sexual holiness. These practices allow a husband and wife to create sexual intimacy with the Almighty as their partner. Moreover, they can even become as Godlike as is possible during this process and create a new life. By sanctifying this intensely physical act, Jews can bring to fruition part of the divine plan for the universe, while fulfilling women's needs for pleasurable and meaningful sex.

In general, women search for a spiritual dimension in a physical relationship with men more than men do with women. Women sometimes experience this yearning by feeling exploited or cheated when a physical relationship lacks emotional bonding or spiritual connection. Men may also feel this pain, but they tend to do so less intensely and less often than women do. Women in a strictly physical relationship can feel their souls' pain when they search for true intimacy and it is lacking.

The laws of sexual holiness stress the importance of almost every day in a woman's monthly cycle, and cause her to relate to her husband accordingly. These laws prohibit intimacy with her husband from the time she gets her period until a week after it ends, when she must first immerse in a ritual bath. Doing this provides a framework for making sex holy. Under these conditions, a couple can enjoy having sanctified sexual relations until her next period begins, when this cycle begins again.

Having couples refrain from physical intimacy when it cannot be sanctified gives women the space to replenish themselves emotionally and work on their marriages. This may involve improving nonphysical forms of communicating that might otherwise be neglected. Many women feel spiritually replenished during this monthly process of physical and emotional intensity followed by standing back, appreciating, and developing other aspects of their marriage.

The holiness of marriage and sexual intimacy are considered to be central aspects of Jewish life. The fact that women are given ultimate control over these is one proof of the egalitarianism of men and women in religious matters. The laws of family holiness help insure that women will not be treated as sex objects and that sex will be elevated to its maximal spiritual heights.

It has been suggested that men use external reminders such as *tallit* and *tefillin* to get the added spiritual awareness that women get from the rituals associated with their bodies. The sanctity that women create in this part of life infuses both their marriages as well as their children with this influence.

### Spiritual Contribution of Taking Challah

The second special women's *mitzvah* is that of taking *challah*. When any Jew bakes a substantial amount of bread,[84] he or she is supposed to take a small portion and give it to Jewish priests (*cohanim*).[85] The priests may eat it if they are in a state of ritual purity (which no one is today). It is customary for many Jewish women to bake bread every Friday in honor of the Sabbath.[86] This is one of the special *mitzvot* that women do that bring blessing into their homes.[87] Women baking bread parallels what the Jewish priests did in the Temple every Friday. They baked special loaves of bread, then set them out on a golden table. A week later, the priests ate the bread which miraculously was still warm, satiating and delicious.

Judaism requires us to spiritualize the material world by our actions, not simply by having holy or noble thoughts. We constantly strive to make our mundane behaviors holy, and sometimes use religious rituals to help us do that.

Eating, for example, is part and parcel of many Jewish celebrations. Jews are required to eat special meals every Sabbath and Jewish holiday, when a baby boy has a ritual circumcision, when a child becomes a Jewish adult, and at Jewish weddings. One reason for this is that eating in Judaism is much more than a way of quelling our hunger. We spiritualize eating and use it as a primary way that we connect to the One who gives us life.

It is no accident that the first and primary way that a baby connects to her mother is via nursing. God gave us parents to serve as models of how He relates to us. When a baby is hungry or thirsty, she cries and the mother provides exactly what the baby needs. At the beginning of nursing, the baby is usually thirsty, so that milk is watery. After the baby's initial thirst is quenched, she needs nutrients, so the middle part of the mother's milk is chock full of protein, vitamins, minerals and antibodies. When the baby is almost sated, the last part of the milk is cream, to help the baby gain weight and grow. Through this process of the baby calling to the mother, and the mother lovingly providing in exquisite detail exactly what the baby needs moment by moment, the baby internalizes a message that she is loved and taken care of. When we are older, we can relive this message of being loved by God every time we eat or drink. We do this by focusing on Who is giving to us, and eating mindfully. We prepare to eat by noticing the colors, tastes, textures and delicious aromas of the foods in front of us. When we then eat with a consciousness of connecting to the Giver of such pleasure, we feel loved by and grateful to our Creator throughout our day.

Jews can further sanctify the way we eat by viewing our homes as Temples that house the Divine Presence, our table as its altar, and our food as an offering that brings us close to the One who sustains us with everything we need. Taking *challah* reminds us that we are not supposed to eat only out of hunger, out of a desire to feel physical pleasure, or mindlessly due to instinct or boredom. Rather than live to eat, we eat to live. We respect our bodies by not abusing them in the manner by which we eat, nor by the foods that we ingest.

The pleasure that we get from eating helps us to appreciate the bounty that the Almighty continually gives us. Like a loving mother who nurses her baby whenever he shows that he is hungry, our Heavenly Parent keeps providing us with whatever we need to survive as He holds us in a loving embrace.

God made women in a way that the more the baby nurses, the more milk the mother's body provides. This models for us how the Almighty relates to us. The more we feel dependent on Him and ask Him for what we need, the more He provides for us.

Taking *challah* is a way that we show the members of our household that all material blessing comes from our Creator and should be used to serve God. *Challah* was once a gift that fed the priests who taught Torah to the Jewish people and served in the Temple. Since they didn't own or farm land, it was the responsibility of other Jews to take care of their material needs so that the priests would be free to tend to the people's spiritual needs.

Since the Second Temple was destroyed in the year 70 CE, and the means to remove ritual impurity was lost, all Jews are presumed to be in a state of ritual impurity. Therefore, Jewish priests may not currently eat *challah* that is separated from the dough. Instead, a small amount of dough is baked until it is burnt, then it is discarded.

*Challah* also reminds us that material success is a divine gift. We recognize that it comes from Him, appreciate it, then share our food and material blessing with others.

### Theories about Lighting Sabbath Candles

It has been suggested that women's third special *mitzvah*, that of lighting the Sabbath (*Shabbat*) candles, sanctifies the realm of time. The Jewish day starts and ends at sunset.[88] Jewish women light candles 18 minutes before sunset each Friday to make sure that their homes will have light on the Sabbath. Lighting in advance of the actual start of the Sabbath adds time from the secular weekday to the holy Sabbath.[89]

Lighting Sabbath candles brings full circle the woman's means of bringing spiritual blessing into the world. By observing the laws of family holiness, the woman spiritualizes her (and her husband's) body. When she takes *challah*, she sanctifies material blessing. By lighting Sabbath candles, she sanctifies what would otherwise be mundane time and adds to the spiritual illumination in the world.

When the first woman sinned, she extinguished the tremendous spiritual light that was present in the Garden of Eden. Her descendants, Jewish women, bring back some of this light by kindling Sabbath candles.

When a woman does this, she culminates a process that began long before she ushers in the Sabbath. The first three days of the week, we draw our spiritual nourishment from the sanctity of the prior Sabbath. The next three days, we start filling a new reservoir of holiness—that of the Sabbath to come. We do this by preparing our spiritual treasuries that will be opened on the Sabbath. We invite guests to our Sabbath meals, clean our homes, buy and prepare special foods, all in honor of the Sabbath.

As the day approaches, we feel excited about once again greeting the Sabbath queen. On Friday, we bathe and get dressed in beautiful clothes to honor the Sabbath. We set the table with our finest tableware as the special Sabbath foods fill the house with their aromas. Lighting candles before the Jewish Sabbath actually begins expresses women's excitement about spiritualizing time. By inaugurating the Sabbath before it technically begins, we show that every moment of human existence can be infused with infinite meaning. Every moment that we are alive we can elevate ourselves and the physical world.

Every Friday, Jewish women spiritually illuminate their homes. We usher in an atmosphere of peace, serenity and spiritual blessing as we demonstrate that every moment of time is significant and has its unique spiritual potential to unlock. There is a difference between that which is holy and that which is secular. We can make choices that fill the world with spiritual light rather than choices that obscure the Divine Presence in our lives. There is a difference in holiness between the Jewish Sabbath and the six weekdays. Jewish women show that it in within human capability to take what is neutral or secular and invest it with so much sanctity that one moment of time can be qualitatively different from the next. When women elevate time by connecting it to God, we open storehouses of spiritual blessing that overflow into our homes and the souls of our families.

Through these three *mitzvot*, Jewish women take our internal awareness of time and sensitivity to others, and use them to sanctify the realms of person, place and time. In these ways, we fulfill God's plan in having created the world.

# 4

# Women as Redeemers of the Jewish People

We just saw that there are three types of holiness in the world—that of person, place and time. When we eat kosher[90] food in a sanctified way, appreciating that God is providing for us, we contribute to the holiness of our bodies. When we enter a synagogue where people are praying, it feels holier than walking on a public street. When we observe the Sabbath or a Jewish holiday, we feel the sanctity of time.

Each type of holiness has subdivisions, and their nuances impact our lives. For example, we metaphysically experience the holiness of the Sabbath in three different ways as the day unfolds. On Friday night, we experience the Sabbath as a queen. We receive her passively when we light the Sabbath candles. We experience the romance of being sequestered with our beloved Sabbath on Friday nights after longing for her the prior week.

Saturday morning impacts us as a king affects the world by commanding us to study Torah. We connect to the intellectual side of Torah by studying it during the Sabbath day.

As the Sabbath ebbs away, we experience the holiness of time both actively and passively. We eat a small meal before the Sabbath ends, but are not focused on learning Torah. This final aspect of the Sabbath portends the coming of the Messiah.[91] The messianic era will usher in a time when God's presence in the world will be so obvious and tangible that the world will be in a state of endless Sabbath. At that time, the divine purpose in creating the world will have been fulfilled.

## FULFILLING THE PURPOSE OF CREATION

What was the Almighty's purpose in creating the world, and what is needed in order for it to be fulfilled? As has been suggested, God created the world in order to give man a place to obey His commandments and thereby allow the Creator to bestow treasures of goodness on us. When the first woman got Adam to sin, man and woman lost their opportunity to bring the world to its state of spiritual perfection.

The first couple was created in order to recognize and ratify that there was a singular Creator whose will gave man's life ultimate meaning and whose commandments needed to be done. It became the task of each successive generation to fulfill humanity's original mission. When people put aside their personal desires and drives and do God's will, they prepare the world for the messianic era.

How does this concept apply to men versus women? How does the Torah's view of their different natures fit in with the original plan of Creation?

Adam lived in the Garden of Eden, surrounded by its splendor and lushness. He was created and brought to life directly by the Master of the Universe, and was charged with a singular mission. That mission was to enjoy all of the creations that God had placed in the world—the sights, scents, sounds, sensations, and tastes. Adam had only to restrict himself from taking fruit from one tree and the rest of Paradise was his to enjoy forever, as a reward for restraining himself in this one area.

Within hours of her creation, the First Woman (Chava) ate from the fruit of the tree of knowledge of good and evil, and gave some to her husband. The rest is history. The subsequent years have been spent trying to make up for the imperfection brought into the world by Adam's sin. In order for us to rectify this sin, we have to understand what it was, and what Adam's and Chava's roles with respect to each other were intended to be.

## CHAVA'S DUAL ROLES

Adam was supposed to have reigned over the world as God's appointed surrogate while remembering that the Almighty was the ultimate decision-maker and ruler. By acquiescing to the rule of his Creator, Adam would have sanctified all earthly existence, and shown that its purpose was to serve the Creator. Adam was charged with one *mitzvah*, and his task was to serve God directly by keeping it.

Chava, on the other hand, was created in a different manner than was Adam. She was created as a "a helper against him." God did not directly command her not to eat of the fruit that He told Adam not to eat.[92] Rather, she had two specific roles. Her first role was to be a helper (*ezer kenegdo*) to Adam. She was supposed to be an equal partner to her husband. One of her responsibilities was to help Adam recognize his limitations. The idea that Chava was a "helper against him" is interpreted to mean that she was to help him when he needed and deserved her help, then oppose him when he didn't deserve her help. That implied that Chava, due to her objectivity, could be more aware of God's will than Adam was.

Chava's name also comes from the word *chai*, meaning life. As her name implies, her second role after she sinned was to be the mother of all people. By encouraging Adam to sin, Chava was more of an opponent to Adam than his helper. Since she embodied the souls of every woman who would ever be born, it became the primary task of all of her female descendants to fix her mistake by enabling themselves and their husbands to reach their spiritual goals.

The sages usually translate the term *ezer kenegdo* to mean that a woman is an *ezer* when she helps her husband, and a *kenegdo* when she opposes him. However, *ezer kenegdo* can be translated in a different way. A woman can be her husband's *ezer* when she opposes him, and sometimes help him the most by so doing.[93] Throughout history, Jewish women have opposed their husbands' misguided actions at critical times. This has enabled the men, and at times the entire Jewish people, to attain spiritual heights that they could not have attained otherwise.

Women historically have redeemed the Jewish people by opposing their husbands, and by being mothers. The former role rectifies Chava's sin and both roles exercise women's creativity, love and power.

## Apparent Duality in the World

God made a world that seems to have two distinct forces—that of good and that of evil. Throughout history, nations have worshipped these forces as independent entities. Zoroastrianism, an ancient Persian religion, is a prime example of this. They prayed to one god who did good, and to another god who controlled evil. They prayed to a god of light and to a god of darkness.

By contrast, Jews believe that the world will be redeemed when the entire world realizes that "the Lord is one and His Name is one."[94] The world will be one step closer to redemption when people recognize that there is only one force in the world. Things only happen because there is one Prime Mover who allows or causes all things to occur.

Besides our difficulty believing that our Creator is behind everything that happens, we are also challenged to believe that whatever He does is for our good. When events happen that we perceive are bad—illness, death, pain, suffering, and the like—He intends them ultimately to be good.[95]

In the Torah, biblical man struggles with himself. Part of him wants what he wants, and part of him wants what the Almighty wants for him. The biblical woman, on the other hand, quietly and tenaciously influences and supports men to do what God wants. It is the biblical woman who more readily sees the apparent forces of good and evil coming from the same Godly source. Men have to develop themselves through trials and tribulations with the outside world to get to the same place. In the Torah, Jewish women seem to intuitively understand this message. Several illustrations follow.

## SARAH

Biblical women act behind the scenes, quietly and subtly, to bring the world to the state that the Almighty wants it to be. One of the first biblical accounts of this occurs in the story involving Abraham and his wife Sarah. Here is what the Torah says:

> And Sarah saw the son of Hagar the Egyptian, whom she had born to Abraham, making fun (of Isaac, Sarah's son). And (Sarah) said to Abraham, "Chase out this maidservant and her son, because the son of this maidservant will not inherit with my son, with Isaac."
>
> And the thing seemed very bad to Abraham because it concerned his son (Ishmael). And God said to Abraham, "Let this matter not seem bad in your eyes—regarding this young man and your maidservant. Everything that Sarah tells you, listen to her, because your children will be called through Isaac."[96]

Abraham is called the first Jew because he came to an intellectual understanding that the world had one Creator. He determined that it was proper to worship only that deity and none of His creations. However, Abraham lacked something in his persona that prevented him from fathering the twelve tribes that would start the Jewish nation. It was Sarah who provided a corrective to Abraham's character flaw.

Abraham's overwhelming loving and kind nature prevented him from seeing how corrupt his son Ishmael was. The childless Sarah had initially encouraged Abraham to father a child with her servant, Hagar, with the expectation that Sarah would raise this surrogate child. However, once she was pregnant, Hagar had no intentions of giving this child to her mistress to raise, and she started disparaging Sarah.

Ishmael had been an only child for 13 years when his half-brother Isaac was born. Ishmael realized the threat that this new baby posed to him and he had no intentions of relinquishing his role as Abraham's heir to this intruder.

As time went by, Sarah saw clearly that Ishmael was not interested in following in his father's moral footsteps, and that her stepson was doing things to threaten her baby's life. She told her husband that he had to send Ishmael away or he would be a terrible influence on Isaac's spirituality, and perhaps even jeopardize his brother's life. She understood that Isaac alone was suited to be Abraham's heir, and that drastic measures had to be taken to insure that occurred. Her prophetic insight was greater than Abraham's and she was aware of things that he was not.[97]

Since Sarah's time, Jewish women have repeatedly demonstrated a spiritual fortitude that has enabled the Jewish people to survive and flourish both physically and spiritually. It is the hallmark of the Jewish woman that she can sense God's will and act in consonance with it. She thereby ensures the continuity of the Jewish people as a holy nation and the carrying out of the divine plan for the world.

## REBEKAH

There are many biblical women who devoted their lives to ensuring Jewish survival. After Sarah died, her son Isaac married his cousin Rebekah. They had twin sons named Jacob and Esau. As the boys grew up, Esau became immoral while Jacob strove to sanctify life and serve God.

Before Isaac died, he wanted to bless Esau because he believed that Esau would develop his tremendous spiritual potential. Rebekah understood that this son would never bring his potential to fruition. For this reason, she concocted a plan that resulted in Jacob getting his father's spiritual blessing instead of Esau.[98]

Rebekah came from a home where her brother and father were shady business people. She saw through Esau's pretenses to be holy and his attempts to dupe Isaac into thinking that he aspired to be a spiritually wholesome man. Rebekah understood that he was not a fitting recipient for the spiritual blessing that Isaac wished to bestow on his heir.

Isaac was not as capable as Rebekah of recognizing the danger that Esau's evil represented. She not only rejected Esau's façade, but knew that the only way for Jacob to get what was due him was by using guile. Esau used guile for evil purposes, but it could also be used for good. Rebekah used deception to show her husband and Jacob the power that evil can have when it is harnessed in the service of good. In this case, she convinced Jacob to use subterfuge to get his father's spiritual blessing. Rebekah understood that in such a case, good can achieve even greater spiritual heights when negativity is used with it for a higher purpose.

Jacob couldn't make use of the spiritual energy that is created by overcoming evil until his mother forced him to use apparent falsehood to serve spiritual ends.

## LEAH AND RACHEL

Jacob was the progenitor of the Jewish nation. As such, he was destined to father twelve sons. In one of the most romantic biblical love stories, Jacob fell in love with his cousin Rachel and worked for her father for seven years in order to marry her.[99]

When the wedding day came, Rachel's father Lavan brought his disguised elder daughter Leah to the wedding canopy wearing a wedding gown with a thick veil. Jacob married Leah, thinking that she was his beloved Rachel.

Both Jacob and Rachel had anticipated that Lavan would try to trick him into marrying Leah, so Jacob gave Rachel secret signs by which she could signal him that she was indeed the bride. Yet, when Rachel saw that her sister was being brought to the wedding canopy, she thought, "My poor sister will be totally humiliated when she is discovered to be an imposter." At that point, Rachel ignored her personal pain and gave Leah the secret signs that Jacob had prearranged with her.[100] He did not discover that he had married Leah until the next morning after the marriage had been consummated. A week later, he also married Rachel.

After they were married, Leah had four sons in short order but Rachel was barren. Both women were prophetesses and knew that Jacob was destined to have twelve sons. They recognized Jacob's holiness and each wanted to maximally build the Jewish nation with him. At this point, each wife thought that she might be unable to have more children, and each wanted to contribute to the eternal spiritual mission ahead. So Rachel gave Jacob her maidservant Bilhah as a surrogate mother. After Bilhah gave birth to a son, Leah also decided to give Jacob her maidservant (Zilpah) in order to raise more children with him.

While the biblical text[101] suggests that the sisters were rivaling for Jacob's affection and attention, our sages teach that much more was going on. Each sister wanted to be the mother of as many children as possible who would become spiritual pillars of the world. Each wanted to raise as many children as she could to have an intense relationship with God.[102] They poured out heartfelt prayers asking the Almighty to grant them children who would carry on the mission of the Jewish nation and fulfill the divine plan for the world. Each in her own way paved the path for future Jewish women to pray with intensity, sincerity and selfless motivations.

## Rachel's Uniqueness

Rachel, who was raised in an idolatrous culture by a dishonest father, had an unquenchable desire to bear and raise children who would serve God. Despite her deepest yearnings, she only gave birth to two sons, dying in childbirth as the second one was born.

The Talmud says that the First Temple was destroyed and the Jews were exiled from the land of Israel because Jacob's descendants later committed idolatry, bloodshed and sexual immorality.[103] Instead of destroying the Jewish people for forsaking their mission to be a spiritual light to the nations of the world, the Almighty allowed His House of Worship to be destroyed and the Jews were exiled from the land of Israel. As they went into the Diaspora, they passed by Mother Rachel's grave.

There is no point to Jews living in the land of Israel if they behave like other nations. They were given the Holy Land as an inheritance because the Creator wanted them to live there as a holy people who follow the Torah. When they do this, they model to the world how to have a relationship with a God who expects us to be moral and to create a just society that others admire and respect.

When the Jews were exiled during the First Temple period, the *Midrash* says that the prophet Jeremiah summoned the souls of Abraham, Isaac, Jacob and Moses. He asked each to plead with the Almighty to bring the Jews back from exile.[104] Abraham tried to invoke the merit of having been willing to sacrifice his son Isaac at God's request. God had promised Abraham that Isaac would be his heir, yet He asked Abraham to offer his 37-year-old son to Him on Mt. Moriah.[105] In the end, God told Abraham that He didn't want Abraham to actually sacrifice his son.[106] He only wanted Abraham to follow His commands instead of using his own logic and emotions to decide what is right and wrong.

Abraham's seeking out and believing in one God, and his willingness to do whatever was asked of him led to the Almighty making an eternal covenant with him and his descendants. That promise included giving the Jewish people the Torah and the land of Israel. Nevertheless, our first forefather did not convince the Master of the Universe to change His decree and bring his descendants back to their land.

Isaac then pleaded with the Almighty to redeem the Jews in his merit. After all, he had been willing to be sacrificed by his father at God's command. Isaac's supplication was also rejected.

Jacob then beseeched the Almighty to redeem his descendants. He invoked the merit of overcoming many challenges to build the Jewish nation while keeping his faith in God. He asked God to have mercy on his descendants, yet his words had no effect.

Finally, Moses pleaded in the merit of having shepherded the Jewish people for forty years. Even after they repeatedly challenged him and God, he stayed their advocate and didn't desert them. Yet, his words did not get the Almighty to relent.

Then, Rachel's soul presented itself before her Creator and pleaded her case. "Master of the Universe," she cried, "my beloved husband worked for me for seven years. When those years finally ended, the day of our marriage that we yearned for so much came at last. To my horror, I watched as my father led my disguised sister Leah to the wedding canopy instead of me! I could not bear to see her be humiliated, so I gave her the secret signs that Jacob and I had prearranged so that he would marry her. I even stayed under their nuptial bed all night speaking to him when necessary so that he would not know until morning that he had married Leah and not me.

"I am only flesh and blood, dust and ashes, whose nature it is to be jealous, yet I was not jealous of my sister when I gave her the secret signs that allowed her to marry my husband. I overcame my personal feelings of jealousy and had pity on her for the shame that she would suffer if she was exposed as an impostor.

"Don't you think, God, who are so merciful, that You can overcome Your 'jealousy' that the Jews are unfaithful to You when they worship other gods? Can't You allow Your mercy and pity to overcome Your 'jealousy' and allow Your children to come out of exile and return home?"

Her plaintive cries moved the Almighty to pity, so to speak, and He replied, "Rachel, stop crying. For your sake, I will return the Jews to their homeland."

Our Heavenly Father only allowed himself to be entreated by Rachel, who overcame the most natural of feelings. She expressed extraordinary self-sacrifice for another Jew—in this case, the person for whom she would naturally feel the most jealousy. Her act had far-reaching repercussions that aid the Jews until today.

God told Jacob to bury Rachel far from where he would be buried so that she could plead on her children's behalf when they would go into exile. It will be in her merit that Jews will be gathered in from the Diaspora and return to our land.

*Leah's Uniqueness*

Leah was destined to give birth to seven of Jacob's twelve sons.[107] Had this happened, Rachel would have given birth to only one. Feeling compassion for her sister at a time when Rachel had but one child and Leah had six, Leah prayed that God should have Rachel bear a second son,[108] even though this meant that Leah would be the mother of one less tribe. Leah's prayers spared Rachel the humiliation of having fewer children than the maidservants had, since each of them had two sons. She showed Rachel compassion in the same way that Rachel had cared for Leah's dignity on what should have been Rachel's wedding night.

Leah became a spiritually great woman in her own right, perhaps partly due to the challenges that she had in her marriage. She gave birth to Levi, the progenitor of Jewish priests and Levites who served God in the Tabernacle and Temples. Her fourth son, Judah, was the progenitor of Jewish kings, including King David and the Messiah.

## DINAH

After giving birth to six sons, Leah gave birth to a daughter, Dinah. Some years later, Dinah was abducted and raped by a local non-Jewish prince named Shechem.[109] One explanation as to why this terrible incident occurred is that Jacob had hidden Dinah when his entire family met his brother Esau after not seeing each other for many years. Jacob hid Dinah because he was afraid that if the evil Esau would see her, he would marry her and corrupt her.

The *Midrash* says that Jacob should have let Dinah marry Esau because rather than her falling prey to his evil, she might have influenced him to become righteous.[110]

Here again, a biblical woman's virtuousness was viewed as so powerful that it could influence men to actualize their spiritual potentials and become great. Left to their own devices, these men would not, or could not, have developed their potential goodness.

## TAMAR

Some years later, Jacob's son Judah was involved in a disturbing incident with his daughter-in-law Tamar.[111] Judah had three sons. His oldest son, Er, married a woman named Tamar. Er didn't want to mar her beauty by getting her pregnant, so God took his life. According to biblical law, the brother of a man who died childless was supposed to marry the widow. The child of that union was then "credited" to the deceased. In Tamar's case, Onan, Er's younger brother, was supposed to father a child with Tamar who would carry on Er's name.

Although Onan married Tamar, he refused to get her pregnant because their resulting child would not bear his name. God killed him as well. The responsibility of fathering children with Tamar then fell on the third brother, Shelah, who was too young to marry her at that time. Judah asked Tamar to stay a widow until Shelah was old enough to marry her.

In actuality, Judah was just stalling for time, as he did not want his remaining son to marry Tamar. After losing two sons shortly after marrying her, Judah worried that Shelah's marrying her would cause Shelah's demise as well.

When Shelah grew up, Tamar realized that Judah was evading his responsibility to have Shelah marry her. She took matters into her own hands. She disguised herself and seduced Judah into getting her pregnant. The male ancestor of no less than King David was born from this unorthodox union.[112]

Tamar's righteousness in acting out of loving kindness for the deceased, with no ulterior motives, transformed what could have been an act of prostitution into a holy sexual union. The souls of her resulting twin sons were endowed with great spiritual potentials. One son became the progenitor of the kings of the Jewish people, who would likewise act for God's honor without having selfish or ulterior motives.

## JEWISH WOMEN IN EGYPT

The book of Exodus gives an expanded picture of what biblical Jewish women were like. At the end of the book of Genesis, a severe famine forced Jacob's family to leave the land of Israel and settle in Egypt, the breadbasket of the Middle East. Egypt was a world superpower and a center of cultural and scientific sophistication. Their panoply of gods and licentiousness were of equal repute.[113]

Twenty-two years prior to Jacob's family going to Egypt, his sons had sold their 17-year-old brother Joseph into slavery. Through divine providence, Joseph was now the viceroy of Egypt. He attained this powerful position by engineering a brilliant plan to save and store grain during seven years of plenty. He later distributed it to the starving Egyptians during the ensuing famine. His brothers ended up coming to Egypt during the famine to buy grain, and eventually the viceroy revealed himself as their long-lost brother. Joseph then invited his extended family to come to Egypt where he could insure that they had food to eat. He settled them in an area called Goshen, where they could live as moral people in a sheltered environment and be unaffected by the immoral environment of Egypt.

The men became too comfortable in their new residence, and began to spread throughout the country. They became materially prosperous and considered Egypt their home. The women did not want to trade the spirituality of the land of Israel for the prosperity in the new, immoral environment. What had seemingly started as a temporary remedy to a few years of famine became a 210-year-long exile from the land of Israel.

During that time, after Jacob and his sons died, the Egyptians enslaved the Israelite men. The slavery became ever more oppressive, until the men were so beaten down that they had no time or energy to be intimate with their wives. The wives were determined not to let the Egyptians destroy their nation's morale and future. They prepared food to feed the men who did backbreaking work in the fields. The women also took copper mirrors with them, which they encouraged the men to gaze at in order to admire their wives' reflections. When the men saw how beautiful their wives looked, they became intimate with them, and the women conceived from these unions.

The women did this so that the slavery wouldn't diminish their nation. Through these women's efforts, not only did their husbands survive, but the nation increased from a mere seventy individuals when Jacob went to Egypt, to at least three million people when the Jews left

Egypt 210 years later.[114]

God formally recognized the women's accomplishments when the Israelites who left Egypt during the Exodus built a Tabernacle in the desert. At that time, Moses asked every person who wanted to contribute materials for its construction to bring them. The women donated their gold jewelry that they had formerly refused to contribute to the building of a Golden Calf,[115] as well as the copper mirrors that they had used for procreative purposes in Egypt. Moses didn't want to accept the mirrors because he felt that they had been used for vanity (women putting on makeup). As such, he saw no place for them in God's House of Worship.

The Almighty told Moses, "Accept the mirrors. They are more precious to Me than any other contributions (to the Tabernacle). It was because the women used these mirrors in Egypt that they had many children and the Jewish nation was so large by the time of the Exodus. What the women did with these mirrors was very holy. They seduced their husbands so that they could fulfill the commandment to father children and bring many Jews into the world."[116]

The copper mirrors were made into the laver and washstand used to wash the priests prior to performing their divine service every day.

Our sages tell us that the Israelites were only worthy of being redeemed from Egypt due to the merit of the Jewish women, who were more righteous than the men during the many years of enslavement.[117] The men had become almost as unholy as their Egyptian neighbors whereas the women had not assimilated into the Egyptian culture as much as the men had.

### Shifra and Puah

As the Israelite population in Egypt grew, Pharaoh worried that he would be overthrown. He decreed that all Jewish male newborns must be killed at birth. There were two Jewish midwives—Shifra and Puah—who were especially charged to carry out this royal decree.[118] These two brave and crafty women not only refused to tell the mothers, "I have to kill your baby. I'm only following orders," they helped the babies thrive. They risked their lives by lying to Pharaoh and saved Jewish babies under his nose.

### Miriam

Perhaps the most brazen rescue of a Jewish baby under Pharaoh's nose was that of Moses himself. When Amram, a renowned leader of the tribe of Levi, heard Pharaoh's murderous decree, he divorced his wife Yocheved. Amram did not want to father children if they would be killed at birth. The rest of the Jewish men promptly followed his example and also divorced their wives.

Amram's daughter Miriam chided her father for his lack of faith. She told him that his decision was worse than Pharaoh's. After all, Pharaoh only decreed that male babies should die. Her father's actions precluded the possibility that either males or females would be born.

Amram took Miriam's words to heart, remarried Yocheved, and the other Israelite men did likewise with their wives. Just as Amram feared, Yocheved soon gave birth to a baby boy. They did not know at the time that this child, later named Moses, was destined to lead the Israelites out of Egypt some 80 years later.

When Moses was three months old, he could no longer be hidden at home. His mother put him in a basket and placed him near the Nile, semi-complying with Pharaoh's sadistic decree that all Jewish male babies should be thrown into the river. Miriam watched over him from a distance to see what his fate would be.

Soon, none other than Pharaoh's daughter discovered the child, and had compassion on him. She knew that she would need a wet nurse to feed him. At just the right moment, Miriam appeared and generously offered to find such a woman. The princess agreed, and Miriam took Moses back to his own mother to raise him until he was weaned! In this ironic manner, the future redeemer of the Israelites grew up with his family until it was time for him to be raised as Pharaoh's grandson in the royal palace.[119]

## THE GOLDEN CALF

The Almighty gave the Jews the Ten Commandments seven weeks after their Exodus from Egypt. Prior to giving it, He made sure that the women would all be present and would witness the event with the same immediacy as did the men. This was to make sure that the mistake that Chava made in the Garden of Eden would not be repeated.

Adam, rather than God, apprised his wife of the prohibition against eating from the tree of knowledge. Had she heard the command directly from her Creator, she would not have sinned.[120] Therefore, it was imperative that the Israelite women hear the Torah directly from God. This would enable them to observe its laws better, as well as give them the necessary tools to properly influence their children to carry on their Jewish heritage.

The divine revelation that occurred through giving the Torah on Mount Sinai replicated the relationship between God and Adam before man sinned. Giving the Torah after the Jews were redeemed from Egypt paralleled God's giving Adam his commandment not to eat from the tree of knowledge of good and evil.

When God gave Jews the Torah, the Jews agreed to observe both the Written and Oral Laws.[121] Their accepting God's absolute sovereignty over them allowed Him to reinstate the same relationship that He had had initially with Adam. Through the revelation at Mount Sinai, God wedded Himself to the Jewish people, so to speak, with the Torah serving as the marriage contract. When the Jews accepted the Torah, it was as if they agreed to be God's wife, and they pledged themselves to an exclusive relationship with Him.

Unfortunately, this proved to be a short-lived marriage in some respects. Forty days after God revealed Himself by giving the Torah, some of the men insisted on making a golden calf. The women did not participate in this.

The Jewish women decided to do what the Almighty told them to do rather than following the men's impulses. Through their behavior, the women achieved a spiritual level that was worthy of bringing the Messiah.

They commemorated the spiritual elevation that came with their refusal to get involved with the Golden Calf by accepting the monthly celebration of the New Moon (in Hebrew, *Rosh Chodesh*).[122] It has been a custom since the time of Moses for women not to do everyday chores on *Rosh Chodesh*, in recognition of the holiday's special significance for them. Thus, they do not launder clothes, iron, sew, or weave on *Rosh Chodesh*. (Employed women do work at their jobs.) It is also considered desirable for Jews of both sexes to eat larger meals than usual on *Rosh Chodesh*, preferably with bread, in honor of the day.[123] Some women also wear special clothes on *Rosh Chodesh* to honor its significance.

## THE SPIES

The men who participated in the Golden Calf incident repeated the same kind of mistake that Adam made by substituting their judgment for God's. They sinned again in a later incident by insisting on sending twelve spies prior to the Jews' entry into the land of Israel to see if the place was as good as God had said it was. After touring the land for forty days, ten of the spies brought back an evil report and convinced the rest of the Jewish men that they would be unable to conquer the land's inhabitants. Despite the efforts of two of the spies to convince the men that the land they were about to enter was good, the Israelite men told Moses that they didn't want to go into the land. This resulted in that generation's adult males (excepting the two spies who brought back a good report[124]) dying in the wilderness over the next 38 years.

The Torah refers to the ten spies who discouraged the males from following the divine plan to enter the land as an evil *eidah* (congregation). Later, the Torah says that the Almighty should be "sanctified in the midst of the Israelites."[125] We learn from the Spies narrative that an *eidah* consists of ten adult Jewish men. That is the basis for a *minyan*, a quorum for public prayer, minimally requiring ten Jewish men. Some other public events require the same minimal quorum of ten Jewish men because of the requirement to sanctify God in the midst of an *eidah*.

A possible reason why ten men constitute a *minyan* and women do not is because the entire need to have a quorum to bring down the Divine Presence only applies to males. Women are considered to each be sufficiently holy to not require a group of them in order to say special prayers. This is why the entire idea of public prayer and certain types of sanctification of God's Name are primarily associated with men.

The Israelite women in the wilderness did not listen to the spies' maligning the land of Israel. They wanted to enter the Promised Land. Due to their righteousness, they did not die in the desert, as did the males. Due to their love of the land, the women all[126] entered the Holy Land under the leadership of Joshua.

In this and other incidents, the Israelite women showed that they loved God and were receptive to His will. Their behavior was so exemplary that had the men acted as the women did, the Messiah would have come during the era of the generation of Jews who left Egypt.

## DEVORAH AND YAEL

Devorah and Yael were two special women who are mentioned in the Book of Judges.[127] Devorah was the only female judge in all of Jewish history. She was also a prophetess, and the greatest Jew of her generation (the *gedolah ha-dor*). She lived between the time the Jews entered the land of Israel and the establishment of the Jewish monarchy. During most of that time, male judges ruled the nation. However, since no men of her era were qualified to be judges, the entire Jewish nation came to her to be judged.

It is interesting that Devorah's husband was an ignorant, simple man. She encouraged him to apply his spiritual potentials in the best way that he could so that he would have a share in the Hereafter. To this end, she made very thick wicks for the candelabrum (*menorah*) in the Tabernacle, and asked her husband to take them there.[128] She made the wicks in a special way that enhanced the light of the flames that were lit for God's glory. As a reward for this, the Almighty caused her spiritual light to shine over the entire Jewish people by her being a judge.[129]

During her rule, the Canaanites oppressed the Jews for twenty years, led by a captain named Sisera. God ordered Devorah's husband, Barak, to choose an army of 10,000 men to fight the enemy. Despite God's promise that Barak and his army would be victorious, Barak was afraid to go. Devorah was the only one who was able to motivate the Jewish men to fight the Canaanites. She did this, in part, by promising Barak that she would accompany him in battle. However, since Barak didn't have enough faith in God on his own to do as he was told, he lost the opportunity to be the main agent of the military victory. Two women, Devorah and Yael, got the honor instead.

When the Jews fought the enemy, they killed all of the men except for Sisera. The army commander fled and found refuge in the tent of a woman, Yael, whose family[130] was friendly with the Canaanite king's family. Yael had sex with Sisera in order to exhaust him, and then she plied him with milk to get him to sleep.[131] Even though such relations were normally forbidden, Yael did so in order to save the Jewish people.[132]

Before falling asleep, Sisera asked Yael to be his sentry and tell anyone looking for him that he was not there. After he fell into a deep slumber, Yael took a tent pin and hammered it into his temple, killing him. Soon afterward, Devorah sang a song lauding Yael for her role in the Jews' salvation.[133] Thus began a forty-year period of peace for the Jews. Yael's selfless actions resulted in her meriting having the great rabbinic scholar Rabbi Akiva as one of her descendants.

It is noteworthy that when Devorah sang her song of praise to God for the victory, she referred to herself as "a mother in Israel."[134] Even though she was brilliant, a prophetess and a judge, the greatest role she saw for herself was as a mother of the Jewish people. As such, she prayed for her people,[135] had pity on them,[136] and reproved them for their misdeeds so that they would correct their ways.[137]

# RUTH

The events in the Book of Ruth occurred several hundred years after the Israelites entered the Holy Land. The book begins with a man named Elimelech leaving the land of Israel with his wife Naomi and their two sons, and settling in the land of Moab (Jordan of today). Elimelech was a leader of his generation, both economically and spiritually. Many commentators say that he left Israel during a famine so that he could preserve his wealth and not have to support the ubiquitous poor who might knock on his door asking for charity. He could have constructively dealt with feeling overwhelmed by the devastation wreaked by his people's poverty in several ways. One, he could have helped some by giving them some of what he had. Two, as a leader of that generation, he could have told people, "Don't just ask me for money. Pray to the Master of the Universe to end the famine." Three, he could have told people that famine in the land of Israel was a sign that the Jews weren't living the kind of moral life that they were supposed to, and encouraged them to think about how they needed to improve their behavior. Instead of doing these, he left the country.

Not surprisingly, after living in the land of Moab for a while, his two sons married local princesses. Elimelech died, either as punishment for leaving the land of Israel, or for evading his responsibilities to his fellow Jews. His two sons also died, either as punishment for intermarrying, or for not returning to the land of Israel once their father died, or both.

The Book of Ruth concerns itself with how Elimelech's wife Naomi and their daughter-in-law Ruth rectified the failings of their respective husbands. Those failings included the same failings that the generation of Israelite men showed after they left Egypt.

One of the first things that these women did after becoming widowed was to return to the land of Israel. This parallels how the Israelite men who left Egypt criticized the land of Israel, while the women insisted on entering the land and settling there. Elimelech and his sons were punished severely for spurning the land of Israel, while two of their wives returned to the land as soon as they could.

Elimelech's second shortcoming was his refusal to support his poor brethren. By contrast, Ruth unhesitatingly supported her mother-in-law by gleaning in fields when they went to Israel. She also abandoned her homeland of Moab, where she was a princess (the daughter of King Balak), and prepared to live a life of poverty among Jews.

Had Ruth only done these, it is doubtful that she would have had a legacy of greatness. It is likely that her tremendous desire to join the Jewish people by converting, plus her selfless kind deeds for her mother-in-law and deceased husband, earned her an eternal place in our Bible.

Ruth returned with Naomi to the land of Israel after their husbands died. Ruth immediately started to glean in the field of Naomi's relative, Boaz, in order to procure enough food for both women to eat. By the time the harvest season ended, Boaz had enabled Ruth to get food for her and Naomi without getting harassed by his male workers. Naomi, however, had higher hopes for Ruth than that.

In the style of Tamar before her, Ruth set out to insure that Boaz, her deceased husband's relative, would marry her and father a child with her to carry on the memory of her first husband. Like Tamar, she was motivated not by her personal desire to have a child, but by wanting to memorialize the name of the deceased.

In the Book of Ruth, she repeatedly refers to Boaz as a "redeemer." Her unorthodox way of stalking him was only in order to serve God. She wanted her husband's name to continue by having a legacy among the Jewish nation, and wanted to be a mother to a Jewish child.

Through her maneuverings, Ruth operated as an *ezer kenegdo*—a helper—to Boaz. He did not need much convincing once he realized Ruth's altruistic motives in wanting to marry him (as opposed to marrying this rich man for his money). However, had she not initially encouraged him to marry her, he might not have done so.

The result of Boaz' and Ruth's marriage was a child who became the grandfather of King David. For this reason, Ruth is known as the "mother of royalty."[138] She merited living until the reign of her great-great-grandson, King Solomon. At the beginning of his rule, she sat on a special seat to the right of his throne.

Ruth was yet another virtuous woman who enabled a man to live up to his potential by her being a mother in Israel and an *ezer kenegdo*. These women acted with no thought of personal reward. Their sole desire was to help men and themselves further God's plans to bring the world to perfection.

## CONTEMPORARY WOMEN

How can modern Jewish women redeem the Jewish people without seducing men into levirate marriages, or without getting their husbands not to play favorites with their children? First, they can encourage their husbands to spend extra time learning Torah. Some women work part- or full-time, or do extra domestic chores to enable their husbands to have time to learn.

The internet, Skype, and a plethora of English books on Jewish topics make it possible to access Torah classes anywhere in the world. Men in some cities study Talmud together (*daf yomi*) as they commute by train or bus to work, while other men who can't make it to a live class listen to it on the internet. People listen to Torah on MP3s on their way to and from work, while jogging or driving, at home, or even on vacation. Even soldiers stationed in the far reaches of the world are able to learn, thanks to technology!

Of course, women should also learn Torah and stay inspired as their free time permits.

Some women use their domestic talents to encourage others to experience Judaism. They invite Jews to their homes to enjoy a home-cooked Shabbat or holiday meal. So many people grow up in homes where their family does not regularly eat meals together that they welcome spending time in a wholesome family atmosphere. When guests feel the harmony and holiness that pervades a Jewish home, they may want to learn about the Torah that facilitates that way of life. It is unusual for many people to enjoy a meal together, where people talk to one another without the distractions of computers, television or phones. Sharing Jewish ideas that are appropriate for guests while they enjoy a delicious meal is often a stimulus for newcomers to learn more.

Women can also organize Torah classes in their community. If a community doesn't have anyone who can teach relevant Torah topics in an interesting way, they can arrange for speakers from elsewhere to give live classes—one-on-one or in groups—by Skype or other technology. Many filmed lectures can be accessed online and viewed by individuals or groups at their convenience.

Many women have the financial means to sponsor Torah speakers. It is wonderful when they do so to memorialize a loved one, or simply care enough about others to spread Torah in their communities.

Women can also organize Torah sessions with study partners. Organizations such as Partners in Torah arrange for a study partner at no cost for any Jew who wants to learn Torah. Teachers are found according to the topic that each student wants to learn, with an appropriate teaching style and personality.

Women also help men to fulfill their potentials by raising Jewish families. The love and moral education that children receive from their mothers are cornerstones of their religious and emotional development.

The home has always been the most fundamental Jewish school, and mothers' interactions with their children affect their personal, social and spiritual development.

A third area where women can excel is in doing charitable work and by encouraging others to do kind deeds. For example, women have initiated and run charitable organizations that feed the hungry, clothe the poor, provide shelter for abused women, educate people and provide vocational training, aid victims of terror, provide meals for the families of new mothers and mourners, and so on. In the past few decades, they have also initiated organizations that provide support and financial help to infertile couples, handicapped children and their families, and to the families of those with extraordinary medical needs.

In Israel, 25% of the Jewish population volunteers! There are thousands of religious teenage girls who provide social welfare services for two years after graduating high school, mostly in schools and residential facilities for children. These volunteers tutor children, provide enriching after-school activities, visit children undergoing cancer and other serious medical treatments, spend time with and help elderly shut-ins, and more. It is common for some religious girls to grow their hair for two or more years, then they cut and donate it to make wigs for children undergoing cancer treatments. Instead of focusing mostly on themselves, such girls are raised with a consciousness of giving to others, and feeling the satisfaction that goes along with that.

Women's kind acts are an important way that we help bring the Messiah. Inviting guests who have nowhere to go to our homes on the Sabbath and Jewish holidays, teaching unaffiliated Jews about the depth and beauty of Judaism, encouraging those around us to learn more Torah, modeling and encouraging others to give to those who need help, raising children to care about God and to have a strong moral compass, visiting the sick, and comforting the bereaved and those who need a listening ear are all ways that modern women redeem the world.

It says in the *Chapters of the Fathers*, "The world stands on three things: on Torah, on prayer, and on deeds of loving kindness."[139] Every day, Jewish women (and their families if they have one) should learn Torah. Every day we should pray. These combine with a third pillar—doing selfless, kind deeds (*chessed*, in Hebrew).

We read the book of Ruth on the holiday of *Shavuot*. On that day, God gave the Jewish people the Torah—our GPS for life. The pairing of these two suggests that the world can only thrive when people not only learn but also live Torah, which requires us to act with the kindness of

Ruth, Naomi and Boaz.

Our Creator wants us to imitate Him. He continually nurtures and sustains the world out of love and selflessness. When we act out of love and help others to reach their spiritual potentials, the Almighty won't have to act in a supernatural way to redeem us. Women, with men, can join forces and build an everlasting world of kindness.

If we do our utmost to practice loving kindness, the Messiah and the Divine Presence will want to join us as we bring redemption to a troubled world.

# 5

# Clothes Make the Man–Are They Woman's Undoing?

It is well-known that we project our personalities through our body language and the way we dress. Both make personal statements that reveal our inner character, feelings, and attitudes. Therapists may even diagnose patients before they say a word by noticing their demeanor and what they are wearing. It doesn't take a rocket scientist to understand that a woman who dresses flamboyantly, with multicolored hair, many rings, and intense makeup is looking for attention. That and more can be said for a woman who wears skimpy clothes and is blatantly seductive. We can surmise that a woman who looks sad, sits hunched over, is unkempt, and does not care about her appearance is depressed. A fourth woman wearing a dark suit is a corporate stereotype with her low heels, reading glasses, hair pulled back in a bun, and subtle makeup.

Whether we like to admit it or not, we all make statements to the world via our clothes and body language. There was a time when popular books taught people how to "dress for success." For hundreds of years, costume designers have dressed actors and actresses for their stage roles. Today, dating coaches advise female clients how to dress and use makeup to attract the kinds of men they want to date. Specially trained psychologists advise lawyers how their clients should dress to win a favorable verdict at a trial, and advertising agencies make billions of dollars by knowing what kind of look will sell a product.

Western society is very fashion and image-conscious. For women, being fashionable often involves revealing and displaying their body for the world to see. If we've got it, we are supposed to flaunt it. Privacy is considered to be an antiquated value.

It is sad that many young girls are socialized to see themselves as sex objects from a very young age. A 2012 study showed that 68% of American girls ages six to nine wanted to look like sexy dolls, while 72% said that the sexy dolls were more popular than non-sexy ones.[140]

If we don't live up to others' expectations of how we should dress and display ourselves, we might pay a price. Here are a few examples:

Amy was a smart high school student who didn't want to wear the skimpy, revealing clothes that were in fashion. She wore modest outfits instead, wanting her body to be private and shared only with the man she would someday marry. Her classmates shunned her for her old-fashioned views.

The author was waiting one night to ride the train from Manhattan to the North Shore of Long Island. Moments before the train left the station, two attractive women in their twenties entered and sat facing her. Each wore a black pantsuit with a plain white top, little makeup, shoulder-length hair, and dark shoes with low heels. As soon as they sat down, the author pegged them as lawyers who had just finished their day's work in a mid-town Manhattan law firm. The blonde confirmed this when she told the brunette, "Did you hear how Judge Goldstein berated and then threw Mary Ellen out of court yesterday for wearing a frilled blouse and short skirt? He told her that the next time she came to litigate a case in his courtroom, she'd better look professional and not like she's going to a party!"

Then there was Lindsay. She was a beautiful woman with a voluptuous figure who always wore tight, low cut shirts and very short dresses or tight leggings. Her bright red lipstick completed her look. She lamented to her therapist how men she passed on the street kept trying to solicit her, and she couldn't understand why she was singled out for such unwanted advances.

We choose whether or not to dress according to prevailing fashions. Our responses say a lot about who we are, how we see ourselves, and how we want others to see us. If a woman wants people to see her a certain way, but they consistently see her in a way that she feels disparaged, her intentions are irrelevant. She will be misunderstood until she appreciates and is responsive to others' points of view.

Most women want to feel sexy and desired and may not realize how strongly men are affected by how they project that aspect of themselves. Not infrequently, the men don't notice other parts that the women want to be appreciated. Men react very strongly to the way women look (isn't that nice?), whether at work, in social situations, or in intimate settings. They don't compartmentalize themselves the way some women think by totaling tuning out the part of their brain that gets excited when it focuses on a sexy woman. Therefore, if a woman wants a man to focus on her work talents, personality, intellect, or the totality of who she is, she should tone down how distracting her looks are.

There is a presumption in Jewish law, as well as a societal reality, that men find it difficult to remain unaffected by a woman who displays her body. Even when men try not to notice, it is difficult when a woman's body is flaunted.

A religious man was teaching summer school classes at a religious college to a dozen secular female students. Most of the women wore very revealing clothes that he found inappropriate and distracting. This was compounded by the fact that they sat close to him in a small classroom. He requested that when they would come to future classes that they wear tops that covered their torso.

When he came for the next class, some of the women were still scantily attired. He felt very uncomfortable and made his request again. The next week some of the students again ignored his plea. The following week, he brought in a platter of freshly baked, fragrant chocolate chip cookies and placed them on a chair in front of the offenders. He told them at the beginning of the two-hour class, "You can look but you can't have any."

Before the class was well underway, one of the students complained, "What you did wasn't fair. You shouldn't entice us with cookies, put them down in front of us where we can see and smell them, and tell us that we can't have any."

He responded, "Now you know how I feel."

From then on, none of the women came to class wearing clothes that left too little to the imagination.

## MEN'S AND WOMEN'S BODIES

The Almighty created men in a way that they are attracted to women so that those feelings would be used productively in marriage. There is beauty in the idea that a woman should not want every man to find her sexy. She can feel that she is sexy, yet keep her body reserved for one special person to admire. When a woman's body is exposed to the public, it cheapens her beauty rather than enhancing it. Our bodies are our packages, not our essence. A woman who feels that she should display hers may see herself largely as an object, and broadcasts to others that her body is what's most important about her. Men then relate to her accordingly. If she downplays the physical aspects of herself, she may worry about who she will be and how others will notice and relate to her. If a woman wants to discover her soul, her inner essence, and what is real and lasting in herself, and have others see beyond her façade, she should downplay her sexuality. Otherwise, her body may simply be too distracting.

As was mentioned, Judaism tells us that the differences in the anatomy of men and women are not biological flukes but were intentionally designed by our Creator. It has been suggested that they were meant to reflect differences in the way that people can express their respective souls' potentials. One theory suggests that men's anatomy reflects their being more outer-directed than women. If men are especially attentive to the details of the world around them, this implies that they will be attracted to women's external appearances. This attraction can strongly influence their decision to further a relationship, or can motivate a man to use women for self-gratification. Women's anatomy, on the other hand, reflects their tendency to develop relationships based on inner qualities and then to generalize those feelings to externals. This suggests that women often find men emotionally appealing and then become physically attracted to them.

Businesses capitalize on the presumption that men are very susceptible to sexual influences and physical appearances. For instance, American advertisements frequently include sexual messages, even when the advertised product or event has little or nothing to do with sex. Soft drinks, liquors, cars, boats, vacations and even cigarettes are sold with suggestions of sex, or at least with beautiful women in tight or revealing outfits alongside them. By contrast, women's products are advertised with the message that if women use them, they will become beautiful and/or loved by a man. The subtle difference between these two approaches results in partially clad women appearing in ads for men's products, whereas scantily clad men rarely market women's products. Advertisers know that the promise of sex sells products that men use, while women buy products that promise to make them feel beautiful or loved.

Another phenomenon that reflects differences between men's and women's attraction to sexual stimuli is prostitution and interest in pornography. There have been prostitutes from time immemorial, and modern pornography is a booming industry. It has been estimated that

66% of American men view online pornography at least once a month.[141] This suggests that many men seek purely sexual interactions with women and use women as objects for their pleasure. Many men are even willing to pay for both.

The media frequently portrays females as sex objects and sex outside of marriage as desirable. (In Judaism, sex is only permitted when a man commits himself to taking care of a wife.) Portraying females in these sexual ways has many devastating consequences. Among them are the fact that one in five American females is sexually assaulted; twelve percent of them aged ten or younger, and 50% of them before age 18.[142]

Jewish law presumes that men will be sexually attracted to women's bodies and requires women (and men) to downplay their sexuality in public. It is forbidden for men to treat women as objects. This makes it easier for men to take women seriously and better appreciate their nonsexual attributes. Another consequence is that many employers like to hire religious men and women because there is little sexual harassment and flirting and work time is used more productively.

## PROJECTING A GODLY SELF-IMAGE

Judaism teaches that how we dress not only affects how others perceive us, it affects how we see ourselves and how we relate to the world. For example, the Talmud advises that when we pray, we should dress up as if we are addressing a king who has the power of life or death over us.[143] Wearing formal clothes (as opposed to pajamas or a bathing suit, for example) helps us to see ourselves as important and makes it easier to pray as if we are truly addressing a King of Kings.

Modern research also supports the idea that our mode of dress affects the way we think. For example, subjects who took cognitive tests while wearing suits and other formal clothes used more abstract thinking than peers who wore casual clothes.[144] The researchers concluded from the results that the clothing we wear "influences cognition broadly, impacting the processing style that changes how objects, people, and events are construed."[145]

Another study showed that when people wore what were described as white doctors' coats they were more attentive, detail-oriented and accurate when doing tasks than when they were told they were wearing painters' coats.[146] It seems that we try to live up to the messages our clothing gives us. If our clothes symbolize higher-level performance, we perform, feel and behave better.

We can conceptualize the way Judaism asks us to dress in the context of how we should relate to the world. The world in which we live is called "*olam*" in Hebrew. It comes from the word *he'elem*, which means "hidden." In our world, the Divine Presence is always hidden to some degree so that He can reward people for searching for and finding Him.

If our job in life is to seek and find our Creator, how do we dress for such a mission? What uniform do we wear to put ourselves into the proper mindset? Presumably, we should wear outfits that downplay our material/superficial self and help our hidden spiritual essence to emerge.

The Hebrew word for modesty is *tzniut*, which means "hidden in its proper place." It has been suggested that the Jewish laws of modesty were enacted so that people would let their internal essences emerge, rather than being focused on their physical coverings. Covering the body reminds us that our external, physical appearance is not our essence. Valuing our bodies in their own right is like buying a box of shoes, then throwing away the shoes and wearing the box! Just as it is the shoes inside the box that are important, so it is with our essence being inside us. Jews are supposed to look for the divine image behind the screen of the physical and material world. We must seek the divine image inside us and others.

Our Creator gave us bodies as vehicles by which we express our souls, and did not intend for us to view them as ends in themselves. The more we focus on our body as if it were our essence, the harder it is to value and project what is really us—our souls. Focusing on our body's looks also makes it hard to maintain a mindset of relating to a God who is totally spiritual, and distracts others from this goal.

This concept applies equally to both sexes. Judaism obligates both men and women to present ourselves in a way that we take responsibility for how others view us and the messages that we give. This includes presenting ourselves in a way that others notice our inner Godliness rather than focusing on our superficialities.

If we dress in a revealing way, others can misinterpret what they see as representing our essence. We must remember that bodies are merely the external garments that clothe our souls.

## WHY WE COVER THE BODY

The first time the Torah speaks about the need to cover the body is after Adam sinned in the Garden of Eden.[147] After he ate the forbidden fruit, thereby showing that his physical drives controlled his spiritual ones, he hid from God. When He asked Adam where he was, Adam replied that he hid "because I knew I was naked."

Prior to eating the forbidden fruit, Adam and Eve were both naked, yet the Torah says that "they were not ashamed." This is because, prior to sinning, their bodies had only one function—to serve God. Once they indulged their physical drives in a way that was at odds with their spiritual mission, they internalized desires to get pleasure independent of serving their Creator. That made it possible to misuse their bodies to fulfill their animalistic drives. Once they split off their physical desires from their spiritual drives, they had to cover their bodies. They needed a constant reminder that they should use their bodies to accomplish their divine missions, rather than seek physical pleasures as ends in themselves.

The Almighty would not have allowed the first couple to remain naked from the time they were created until they sinned if bodies were inherently sinful or distasteful. Clothing only became necessary once people showed that they would misuse their physical desires if they weren't restrained. When God expelled Adam and Eve from Paradise, He made them clothes. This suggested that once people could potentially misuse the body as an end in itself, they would need reminders to use it properly.

An interesting *Midrash* addresses the changes that came about due to Adam's sin. Adam initially had tremendous physical and spiritual stature. After he sinned, the Almighty diminished his physical stature to reflect his diminished spiritual greatness. The only part of Adam's body that did not stop reflecting his spirituality was his face. To this day, people's faces and especially their eyes reflect their souls. Perhaps this is one reason why the Jewish laws of modesty never required a woman to cover her face, even though wearing a veil was a common practice in the Middle East. Perhaps when a soul can be glimpsed behind the body's façade, we don't need to cover it. Our body won't obscure our soul when our soul is projected on our faces.

Thus, one outgrowth of the Jewish laws of modesty is that they help us to project a proper self-image—one that reflects our divine potentials and mission—to the world. Western media, culture and fashion want us to project the contours of our body instead and think that is the real "me." The more our image is one that identifies with God's attributes, the more we will act in accordance with it instead of seeing ourselves as objects whose animalistic desires need to be fulfilled

.

## COVERING WHAT IS PRECIOUS

A second suggestion as to why the body must be covered has to do with accentuating its preciousness. When we own something valuable, we shouldn't flaunt it because the more we show it off, the more we cheapen it. Someone who owns beautiful silver, exquisite jewelry or a family heirloom only displays them on rare occasions. If we exhibit our family jewels all the time (imagine wearing them every time we take out the garbage), they will cease being so special. Just as some people find it exciting to go to one black tie affair once each year, most find it a social chore to have to go every month.

Just as familiarity can breed contempt, or at least dampen our excitement about material objects and events, the same can happen in religious domains. Many Jewish laws remind us to stay aware of the sanctity of various objects. For example, we keep prayer books closed when they are not being used, and men cover their *tefillin* and put them away in a cloth bag as soon as they finish wearing them every day. These actions help preserve our reverence for these objects. The holier something is, the less casually we are allowed to treat it.

People had this kind of reverence for the Holy of Holies in the Tabernacle and Temples. It was the holiest place in the entire world because God's presence was most easily felt there. The Torah set down rigorous restrictions as to who could enter it and when. Only the High Priest could enter it on Yom Kippur after he had ritually immersed himself and undergone stringent preparations. Perhaps because the body houses a spark of God, we cover much of it so that its sanctity is unlikely to be degraded and diminished.

The Temple was a holy place, and those who served there had to maintain the highest standards of modesty. The priests ascended its altar via a ramp rather than steps so that their garments would not be displaced when they placed offerings there. The priests' robes also had to cover their entire bodies, with the exceptions of the face, hands and feet. These laws suggest that the closer someone is to God's manifest Presence, the less one is permitted to expose him- or herself. The greater potential holiness there is, the more we must take care to insure that the body acts in concert with that.

Another example of the value of modesty occurs when a man wears a prayer shawl (*tallit*). It normally covers at least the upper half of his body, from his shoulders to his hips or below. When a man prays the *Shemoneh Esrai* or gets an *aliyah* to the Torah, he typically covers his head as well with his *tallit*. Whenever a man or woman approaches greater holiness, we protect ourselves with extra humility and modesty.

This idea is not limited to behavior in the Temple. The *Code of Jewish Law* says:

> It is written, "You should walk modestly with your God."[148]  Therefore, it is every person's duty to be modest in all of his ways...(even when getting dressed or undressed) one should be careful not to expose the body unduly....One should never say to himself, "I'm all alone behind closed doors— who can see me?" For the glory of the Holy One, blessed is He, fills the universe and darkness and light are the same to Him.[149]

This means that we should constantly see ourselves as being in God's Presence[150] since He is aware of us at all times and in all places.

There are thirty-two commandments we may fulfill every day by merely thinking about them. One of these is to make ourselves a throne and a sanctuary for the Divine Presence.[151] This is based on the verse, "You should make Me a sanctuary and I will dwell within you."[152] Among other things, this requires us to act modestly.

## THE CENTRALITY OF MODESTY

The Jewish concept of modesty is unrelated to the secular idea that modesty means having poor self-esteem, repressing one's feelings, or being incompetent. Judaism views modesty as a combination of being humble while valuing privacy—knowing what to reveal and when, and what to keep hidden. In today's world, it is shocking how quickly people share the most intimate details of their lives and bodies with total strangers. People create the illusion that displaying themselves and getting attention means they are important, regardless of how tasteless or inappropriate their behavior or dress is. We should want to be valued for meaningful achievements that we have worked hard to accomplish. We need to develop the self-esteem not to need attention as an end in itself.

Modesty is a prerequisite for men and women to be truly religious. The prophet Micah expressed this by saying, "What does God ask of you? To love doing kind deeds, to act justly, and to walk modestly with God." A Jew must be modest in order to observe the Torah's commandments in a way that pleases the Master of the Universe. This includes being constantly aware of His presence.

A second reference to the centrality of modesty says, "When a person does a premeditated sin, the result is shame, but with modesty comes wisdom."[153] This means that we can only relate to the essence of life if we have the humility and dignity that come with knowing that we are always standing in God's Presence. Such modesty helps us to continually think about how to make our lives most meaningful.

It is easy to live life superficially. For example, many people care more about doing what gets people's approval instead of doing what is right in God's eyes. It is a challenge to relate to life in terms of its transcendent value. The more we try to get self-esteem from others' approving of us, the less self-control and security we have and the less meaning our lives have. Since we can't please everyone, pleasing some people necessitates displeasing others. And if we stand for certain values, there are sure to be others who don't like us for our beliefs. When we develop a sense of modesty, it helps us refine our inner values instead of depending on external circumstances and others to make us feel good. Modesty teaches us how to transcend our egos to search for the deep, inner values that are the lifeblood of the Jewish soul.

## WOMEN'S UNIQUE CONTRIBUTIONS

Judaism believes that God gave women unique qualities so that we will bring them into the world. One of these is modesty. Chava was purposely created from Adam's rib—a part of him that was concealed and internal.[154] Perhaps this was so that women would have the ability to bring "innerness" (modesty) into the world in a greater way than could Adam and his male descendants. It has been suggested that not only did Chava's physical structure reflect her greater potential for modesty, but so did her emotional and intellectual endowments.

Women can only use their extra *binah*[155] (understanding the inner workings of people and things) if they see beyond people's externals into their true selves. We can do that best when we have learned to see beyond our own external trappings.

*Binah* is essential for being a good mother, and therapists use *binah* all the time. In fact, it is the quality they rely on most when working with patients. This is because therapists must be able to empathize with others and understand where they are coming from. Once they appreciate someone's background, thoughts and feelings, they can understand how and why they deal with situations and people the way they do. Then, the therapist can teach people how to modify their perceptions and reactions so that they can lead a more meaningful and productive life.

Therapists need to understand what goes in their own minds and hearts before they can be wholly effective with others. Just as a therapist must introspect to understand what his or her deepest desires, emotions and conflicts are, and how these affect their interactions with patients, so must we understand how our inner workings enhance or impede our spiritual growth and affect our interpersonal relationships.

A Jew who embodies true modesty has already developed an inner sense of security, self-esteem, and meaning in life. These traits are based on internalizing the belief that we were created in the image of God as we try to live up to that calling.

## LAWS OF MODESTY

The Jewish laws and attitudes about modesty pertain to several areas of life. Both men and women are required to act and dress modestly; however, the details differ as to what each should and should not do. Both sexes are supposed to dress and act modestly and to speak in a refined and dignified way.

Men are prohibited from being in situations where they can view women who are immodestly dressed or who are behaving immodestly.[156] Women are similarly enjoined from watching men to whom they are not married who are sexually provocative or stimulating. Men may not even pray in the presence of anyone whose "nakedness" (*ervah*, in Hebrew) is exposed,[157] be it another man, woman, or even the man himself. A woman's *ervah* includes any exposed body parts that she is normally required to cover—the upper arms, thighs, and torso. Men are also prohibited from reading or thinking about things that will stimulate them sexually. The sole exception is that a man may think about his wife and allow himself to be aroused in her presence, provided that she is sexually available.

The laws of modesty require women to wear clothing that covers their arms down to the elbows, with necklines not much lower than the collarbone, and with hems that reach to the middle of the knee joint or below.[158] These areas must remain covered in the presence of men besides her husband even if she is bending, reaching, sitting, and so on. This means that if a dress will not continually cover the requisite areas during the course of her day, it should not be worn. This rules out skirts that cover the knees while standing, but which hike up when sitting or bending over, as well as short-sleeved tops that expose the upper arms while reaching. Thus, when choosing clothes, women must consider not only what they look like in the dressing room, but also what they will look like during their daily activities.

The Torah requires married women to wear something that covers their hair,[159] such as a hat, scarf or a wig. (Technically, this law is independent of the laws of modesty; however, it is a generally accepted extension of modern laws of modest dress.) It is also a custom in many communities that women wear knee socks or stockings.[160] In some communities, women don't wear pants because they are not considered to be modest.[161] Nevertheless, there are many communities where observant women do not make a point of wearing stockings and do wear modestly tailored women's pants.

Women also may not sing individually in the presence of men other than their husbands.[162] Some authorities understand this prohibition to extend as well to two or more women singing together in the presence of men. As a general rule, women are required to act in a manner that is not sexually suggestive or arousing in the presence of men besides their husbands, and men are expected to do likewise with women. Both sexes' demeanor and speech is supposed to reflect the dignity that comes with being created in God's image.

A Jewish man is required to cover his head as a sign of modesty. One interpretation of this is that a man needs to know that he is finite, with limited abilities and knowledge. He is supposed to be aware constantly that there is a Divine Being above him. A wig (or hair covering) serves the same purposed for a married woman.

Some people ask what a married woman accomplishes if she is more attractive wearing a wig than when exposing her real hair. There is no reason that women should not look attractive; they are prohibited from looking *attracting*. As long as the wig enhances her attractiveness without being seductive, it can still make her more aware of the One Above. This, in turn, encourages her to act modestly and accentuate her spiritual beauty at the same time that her physical beauty is apparent.[163]

While many Jewish laws govern how women should dress and act in the presence of men, modesty also applies to the way women relate to one another and to God. The laws of modesty are guidelines that help women present themselves with dignity to the world. Just because a woman isn't in a man's presence doesn't mean she shouldn't be dignified.

Technically, the laws of modesty permit a woman to expose body parts that are normally covered as long as men other than her husband don't see her. Yet some women become sensitized to the idea that their bodies are temples that house God's image and they don't display them even to other women. For this reason, some women cover their hair, as well as other normally covered body parts even they are in the privacy of their homes. Such women (and men who act similarly) imitate the Temple priests who were careful never to expose their bodies in the Almighty's presence.

Overall, the Jewish laws of modesty help us to internalize and project a dignified image to others that helps us to be taken seriously.

## DETAILS IN MODESTY

Critics of the laws of modesty claim that they are obsessed with details and bogged down in minutiae. For example, they ask, "What difference does it make if a woman wears sleeveless blouses rather than sleeves that cover her elbows? Did the rabbis really think that men would get sexually aroused by seeing a woman's biceps?"

One response to this question is that every *mitzvah* is designed to create certain spiritual effects, and sometimes emotional, intellectual, and spiritual ones as well. We rarely know what all of these effects were meant to be. We can measure cause and effect in the physical world, but not in the spiritual one.

Imagine going to an opera, ballet, or musical where all of the performers' costumes are several inches too short. Does it really matter? Does the performance look the same as when every detail is tailored to the mood that is supposed to be created? Do the singers, dancers and actresses perform differently when wearing inappropriately short costumes?

Many years ago, the author went backstage prior to a performance of American Ballet Theatre at Chicago's Opera House. Someone had pinned one white pointe shoe to the bulletin board with a sign on it for one of the workers: "Make sure this is dyed light pink before tomorrow's performance."

The exquisite attention to detail in the performing arts is what makes the difference between a mediocre performance and one that warrants a standing ovation. We accept without questioning the importance of details in biology, chemistry, physics and medicine because we believe that the physical world is real. The difference between 0.1 milligram and 1 milligram of a drug can mean life versus death. In the world of computers, a misplaced period, hyphen instead of underscore, or added letter means the difference between successfully getting an important email message to a recipient versus causing a disaster. Spirituality is even more real than all of these. Even if we can't see the effects that details cause, we can know they exist.

It matters a great deal how people dress in certain work environments. A store does not display a dress unless the sleeves complete a certain look. A movie director does not shoot a scene until every detail of hair, clothing, and makeup are in place. Actors and actresses try to prepare themselves for their roles by walking, dressing, and carrying themselves in ways that are consistent with their characters. This allows them to identify as fully as possible with the person whom they are trying to portray.

We live in a world where women are encouraged to wear the most revealing of clothes in order to be popular and desirable, and where sex is often degraded. The more women dress as objects to be viewed, the more they identify with that role. The laws of modesty help us to maintain a persona that is dignified and that doesn't succumb to peer pressure. In order for Jewish women to have believed for the past 3,300 years that we are Godly souls inside a body, the laws of modesty had to be very specific and not subject to prevailing fashions. These guidelines have ensured that the body's degradation by our surrounding cultures did not have the same effect on the Jew.

Any legal system, Judaism included, has rules as guidelines. Yet, its adherents must also extrapolate from the letter of the law to the spirit of the law. The legalities are important in their own right, but they also protect the spirit of the law and the effects they foster.

It has been suggested that women, with their extra *binah*, have intuitive sensitivity about what types of non-legislated behavior and clothing are or are not modest. It is certainly possible for women to wear clothes that cover the requisite parts of the body, yet attract attention in a way that is anything but modest. Provocative clothes can cover the major parts of one's limbs while being very seductive.

There is no reason for observant women to look ugly or unattractive. There may be specific items of dress, such as a beautiful wig or makeup that enhance their physical appearance. These are permitted as long as they don't make women look attracting.

The laws of modesty have at least two effects—one for the woman herself and one for men who might see her. Certain men may find women more attractive when they see less of a woman's body than when nothing is left to the imagination. Other men may find women more attractive when they wear wigs rather than showing their own hair. In any event, women project less dignity and self-respect and develop less awareness of their inner essence when they wear skimpier clothes.

## MODESTY IN ROLE

Jewish law tells us what parts of the body we must cover, and this gives us a sense of modesty about our physical selves. Similarly, there are laws that help create a sense of modesty about a woman's role. The job of men and women is to be holy and to bring holiness into the world. Men have roles that bring holiness to people, places and objects in the public, external world. Women's roles emphasize bringing holiness into realms that are hidden from public view. This implies that we should develop roles for ourselves in which our inner self is active.

We each have a finite amount of energy and time. The more we develop our outer self, the less time and attention we have to develop our inner self. The more we are preoccupied with how we appear to others and with what they think of us, the less time and emotional energy we have left to focus on what is really important in life. The more we notice and work on how we are doing spiritually, the less we will concern ourselves with getting attention and approval from others.

When society relegated women mostly to the home, men had most of the positions of public power. Judaism discourages both men and women from working in jobs where public honor or prestige is a perquisite of the job. Perhaps this is because modesty and humility are virtues for both sexes. The more people's roles encourage them to see themselves as important because of the honor people give them, the less awe of and obedience to God they are likely to have.

Traditionally, men almost invariably held the Jewish public religious positions (such as being rabbis and rabbinical judges) although there were occasional exceptions to this (such as the judge Devorah). Women were not exempted from public office because they were deemed too unstable, stupid, or incompetent to make decisions that affected society. It might be because Judaism believes that women should develop their abilities to influence people using their personal, internal qualities, and not value themselves according to how much external power they wield. Women were dissuaded or prohibited from powerful external roles so that they would focus on developing their essential internal influences and use them to further the spiritual development of the Jewish people.

As society changed, and women became much more active in its social, economic, and political fabric, many of the traditional roles women occupied expanded beyond their domestic realms. Nowadays, there is no religious reason why women cannot occupy any role in secular society they wish as long as it allows them to preserve their adherence to Jewish standards of morality and ethics. (The same applies to men.) Thus, women can be secular lawyers and judges, businesswomen, physicians, politicians, and the like as long as their chosen professions do not compromise their adherence to Jewish law. In the religious world, it is accepted that women can teach Jewish subjects, even to male students, and can render decisions about Jewish law if they are sufficiently knowledgeable in such areas. As an example, the biblical scholar Nechama Leibowitz, of blessed memory, lectured in many *yeshivot* in Israel during her career that spanned decades.

When men or women gain positions of power or prestige, they need to ask themselves how they can serve God through these roles and be exemplary models of how Jews should live. The more privileges societal roles confer, the more a Jew in that position needs to be careful to sanctify God. He or she shouldn't value their positions as opportunities to get personal respectability and power because others give these roles credence.

One theory about why women are excluded from certain roles of visible power and prestige in synagogues and religious organizations is because these roles disproportionately affect men. For instance, the policy-making of most synagogues primarily affects male worshipers, since they tend to attend in greater numbers and more frequently than do women. It would be inappropriate for women to have an equal say with the men about such policies. However, insofar as synagogues or organizations spend money on programs that equally affect both sexes, there is no reason why women cannot be their treasurers or other policy makers in areas that don't decide ritual observance.

## INTERNAL POWER

The process of psychotherapy recognizes how much one person can affect others, especially parents in a child's early life. God gave parents a great deal of "internal" power—the ability to use their personal influence to mold children for the rest of their lives. The seeds for adult patterns of thinking, feeling, and acting are set down in early childhood, and it is often the mother who profoundly influences them. This is so true that if one asks a roomful of people who influenced their lives the most, chances are good that mothers will be the predominant force. Similarly, many studies have shown the potency of personal relationship in the success of psychotherapy. A therapist's good relationship with the patient is more responsible for facilitating change than any other variable.

The use of one's personal influence (internal power) to affect someone's life is very powerful, yet different from the type of power that occurs at corporate or political levels. People can wield tremendous power if they help others recognize their potentials and assist them in actualizing themselves.

The Almighty granted women the preeminent positions of molding the lives of their family members on an individual basis in the home; men were granted the positions to do so on a societal level. Both use their abilities to influence others through teaching and role modeling.

## FINDING OUR INNER GODLINESS

In today's world, many Jewish women will not get their main fulfillment as wives and mothers. Some women marry late, others won't marry at all, and many stay childless. No matter what our marital or family status, we all need to express ourselves in a modest and fulfilling way. Neither Jewish men nor women should be satisfied living only for ourselves and feel content with secular career and material achievements. Our greatest achievements are in sharing our Godly essence with others and helping them to express their essence. It takes effort to design our lives to continually think of others, but it keeps us from stagnating personally and spiritually. We can't simply wait for these opportunities to fall into our laps—we usually have to make them happen.

Many women do this by reaching out to others, such as by inviting unaffiliated Jews from their workplace or neighborhood to join their Shabbat or holiday meals. They visit sick Jews in local hospitals and comfort the bereaved by making *shiva* visits. As well, they offer a place for out-of-town families to stay when they need local hospitality. Women cook and deliver food to the families of new mothers and for those who are bereaved. Some women without family obligations babysit children whose parents can't afford to hire help and who need a respite. Religious high school girls often help overwhelmed mothers a few hours a week, or go to nursing homes to visit residents who don't otherwise have many visitors. All of these pursuits require sensitivity to the needs of others.

*Choosing a Career*

When the author was in college, she was frustrated by her inability to choose a career. After taking stock of her talents, abilities, interests, and how she could use that combination to work part-time while raising a family, she drew a blank. Finally, she was praying one morning and she read a selection from the Talmud:

> These are the things that a person enjoys the interest from in this world, and the capital remains for him in the World to Come: They are honoring one's father and mother, doing acts of kindness, getting up early to go to the study hall in the morning and attending in the evening, giving hospitality to guests, visiting the sick, providing for a poor bride, escorting the dead to the grave, praying intently, bringing peace between a man and his friend, and between a man and his wife—and the study of Torah is equal to them all.[164]

At that moment, she realized that becoming a psychologist who specialized in doing couples' therapy would be a great career for her. And it was!

Many women can express their Godliness at work by following Jewish ethics, eating only kosher food no matter how tempting the office party food is, leaving work early on Fridays and not working on Jewish holidays or Shabbat. Not only at work, but everywhere, we should strive to treat others respectfully, not lose our tempers or have angry outbursts, and speak only with refined words, no matter how acceptable it is in our environment to do otherwise. By dressing and speaking modestly, we do the best thing possible—we sanctify God's Name. We are walking advertisements for Judaism when people see that we live up to our divine calling.

A Christian army officer visited his Orthodox Jewish accountant in Brooklyn. When they finished their meeting, the men walked to the officer's car as the religious Jewish girls' school across the street ended classes for the day. The officer stood on the sidewalk watching the modestly dressed girls for a few moments, then turned to his accountant and said admiringly, "You can see God in those girls."

Whether we are doing office or professional work, teaching, or working in any other fields, our job is to help others to see God in us.

In both our work and personal lives, being good listeners is also an expression of modesty. Many people today talk, but far fewer listen. We shouldn't be spilling out all of the details of our lives, replete with photos and private information, to hundreds of "friends" in the social media. There is great beauty in being secure enough with ourselves that we can be good listeners to others and not have to invest so much energy getting attention from others, including strangers.

The more spiritually developed we are, the more worthy we feel that

God put part of Himself within us. The Torah says that God breathed into Adam's nostrils *nishmat chaim*—a soul of life.[165] We each have some divine essence that keeps us alive. The more we appreciate our intrinsic self-worth thanks to the divine image in us, the more we can appreciate others' essential worthiness because of the divine image in them.

Modesty helps us find the Godly spark in ourselves and in others. The manner in which women dress, speak, and conduct ourselves facilitates this process. When we try to emulate the One Above, we can connect to our divine soul and use our inner resources to nurture our spiritual growth. Once we identify our inner needs and nurture them in a healthy way, we can do the same for others.

When we transcend our self-absorption, and help others get in touch with their divine image, we expand modesty into a role. Many women do this as wives and mothers, by working in the helping professions and medical fields, and holistically helping others to regain their health with compassion and empathy. When we tune into our divine image, we can appreciate that we were not put here to take center stage. By putting the Almighty into the center of our lives, and being His partners in giving to others and affirming their value, we become much greater than by simply being noticed.

# 6

# *Making Traditional Prayer Relevant*

Ⅰt is difficult for most modern Jews to relate to traditional Jewish prayer. First, the prayers were written in Hebrew, which many Jews can't read or understand. Second, some of our prayers refer to our ancient forebears and to ancient events like the Exodus from Egypt, or to our Temples that to some are irrelevant relics of the past. Third, modern Jews often think that the content and goals of these prayers don't relate to their lives.

It is easiest to address these issues by first understanding what prayer is and what it isn't. Many people think that prayer is a way of getting God to do what we want. If we get the results that we hope for, we think that our prayers were answered. If we don't, we often assume that the Almighty didn't hear our prayers, or that it is pointless to pray. This is the "online shopping" approach to prayer. We submit the shopping list to the One Above and expect Him to deliver what we order in a timely way. If we don't get what we want, we don't patronize that vendor again.

Unfortunately, many people assume that God does not exist if He doesn't respond to us in the way that we want. Others only pray when they are in a proverbial foxhole because they think that the Master of the Universe has better things to do than to deal with our seemingly petty problems. Judaism teaches that neither of these attitudes is correct.

The Almighty put us in this world in order to have an intimate relationship with us, both in this world and in our spiritual afterlife. We partly develop that relationship through prayer. Lacking things such as health, children, a marriage partner, money, and the like can motivate us to draw close to Him when we realize that we require His help to get what we need or want.

Talking to our Creator from our hearts is never useless. He always hears our sincere prayers. Sometimes He gives us what we want, and sometimes He doesn't. But no sincere prayer is ever wasted, because it always succeeds in creating spiritual goodness in the world and brings us close to the Almighty. That is valuable in and of itself.

This is similar to what happens when a parent and child have a loving relationship. The closeness between them is valuable in its own right. There are times when a child tells the parent about difficulties that she is having and the parent knows that it won't be good for the child if the challenge is taken away. The child needs that challenge to develop. In such instances, the parent gives love, reassurance and a listening ear instead of resolving the problem.

We have to develop a similar kind of childlike trust in God. Since He made the universe and has a plan for each of the billions of people in it, as well as for humanity as a whole, we need to accept that He knows what is best for us and the world. If He withholds giving us what we ask for, He must have a good reason for so doing.

At times, He eventually reveals to us why what we thought we needed was not in our best interest, or wasn't good to have happened at that time. At other times, we simply need to have faith. Successful prayer is not about our learning how to manipulate the Creator of the world. It is part of a process where we strive to understand how we are supposed to live and become who we were meant to be. Developing the faith to accept God's agenda when it clashes with ours is an important component of this.

## WHAT IS PRAYER?

The Hebrew word for prayer is *l'hitpallel*, which means "to judge oneself." When we pray, we are supposed to think about why we should get what we are requesting. If we get it, will we use it to further God's plans for the world or only our own? When we pray, we are also supposed to introspect about how we have used the gifts that the Almighty has already given us, and modify our attitudes or behavior if we are not using them for a spiritual purpose.

It is legitimate to ask our Heavenly Parent to provide us with what we need; however, if we pray so that we can get Him to do what we want, without being interested in what He wants, that is not prayer. Prayer is supposed to forge a relationship where we yearn to connect with the Being that gave us life so that we will have the pleasure and reward of having a meaningful closeness with Him.

Since the process of praying meaningfully is difficult for most people, it is very tempting to take the easy way out and either not pray or just give lip service. We are supposed to devote time and energy to trying to develop a personal relationship with the One Above. To do that, we normally use the same kinds of skills (such as communication and learning about the other) and overcoming the same kinds of challenges that we have in our human relationships. Some people prefer to view a rabbi, cantor or religious teacher as their surrogate in this process. Just as we can't appoint someone else to be the husband or wife that we were meant to be, we have to invest the time and effort in our relationship with God for it to be meaningful.

For traditional prayer to be meaningful, one has to study what the words mean, why the structure of the daily prayers is what it is, and the significance of the things that we mention and ask for. While a person can pray in any language, and it is good to speak to our Creator from our hearts, the standard Hebrew prayers have a special metaphysical impact on the world. If one reads a book that explains the Jewish prayers, it will usually turn traditional prayer from a baffling and frustrating experience to one that is meaningful and inviting.[166]

Our morning prayers begin with our recognizing and appreciating many of the good things that God does for us that we typically take for granted. He gives us life, bodies that function, clothes that protect us, and much more. It is important that we recognize the Source of everything that we have as well as the many kindnesses that He does for us 24/7. We reciprocate His continual gifts to us by observing the   Torah.

Just as some mothers hope that their children will make the world a better place, so does the Almighty put us here with similar intentions. If a child doesn't appreciate what his parents do for him, and misuses what he is given, a wise parent will stop giving to him. Until the child is willing to use what he gets in a constructive way, a parent would be irresponsible to keep acceding to the child's request to give him things. Sometimes God acts similarly.

Our Heavenly Parent wants each of us to look for, and find His Presence in every facet of our lives. He created a world whose materialism can obscure how He acts behind the scenes in our daily lives. He directs what happens to us moment by moment, yet still gives us free will to find Him and live in a way that will bring spiritual blessing to the world—or not.

Human beings are the crowning achievement of the universe that the Creator put here. When we take what He gives us materially, intellectually, physically and emotionally and use those gifts to serve Him, we bring His goals for Creation to fruition. If we pray for Him to give what we want with no regard for how it can serve spiritual purposes, we may be asking the Almighty to help us be happy while we destroy ourselves or others spiritually.

This is one of many reasons why our prayers are not always answered in the way that we would like. We often ask for things that are not ultimately in our best interests. We also have no idea how others will be affected by our getting what we want.

For example, if we pray to win a lottery, who will we be if we become rich? Will we use our newfound wealth to create a closer bond with God? Will we use the money to become more dedicated to observing the Torah? Will we become more conscious of God's Presence in the world and use the money to help others? Perhaps He doesn't allow us to win the lottery because He knows that a year after winning we will be overly focused on ourselves, take credit for our choice of the right numbers, and forget the Being who made our wealth possible. It could also be that we don't win a competition because someone else needs the prize more!

When God's answer to our prayer is "No," sometimes it is a message to us that we are not yet ready to receive what we think we need. If we work on ourselves to receive more appropriately, we may make ourselves worthy of getting what we prayed for at a later time.

For example, a woman could be childless and want a baby so that she won't feel lonely, or so that she can be like all of the other women that she knows. Meanwhile, she doesn't have the patience and is too self-centered to be a great mother. If the Almighty makes her wait, she might decide to work on her character traits and prepare herself for the challenges of motherhood. By the time she gives birth, she will be in a much better place to raise a child.

## GOD'S INVOLVEMENT IN OUR LIVES

God runs the world according to principles of general and specific supervision, and responds to our prayers accordingly. The Creator not only made the world, but continually supervises it in a general way. This is necessary because He has an overall plan for it that needs to occur by a certain time. His goal is for every person to recognize His Presence in all aspects of our lives.

He also guides the details of what happens to every Jew. He confronts us with specially designed situations every day, many of which are inherently neutral. If we are spiritually tuned in, we will use those opportunities to grow spiritually. If we choose otherwise, those opportunities will be lost, and we may even use them destructively.

To illustrate this idea, suppose that someone gets a good job. Some people would attribute this to their abilities, good references, impressive interviewing skills, and so on. Observant Jews, however, believe that one's abilities are factors, and we must make appropriate efforts to secure a job. Ultimately, though, it is God who determines the outcome.

Once we have a job, we can immerse ourselves in work, career advancement, and making money as ends in themselves. Instead, we should continually ask, "Why did the Almighty help me get this job? How can I use my work to further the Creator's purposes? How should I use my job to further my spiritual growth? How would my Creator like me to show that I appreciate this gift?"

Ideally, we should view a good job as a divine gift that enables us to give more money to charity, spend more time or give us peace of mind to study or teach Torah, or serves other spiritual ends. The job might allow us to set an example to our Jewish and gentile co-workers of what it means to live a moral life and be a good person. Our co-workers can see that it is possible to eat only kosher food, to refrain from gossiping about others, to honor the Sabbath and Jewish holidays by not working on them, to be honest in business, and to keep proper boundaries in interpersonal relationships.

Sometimes God uses our job to challenge us spiritually. Will we keep our religious resolve when we are pressured to enjoy non-kosher food during social functions? Will we accept a job that requires us to work after sunset on Fridays and on Jewish holidays? Will we refuse to engage in unethical practices at work, even if it is common practice to lie, cheat or bill clients in that way?

We sometimes think that getting what we want must be a blessing. Sometimes it is and sometimes it isn't. Its ultimate goodness depends on how we use it. If we use a gift to destroy ourselves spiritually, it is no blessing. To quote Oscar Wilde, "There are only two tragedies in life: one is not getting what one wants, and the other is getting it."

People often think that vocational or financial success is the key to a happy life. Studies have shown that once people can afford basic food, shelter and clothing, having more money does not make people happier. Sometimes people have affluence and great jobs, but learn the hard way that it took them away from their loved ones and from what was really important in life.

Developing the attitude of being thankful and satisfied with what we have makes us happy. Not only isn't it a good investment strategy for God to give money to people who don't use it to help others, having money sometimes facilitates people becoming arrogant and self-centered. The more blessing we get, the greater is our responsibility to use it properly. When people misuse it, the Giver may decide to bestow His blessing elsewhere.

When we use the gifts that the Almighty gives us as means to lead a Godly life, He may then give us more of what we ask for. He may see that we will develop ourselves spiritually through ease, not only through hardship.

With these ideas in mind, we can now appreciate that prayer is our way of verbalizing to our Creator that we recognize and appreciate the many things that He does for us. Also, we create and deepen a relationship with our Heavenly Parent via prayer. Realizing our dependence on Him encourages us to ask Him for what we need to grow spiritually. When He responds to our requests, it makes us love and have faith in Him even more.

Still, like a child who doesn't have the experience or wisdom to know when what he's asking for won't be good in the long-run, we have to accept "no" as a legitimate divine answer. King Solomon, the wisest man who ever lived, stated this when he dedicated the Temple.[167] He prayed that God would listen to the prayers of individuals according to His knowledge of what they truly needed, not based on what they prayed for. This is because people sometimes ask for things that aren't in their best interest. This was elucidated to mean that Solomon asked God never to give Jews what they ask for when it won't be good for them. On the other hand, he prayed that the Almighty would always grant non-Jews their requests since they sometimes traveled long distances to offer sacrifices in our Temple. They would not believe in the true God if they didn't get what they asked for.[168]

Even when God says no, we can know that He has heard us. At such times, our greatest growth is in accepting that He has a good reason for His decision.

## THE RELEVANCE OF ANCIENT LITURGY

There are many reasons why our liturgy refers to Jewish historical events and why our prayers were written in Hebrew. The daily morning prayers make us aware of how much our Creator does for us every day. The preliminary prayers underscore how this happens to us personally, and the subsequent prayers highlight how He shows His power and goodness through nature. The latter prayers remind us of how God has intervened on behalf of the Jews throughout history. It is nothing short of miraculous that the Jewish people are still here after spending 2,000 years in exile among the nations of the world. Our prayers remind us that the Almighty kept his promise to Abraham that the Jewish people will be eternal, and that after exile we will live in the land of Israel. The fact that these promises have come true shows us that He has a 3,300-year track record with our nation. We should trust that He is also capable of and interested in giving us what we need in the present, just as He did in the past.

The reason almost all of our standard prayers are in Hebrew (the others are in Aramaic) is because Hebrew is a holy language, whose ideas cannot be expressed precisely in any other tongue. Even if we don't fully understand what we are saying in Hebrew, our prayers can have metaphysical effects and reach Heaven in a manner that no other language can.

It is beyond the scope of this book to explain the meanings of our prayers or the specific reasons why they mention certain historical events. However, we can learn a critical lesson from the fact that our prayers refer to our ancestors' lives.

Since the time of Abraham, our faith in God has been challenged. Our forefathers, foremothers, and the Israelites who left Egypt all had to overcome barriers to their relationships with the One Above. Our ancestors were challenged by the same problems that we have relating to Him. For example, Abraham and Moses were troubled by God's apparent injustice. Our forebears had tremendous difficulties raising children who would be moral and get along with one another. Most of our foremothers were initially barren. Our forebears had to contend with natural disasters such as drought and famine that forced them to relocate. Yet, all of them prayed and developed more mature views of God by having to deal with these challenges. Referring to our forebears reminds us that we don't have such unique problems that we can't talk to our Creator about them. It also reminds us that we can (and should) grow spiritually through the challenges that God puts in our lives.

Our forebears and the sages who composed our prayers all struggled with their own personal tragedies,[169] and in many cases, with national ones as well.[170] Each developed his or her own way of relating to God in times of joy and tragedy. Throughout their lives, each had to come to terms with His ways of running the world and overseeing their lives. Each accepted that His wisdom, love and justice do not require Him to gratify our every desire, hope and demand. Our traditional prayers remind us that we can use the same approaches that our ancestors did to relate to our Heavenly Parent no matter what our life circumstances are.

## CULTIVATING CLOSENESS AND APPRECIATION

There really is no such thing as a sincere prayer that isn't answered. God runs the world in the best way possible to enable us to get the most out of life. Instead of letting us stay in spiritual kindergarten, He continually sends us challenges that spur us to have increasingly mature and accurate understandings of how He runs the world, and that encourage us to grow in our responses to Him.

The Almighty loves the Jews so much that He wanted our ancestors to experience Him as He truly is, not only as people want Him to be. The more you love someone, the more you want to share your essence with the other person and have the other person know you. Similarly, our Creator wanted our forebears to truly get to know Him. To that end, He sometimes revealed Himself to our ancestors as a Being who is loving and kind, and at other times as a Being who is powerful and who metes out justice.

When we were children, we had to learn that our parents could withhold giving us things that we wanted yet still be loving. If we want to have a real relationship with God, we must not misinterpret His not giving to us as His being absent or not caring.

Some people negate everything good that the Almighty does for them when He doesn't give them the few things that they ask Him to give. This is akin to a first grader being asked what his mother does and him saying, "Nothing." If she were asked the same question, she would probably say that she does everything! She takes care of so many of her child's needs— shopping, cooking, cleaning, reading him stories, nursing him when he is sick, taking him to school, carpooling him to activities, helping him with his homework, putting him to bed at night...the list is endless. He takes for granted all of the things that she does and gives her no credit for her actions. She, however, knows that her day revolves around taking care of him.

Just because we don't attribute to our Heavenly Parent the fact that we see, hear, smell, touch, walk, talk, eat, love and have myriad positive experiences every day, it doesn't mean that He isn't intimately taking care of us at every moment.

Part of being a Jew is training ourselves to appreciate what others do for us and expressing gratitude for it. We should do the same with God. He watches over us every night and gives us back our souls every morning. He gives us bodies that function with such intricate and interacting details that they put the most sophisticated computers to shame. He puts all kinds of legitimate pleasures in this world for us to enjoy. The magnificence of nature, the delicious tastes of food, the sweet aromas in the air on a spring day, the enjoyment we get when a baby laughs are all the doing of a Creator who loves us more than we can imagine. The least we can do every day is to think of the pleasures and miracles that He makes for us and thank Him for them.

## THE WORK OF PRAYER

Our sages understood how easy it is to lose our excitement with talking to God if we use the same words to pray every day. That is why they encouraged us to continually imbue new meaning in our prayers.[171] Our standard prayers then become a springboard from which we embark on a personal journey to individual, original prayers, said in whatever language we are most comfortable.

This is why another Hebrew term for prayer is "service of the heart." For us to say the traditional prayers from our hearts, we have to study what the prayers mean, then think about their personal relevance to us. We also have to pray in a milieu, at a time, with a mindset, and in a manner that is conducive to prayer.

Most people can only pray meaningfully if they believe that God wants to hear from them. We need only to look for Him hiding behind the scenes—in nature, in the way that our bodies function, and in the events of our daily lives—to see how much He loves us. Like a loving parent, He always wants to hear what His children have to say. Prayer is our response to Him telling us that He is here.

Some people say that a main way that God talks to us is by our learning Torah. Yet if we listen carefully, we can notice that He also speaks to us through the events of our lives. The strange series of "coincidences"

:d to our meeting our spouse; not getting into the class that we wanted and taking a substitute class that led us to a more fulfilling career path; "accidentally" meeting someone who changed our lives; getting that perfect apartment when there were no vacancies—none of these are coincidences. If we pay attention, we can continually see Him intervening in our lives.

A beautiful story is told about a little boy who was to become a famous rabbi. One day, he played hide-and-seek with his friends. He concealed himself in a wonderful hiding spot, then waited a long time to be discovered. When no one found him, he finally emerged. Much to his dismay, all of his friends had given up searching for him and had left long before.

He went home to his father and burst into tears. His father held him and asked what was wrong. The young boy replied, "I was playing hide-and-seek with my friends, and I hid in a great spot. A long time passed, and I realized that all of my friends had left without finding me. That was bad enough, but the worst part was that they didn't even care enough about me to look.... Now I know how God must feel."

## ELEMENTS OF JEWISH PRAYER

The *Shemoneh Esrai* has three main components. It begins by saying that God is "blessed." This means that He is the Source of all blessing that flows into the world. The Hebrew word for blessing comes from the word *beraichah*, which means "a source of gushing water." When we say the beginning words to any blessing, "Blessed are You, God," we are saying that the Almighty is the source of all blessing who wants nothing more than to let His blessing flow into the world.[172] We begin the *Shemoneh Esrai* by asking Him to let His blessing flow so that we can be conduits for what He most wants to do, which is to give to us. In this sense, saying a blessing is not only praising God. It is also our way of requesting Him to give His blessing so that we can use it for spiritual purposes, such as learning more Torah, bringing peace or comfort to people, or improving our character traits.

We begin every prayer service by praising our Creator. This is not because He is an egomaniac who needs our praise, but because we need to appreciate that He is the source of everything that happens to us. He is the Being to turn to for what we need.

Next, we ask Him to give us what we need, after first making sure that we have tried to become a worthy recipient of His blessing. In the

*Shemoneh Esrai*, we ask for things like knowledge, health, material blessing, and honest, moral leaders. Our asking Him for things implies that we have taken stock of ourselves and can assure Him that whatever He gives we will use to its fullest potential.

The third element of prayer is thanks. We thank the One Above when we conclude our prayers, even before knowing if we will get what we asked for. Doing this shows that we recognize that whatever our Creator does is ultimately for our benefit. Some of this we see quite readily, and some of it we don't. Thanking God before He responds to us transforms prayer from an attempt to manipulate or control Him to showing that we accept how He runs the world.

This kind of acceptance helps us to appreciate and love God even when we feel like He is not responsive to our needs, or is making life difficult for us. The more we trust Him, the more we make it possible for Him to show His love for us in ways that help us to grow more.

## ALTERING OUR PERCEPTIONS OF GOD

There is a story about a man who died and went to heaven. There he met his Maker, who showed him a video of his life. At the bottom of every scene were two sets of footprints in the sand on a beach representing God accompanying the man on his journey through life. From time to time, the video showed the man going through an especially difficult time, and only one set of footprints remained. When the man saw that, he burst into tears.

"My Heavenly Father," he cried, "how could you have abandoned me in my times of greatest need?"

God responded, "My beloved son, I never abandoned you. Where you see only one set of footprints, that is where I picked you up and carried you."

If we approach prayer with the right mindset, we can transform our perspectives about God, the world, and ourselves.

# 7

# Women and Prayer

One of the greatest barriers to modern women exploring traditional Judaism is their perception that they are excluded from any meaningful roles. This seems most apparent in the ways that men and women pray. In an Orthodox synagogue, men lead the prayers. Men and not women are counted in a *minyan* (ten men who are needed to say the public prayers). Men, not women, are called up to the Torah (given an *aliyah*). How are women supposed to be anything but second-class citizens if they are excluded from all of these meaningful opportunities?

The Torah's ideas about women and prayer can only be understood within the overall purpose of being Jewish. Since one possible reason that God made the world was to create opportunities to give to us, both men and women are here because He loves us. We can easily feel this love when we see a majestic sunset over the ocean, smell the fragrance of beautiful spring flowers, or feel a delightful cool, summer breeze on our warm skin. Our Creator "hopes" that we will understand and appreciate that He puts all of these in the world for our benefit. Yet there is much more to life than our getting pleasure for which we give Him periodic thank you's. He also asks us to observe His commandments so that we can earn the goodness that He wants to give us.

One of the major purposes of the Jewish nation is show the world how to live as moral people who do God's will. Each of us is supposed to serve the Almighty with our unique strengths and challenges. Doing this fulfills both our individual and national missions.

Originally, each of the twelve tribes that comprised the Jewish nation used a slightly different version (*nusach*, in Hebrew) of prayer. Each *nusach* was designated as the particular vehicle by which each tribe was supposed to communicate with God.

Today, there are various prayer *nusachs* that were associated with Jewish communities in the Diaspora. For example, *Nusach Ashkenaz* is used by Jews who lived in Western Europe and much of the FSU. *Nusach Sefard* is prayed by Jews who came from many Mediterranean and Middle Eastern countries. *Nusach Ha'Ari* is the prayer version used by Lubavitch Chassidim. These and other versions of standardized prayers derive from the original twelve versions that were said by the Jewish tribes. We are not normally allowed to change from a *nusach* our personal ancestors used to a version that belongs to another group. This illustrates the uniqueness of each tribe's path for gaining access to God.

## DIFFERENT CONTRIBUTIONS

In addition to using different styles of prayer, each tribe had unique strengths with which they served God. For example, two tribes, Yissachar and Zevulun, developed a partnership. Yissachar studied Torah all day while Zevulun supported both of them by engaging in commerce. (The tribe who worked, and thereby enabled his brother to study Torah full-time, earned the same spiritual reward as his brother.)[173]

Another tribe was renowned for its military strength. It made its unique contribution conquering the Israelites' enemies and making it possible for the Jews to settle peacefully in the land of Israel. Judah was the tribe from which Jewish royalty descended. Part of the tribe of Levi became priests and performed the rituals in the Tabernacle and Temples. The other Levites played musical instruments, sang praises to God, and ministered to the priests. Many priests and Levites also taught other Jews Torah.

By combining all of our different strengths and observing the divine commandments that pertain to each of us, Jews can serve God personally and nationally. But things fall apart when people usurp roles that don't belong to them or abdicate roles that do. A priest (*cohen*, in Hebrew) cannot renounce his priesthood because he finds the rules barring priests from contact with corpses too restrictive. (Many observant Jews of priestly lineage avoid becoming doctors because of the prohibition against contact with corpses.) Nor can he decide to abdicate his priesthood if he falls in love with a divorcee and wants to marry her. (Priests may marry widows but not divorcees.) Every priest has a unique contribution to make through his priestly duties as well as his restrictions. Jews who are non-priests are forbidden to perform priestly rituals such as conferring the priestly blessing on the Jewish people, and they may not enter parts of the Temple that are reserved for priests, on pain of death.

It is important to note that Jewish roles that confer status, power, and visibility are always accompanied by corresponding restrictions. (The same is true of rights always being accompanied by responsibilities.) Restrictions insure that the roles will be used as vehicles to serve God, not as means for grabbing greater personal power, prestige, money, or honor.

For example, Jewish kings had one of the most powerful and prestigious positions in Jewish society. Unlike most secular kings, a Jewish king was not supposed to use his position for personal aggrandizement. The king was also held to a standard of moral behavior that was generally more stringent than what the King of Kings applied to people at large. Moreover, the king was divinely punished accordingly for even small infractions. Thus, King Saul lost his monarchy for failing to do one thing that he was instructed to do with an enemy nation.

Special laws applied to kings, such as needing to have two Torah scrolls in their possession, one of which they carried at all times. These laws reminded kings that their power was to bring greater glory to God as they showed the people exemplary moral behavior. Their modeling and leadership also helped the nation maintain high moral standards.

## USURPING OTHERS' ROLES

Judaism stresses the importance of each person making her unique contributions to the world, not somebody else's. We may not fully understand why the One Above chose us to have our role and challenges in life. Yet, we accept that whatever role, challenges, and strengths He has assigned us, we should use to do His bidding.

There were many times that Jews usurped roles that were intended for others. One example occurred more than 2,000 years ago, after the Maccabees won a military and spiritual victory over their Greek oppressors. This war resulted in the holiday of Chanukah. The Maccabees were a priestly family, descendants of Levi, whose role was to minister to God in the Temple. After the Maccabees' victory, they rededicated the Temple that the Greeks had defiled and reinstated Jewish ritual service there. However, they also usurped the monarchy and made themselves kings over the Jewish people.

According to Nachmanides, a medieval Jewish commentator and

brilliant rabbi, once kings from the tribe of Judah reigned over the Jewish people in Israel, members of other tribes were not allowed to rule.[174] This meant that once King David ruled, hundreds of years before the Maccabees, the monarchy belonged solely to Judah's descendants. The Maccabees risked their lives, and in many cases died, fighting the Greeks and their followers. Even though they gave the Jews their independence and rededicated the Temple, those who usurped the monarchy were severely punished. Their entire dynasty perished within several generations for misappropriating a role that did not belong to them.

Similarly, a previously righteous king named Uziah decided that he should burn incense in the Temple as the priests did. Eighty-one priests confronted and warned him to leave for trying to appropriate a role that belonged to the priests. "It will not be an honor for you from the Lord God," they admonished. When he refused to desist from offering the incense, God afflicted him with a serious skin ailment that required him to live in shame and relative isolation. He lost his preeminence as a king and stayed sick until he died.[175]

When Jewish women abandon their given roles and insist on getting recognition and status by usurping men's commandments and roles, they miss the point of what being a Jew is all about. From the Torah's perspective, our actions are only valuable insofar as we follow God's will. By definition, we can only serve Him by doing what He asks of us, rather than rejecting it, no matter how emotionally satisfying doing what we want feels.

## FEELING IMPORTANT

The fact that men are obligated to do more commandments than women does not imply that men are more important than women. Judaism determines status by how well we fulfill the mission that we were given, not how well we do someone else's task.

This equating quantity or visibility of *mitzvot* (commandments) with men's greater importance highlights one of the many clashes between secular values and Jewish ones. Many people erroneously believe that traditional Judaism does not give women status. It does, but not necessarily in the ways that the secular world values. This partly reflects the fact that Judaism doesn't value what the secular world values.

For example, one way that status is determined in the secular world is by how visible or famous someone is. God is not impressed by how many people know or see a person. To the contrary, Judaism urges both men and women to strive to be modest and private, with rare exceptions. A Jew's spiritual heroism mostly occurs in private, as we strive to control our animalistic and egocentric drives and direct them to serve God. Women are supposed to cultivate a private relationship with the Almighty as a primary value while men are supposed to do this as a secondary value.

Jews admire strength insofar as it represents moral fortitude in overcoming our desire to sin. Men's performing priestly functions, leading public prayer, and saying *Kaddish* (a prayer that sanctifies God's Name) are not valuable because they give men public honor and visibility. They are important only because the Almighty wants or commanded men to serve Him in these ways. Women may try to increase their status by being more visible in the synagogue, getting *aliyot* to the Torah with men, or by becoming cantors or "rabbis." Doing these may feel good, but they don't serve God because He didn't ask them to worship Him in these ways.

Our success in praying depends upon how well we forge a relationship with our Creator. This is based on how He wants us to connect with Him. When He invites us to pray, we are not supposed to express our personal feelings in any way we please. Just as there is a protocol for how one has an audience with a mortal king, there are rules that govern how we may stand in the presence of the King of Kings. We should not think that just because He is God, we can approach Him in any way we like and that He will be pleased by our efforts. Nor should we think that just because the way we behave feels good to us that God must think as we do. This is why He gave us Ten Commandments, not Ten Suggestions. He tells us the ground rules of how to have a relationship with Him. We don't tell Him what it should look like. We assume that if He found it necessary to tell us to do things that defy our ideas of what is best, He must have a good reason for wanting us to do things His way.

Our standard daily prayers offer us a regularly scheduled audience with our Creator. There are certain rules that pertain to when we have these meetings. These include how we should dress, when we should say various prayers, where we may not pray, and so forth. If we want to say prayers with a group in a way that it constitutes public prayer, additional rules apply. One of these says that public prayers may only be offered in the presence of at least ten men, known as a *minyan*.

## MINYAN

A *minyan* is a quorum of ten men who are equally obligated to pray publicly. Women cannot be counted as part of this quorum because they are not obligated to participate in public prayer. Various rabbinic authorities state that men are required to pray with a *minyan*,[176] whereas others disagree.[177] Even though it is generally considered to be a rabbinic edict that ten men, and no number of women, constitute a *minyan*, the concept of a *minyan* was based on the biblical episode involving the ten male spies (see Chapter 4). These ten men brought back an evil report about the land of Israel to the other Jews, thereby causing the entire population of men to despair about conquering and settling the Promised Land. As a result, all of the adult men of that generation died, thereby delaying the Jews' entry into the land of Israel by an additional thirty-eight years.

This incident led a leader of the Jews and his court of law to realize that male Jews were apparently deficient in their ability to worship the Almighty, based on their misbehavior when they convened as a group. To rectify this, the Jewish leaders wanted men to train themselves to convene as a group only for holy purposes. This would require the same minimal number of men who had previously gathered in order to do evil. The rabbis prohibited men from saying certain prayers as a way of guaranteeing that men would congregate for holy purposes. The rabbis might also have done this as a way of emphasizing men's degradation and imperfection. After the incident with these spies, men were no longer individually capable of communicating properly with God. Only by gathering together with the force of a group would they be worthy of having their Heavenly Father join them.

With respect to women, however, the Jewish leader and his court said, "You never sinned. You never gathered together in a group to do evil. Therefore, we have no reason to decree upon you that you must gather together to do good. No individual woman has anything inherently lacking in her ability to communicate with the Almighty without anyone else's assistance."

These Israelite women did not sin because each independently decided not to be swayed by public opinion. They did not have to assemble publicly in order to form a group consensus not to follow the men. They saved themselves by individually deciding to leave the mob and return home. Therefore, the decree that requires men to join a *minyan* in order to pray never applied to women.

Over the course of centuries, the original rationale for this decree was forgotten, and people made up all kinds of reasons as to why women were not obligated to pray publicly. One such rationale is that a woman's obligation is primarily to her family. In actuality, women were never obligated to pray in a *minyan*. They retained the original status of being allowed to pray alone, as did our Patriarchs and Matriarchs. Such individuals of great stature prayed individually.

The Talmud expresses this concept by saying that all people were originally created from one individual to emphasize the importance of each person being a complete world unto him- or herself.[178] A woman possesses such holiness and purity that she does not need a *minyan*. It is therefore ludicrous for a woman to want to be counted in one. The decree was enacted on men because ten of them are required in order to fix their original deficiency.[179]

We can readily understand how the value of a *minyan* is not because it makes men visible, ergo important. Its value is that it creates an environment where God promises to hear any member's prayers, regardless of his personal, individual merit.

When any Jew prays with a *minyan*, part of the Almighty's covenant with our people obligates Him to "hear" those prayers. This does not mean that He will automatically do whatever the group asks of Him. However, if an individual is not personally worthy of having the One Above hear his or her prayers, or does not pray with appropriate concentration, God will still give him or her an "ear." This is because a quorum represents the Jewish nation at large, which collectively has merits that exceed those of any individual. These collective merits might allow the Almighty to consider requests that would not otherwise be heard if they were not said with proper sincerity.

Throughout Jewish history, there have been individual men and women who have gained an audience with the Creator through their personal prayers, independent of whether or not they prayed in a *minyan*. However, it is to our benefit to pray in a forum where we are guaranteed that our unworthy prayers will at least be noted.

That it is not men's greater importance that allows them and not women to form a prayer quorum is highlighted by the following situation: If a Jew is ever called upon to choose between violating a Jewish law in private or being killed, he or she must violate the law rather than give up his or her life.[180] On the other hand, if the Jew is told to choose between violating a Jewish law publicly or forfeiting his or her life, the Jew must allow him- or herself to be killed. Under these circumstances where sanctifying God's Name is at stake, many authorities consider that ten Jews of either sex constitute a public group,[181] in whose presence a Jew must die rather than transgress any Jewish law. Thus, there are times when ten women constitute a public group, as a representation of the Jewish nation at large. However, they never do this with respect to prayer. If they were not deemed equally important to men, they would not represent the Jewish nation when sanctifying God is at stake.

## PUBLIC VERSUS PRIVATE

Women were not obligated to perform commandments that are done in public. This may be because such involvement could conflict with their first priority to develop their internal and family roles. Nevertheless, if a woman wishes to pray with a *minyan*, it is laudable for her to do so, provided she has the time and the inclination. Yet, our rabbis felt that women can pray more authentically when they are alone than can the typical man. The Talmud even tells us that God counts a woman's tears, suggesting that He is sensitive to women's feelings even when we do not formally verbalize them to Him. Therefore, when women insist on being counted in a *minyan*, they denigrate their abilities to communicate with God. If He tells us that we have enough merits to be heard when we pray sincerely in private, why clamor to insist that He only hears us when we participate in public prayer?

Since women are obligated to pray, but not in public, secular people often interpret this as a denigration of women's worth. This attitude reflects a lack of understanding of the Jewish concept of obligation and prayer. In the secular world, that which is private has little status. In the Jewish world, we have status when we fulfill God's will. Sometimes our divine mandate is to serve Him in private, and at other times we do so in public.

Judaism sometimes places more emphasis on the importance of serving the Almighty in private than in public. For example, although the Written Law was given in front of the entire Jewish nation at Mount Sinai, the Oral Law was given to Moses in private. God taught it to him during a forty-day "face-to-face" encounter where Moses was hidden inside a cloud. Although the Written Law is very important, it is the Oral Law that explains how the Written Law was meant to be observed.

A second example of the importance of private prayer was reflected in the Yom Kippur services that took place in the desert in the Tabernacle, and subsequently in the two Temples. This was the holiest ceremony of the year, in which the High Priest atoned for the entire Jewish people. The central ceremony of the day occurred in private in the Holy of Holies, where no observers were allowed.

A third area that stressed privacy was in prophetic communication. In most biblical instances of prophecy, God communicated to the recipient when he or she was alone. For example, all of our forefathers and foremothers received prophetic communication from the Almighty, typically when each was alone. Moreover, the women's level of prophetic knowledge was sometimes higher than that of their husbands.

Moses' first encounter with God at the burning bush, as well as most of the subsequent divine communications with him, occurred privately. Even the prophetic visions that each Jew perceived at the Crossing of the Reed Sea and the Giving of the Torah at Mount Sinai can be viewed as private, divine communications to masses of individuals, who received prophecy simultaneously.

Just as prophecy occurred with many individuals, each of whom received a private communication from the One Above, public prayer allows many individuals to pray simultaneously, while each person relates to the Almighty on his or her level. Although the forum for public prayer requires at least ten men, the laws about how both men and women should pray the *Shemoneh Esrai* were derived from the private prayer of a woman named Chana. We emulate her style, which was to pray alone and silently.[182] The Talmud uses her as the exemplar of how to pray the *Shemoneh Esrai*.

## CHANA

Chana was married to a prophet named Elkana. During their many years of marriage they were unable to have children. He then married a second wife, Penina, with whom he had ten sons. Every year on the Jewish festivals, Elkana and his family would make the pilgrimage to the Tabernacle, which at that time was located in Shiloh. Every year the family would celebrate the holidays while Chana felt anguish because she remained barren.

One holiday, Chana realized that her husband had given up praying for her to have a child, and she knew that she could not depend on any intermediary to beseech the Almighty on her behalf. She went to the Tabernacle and prayed for Him to give her a son. She moved her lips in silent supplication and challenged Him: "Did You create me to be an angel or a woman? If I am childless because I am an angel, then I must be destined for immortality. However, since You created me with a woman's body, why don't You fulfill my purpose in having it and give me a child?"

Chana prayed with tremendous fervor, and ended her poignant prayer with the promise that if the Creator would give her a child, she would dedicate her son to lifelong divine service in the Tabernacle.[183]

Not only were her prayers answered by giving birth to the prophet Samuel, but she subsequently had four additional children. Something about her prayer so impressed the rabbis that when they compiled the most central daily prayer, they taught that we should pray it as Chana did. To this day, we say the *Shemoneh Esrai* with our hearts dedicated to God, our lips moving, and with our prayer audible only to ourselves, just as Chana modeled.

The significance of Chana's prayer can be better appreciated after reviewing an incident that involved two of Aaron, the High Priest's sons, Nadav and Avihu. Shortly after God gave the Ten Commandments, some male Jews sinned grievously by making the Golden Calf. The following Yom Kippur, the Almighty forgave them. He then asked the Jews to build a Tabernacle as a central place for them to worship Him. At the consecration ceremony, God sent a divine fire onto the altar to show His pleasure with the Jewish people.

Meanwhile, Nadav and Avihu decided on their own to offer God some incense that He had not told them to offer. Even though Nadav and Avihu had the purest of intentions and wanted to serve God with fervor, the Almighty's response was to kill them instantly.[184]

It seems shocking that God punished these two men so severely for expressing their religious passion this way. We normally think that our Creator wants us to pray to Him from our hearts, with spontaneity and initiative. If this is true, why did Nadav and Avihu elicit such a tragic divine response? We will return to this incident after discussing the meaning of prayer.

## COMMANDMENTS

When we pray to God, even out of love, we are not at liberty to forget that He is the Creator of the Universe, its Master and Director. We are obliged to recognize this in various ways, including following His rules. Just as He made the world with laws of nature that allow it to function, He also put in spiritual laws that allow it to function. When He put us in His world, He gave us an Owner's manual called the Torah that tells us how He wants us to lead our lives. His laws allow us to take everything in the physical world and connect it to Him.

Many people observe parts of the Torah because they make sense or are emotionally appealing. For example, most people don't murder because it doesn't make sense to take an innocent person's life, or because it will destroy the social order, and/or it might land them in prison. Many

Jews enjoy participating in a Passover *seder* because it creates a warm family atmosphere and they enjoy eating the delicious food. Some people observe other Jewish traditions because they lead to a more cohesive family. As satisfying as it might feel to observe Judaism this way, this is not serving God. The latter requires that we obey the divine will, not do things because they feel good or make sense to us.

We are supposed to do *mitzvot* to show that we believe that our Creator has the authority to command us. It is easier to do this when *mitzvot* are emotionally appealing or sensible, but we are still supposed to do them when they don't feel good (like fasting for 25 hours on the Day of Atonement) or aren't overtly rational (such as not eating shrimp, lobster or cheeseburgers). Observing *mitzvot* that we don't like shows that we accept that God has the right to tell us what to do. It also ratifies our trust in Him. If He tells us to do 100 things that make sense to us and that benefit us in appreciable ways, we can assume that the laws that we can't fathom must also be beneficial. When we only observe the laws that we like, and pick and choose among the others, we reduce the Master of the Universe to the level of an enlightened human being who gave us interesting suggestions about how to lead a fulfilling life.

Picking and choosing *mitzvot* to observe is serving ourselves, not our Creator. We are supposed to observe all of the *mitzvot* that apply to us, whether or not we enjoy them or find them intellectually appealing.

## Mitzvot Foster Relationships

There are as well other aspects of *mitzvot*. God created human beings so that we would have a relationship with Him. He gave us human relationships so that we could extrapolate from those how to have a relationship with a deity who isn't tangible. The Torah's *mitzvot* help us to have emotionally satisfying relationships with other people as well as with the Almighty. Since we don't know what is required to have an intimate relationship with a totally spiritual being, the Torah tells us what we must do to facilitate that, and what we must not do so that we don't destroy it. The effects of *mitzvot* go far beyond what we can see and feel in the physical world so we need the Creator of the universe to tell us about them.

Since we have human limitations, we can only evaluate whether or not a *mitzvah* makes sense based on how it overtly affects us or others. Yet there is an entire spiritual realm that is more real than the physical world. We affect it by our actions, speech and thoughts in ways that we cannot begin to imagine.

The root of the word *mitzvah* not only means "commandment," but also "attachment." Every *mitzvah* is a tool that the Almighty gives us to elevate our body and connect our soul with Him. Each person has so many facets to him- or herself. We have our personality, our mind, our body, our way of speaking, our life experiences, and so on. The Torah's many *mitzvot* enable us to connect every facet of ourselves to God.

Imagine a man who gives his beloved fiancée a variety of gifts. Each present acknowledges and draws out a different nuance of who she is and what she likes. Likewise, the Almighty gave us a large variety of *mitzvot* that were designed to help us to appreciate different aspects of Him. They also give us the tools to develop and bring into our relationship with Him every aspect of ourselves.

So, whether or not we observe *mitzvot* simply because God told us to do them, each one helps us to deepen our connection with Him. By accepting that divine knowledge is infinite and ours is not, we can do *mitzvot* whose rationales and effects we don't understand. Often, we will appreciate their wisdom and some of their spiritual effects more as we grow.

We can apply these ideas to how we pray. If our focus in prayer is, "Does this feel good to me? What is this doing for me?" a main function of prayer is missing. We should preface our prayers with the the desire to draw close to our Creator, feel gratitude and humility, and then say words that express our needs.

## PREREQUISITES FOR PRAYER

Prayer requires us to have certain intentions and concentration (*kavanah*). Maimonides wrote that there are two kinds of *kavanah* in prayer. One type requires that we minimally understand the meanings of the words in the first paragraph of the *Shemoneh Esrai*.

The other type of *kavanah* is the consciousness that we are praying before God. If that is lacking, our words are not prayer. Even if we understand the meaning of every word that we say in the Hebrew prayers, we must feel that we are standing in God's Presence or we are talking to ourselves or to the wall.

Praying requires us to think that God is the most powerful force in the world and there is no one else that we need turn to in order to get what we need. He created us and the world and continually supervises both. He runs nature and also makes things happen to us individually, continually responding to our moral/spiritual and immoral choices. Since He created us, we owe Him our very existence, and assume that whatever He makes happen to us is ultimately for our good. When we stand in His Presence, we feel awe for Him, gratitude and humility, and praise Him.

When we appreciate that God wants to give us what we need, we are overcome with love and we thank Him. The more we rely on Him for our sustenance, the more we trust and love Him. Our initial feelings of awe encourage us to praise Him. The feelings that follow encourage us to make requests of Him and to thank Him. Both feelings together enable us to pray.

## WOMEN'S OBLIGATION TO PRAY

Women and men are equally obligated to pray the morning and afternoon *Shemoneh Esrai* every day.[185] The *Magen Avraham* suggests an innovative idea to defend the fact that most women don't pray every day.[186] He attributes women's obligation to pray at least once a day to a Torah law that requires every Jew to pray on a daily basis. According to that opinion, any words that a woman says that praise God, ask Him for something, and thank Him fulfill her daily obligation to pray.[187] However, according to currently accepted opinions, women should say the *Shemoneh Esrai* every morning and afternoon,[188] and they are encouraged to say the *Shema* (Unification of God's Name) every morning and evening.[189]

When Jews had a central court in Jerusalem (known as the Sanhedrin), the rabbis spent nine hours a day praying. At each of the three daily prayer services, they spent an hour meditating and saying preliminary prayers, an hour saying the *Shemoneh Esrai*, and an hour drawing themselves away from the closeness with God that they had achieved and integrating back into this world. Even when they prayed in a *minyan*, each individual underwent a personal and private process whereby he developed his unique connection with his Creator. He appreciated what the Almighty had done for him and acknowledged his personal shortcomings that needed fixing. Then, he asked God for whatever he and the community needed for their survival and spiritual growth. Each person had to work very hard to create and sustain an intense bond with the Almighty every day, thereby exemplifying the "work" of prayer.

## MAKING PRAYER MEANINGFUL

How can modern women develop their connection with God through prayer? Here are four suggestions:

One method requires studying what various Jewish prayers accomplish and learning the specific meanings of their words. One can do this by attending classes, watching online videos or listening to taped lectures online, and/or by reading. Regardless of where a woman prays, if she doesn't understand what she is saying or the relevance of those prayers to her life, she won't feel that they connect her to God.

Second, we must make time to engage in the "work" of prayer. Meaningful prayer doesn't just happen, and it rarely comes easily to people. We have to work on ourselves to relate to the standard prayers. The more time and effort we invest in really understanding what each prayer means, and the more we practice focusing as we pray instead of thinking about the many distractions in our lives, the more meaningful our prayers can be.

Third, prayers in the Temple were accompanied by musical instruments and singing. For people who are moved by music, learning traditional or modern melodies and singing wordless spiritual melodies (*niggunim*) and prayers can heighten our emotional states and bring our hearts into our prayers. Music can be a powerful tool for strengthening our emotional bonds with God in a way that words alone cannot.

Fourth, we need to observe and appreciate how the Master of the Universe set up the world. If we look around us and notice the beauty and intricacies of nature, we will marvel at His Creations. We can see His "hand" in every part of Creation. The diversity of plants and animals and their interrelationships in ecosystems; the miracle of a seed becoming a fruit tree or a towering Redwood, a caterpillar becoming a stunning butterfly; the palette of colors, fragrances and designs of spring flowers; the majesty of mountains and glaciers all express the Almighty's love for us and testify to His involvement in the world. We can partially reciprocate this by showing our wonder and gratitude to Him giving us such wonderful gifts.

When we study the sciences, it can move us to praise our Creator for His genius in making the incredible workings of biology, the laws of physics and chemistry, and marvel at the universe. If we learn about each unique creature, organism, and cell, we realize God's greatness and vast wisdom is far beyond anything that human beings can comprehend. It is especially amazing to appreciate the symphony of all of the parts of our body. It is only their precise coordination every moment of every day that allows us to function. Even if we don't have anything that we feel we need, we can use this appreciation to thank the Almighty for giving us bodies that do such incredible things.

Mothers can use their unique experiences to shape how they pray. They can feel wonder at the gift the Almighty gave them, of creating a fully functioning human being from just two cells. They can feel such intense love for a child and know that it is just a fraction of the love that our Heavenly Parent feels for us. They can feel pleasure each step of the way as their baby develops and expresses her personality, and matures physically and intellectually. Imagine God's joy with us as we progress spiritually! Mothers can appreciate the beauty in the world through a child's eyes, and feel the intensity of a child's emotions that have not yet been stifled. Their unconditional love parallels the unconditional love that the Almighty feels for us.

When a child becomes an emotionally and spiritually healthy adult, a mother rejoices in his successes and accomplishments. This parallels how our Creator feels about our growth and good choices. Conversely, when a mother feels pained about a child's lack of appreciation, his squandering his time and energy in negative pursuits, or his rejection of her, she can extrapolate from this to how our Heavenly Parent feels when we make bad choices or reject Him.

There are many opportunities for mothers to thank God for all of their wonderful moments of mothering and not take them for granted. We witness so many miracles that protect our children from injury or death, and divine protection continually heals them from the many sicknesses of childhood. We can ask the Almighty for the wisdom, stamina and help that we need to raise our children to be emotionally, spiritually and physically healthy. This monumental, decades-long task continually changes as do our families.

We need to appreciate that it is not proximity to the holy ark or Torah scrolls in the synagogue that opens the gates of prayer in Heaven. Rather, it is our appreciating the unceasing divine intervention and His goodness in our daily lives, plus our desire to connect to Him that open channels of communication with God.

We see from Nadav and Avihu that the One Above's main desire is not for us to be zealous and innovate new ways of serving Him. He wants us to pray to Him in the ways that He has invited us to do so, and respect His rules for how to approach Him.

Some women feel that the way the Master of the Universe has asked them to serve Him is not good enough. They can insist, like Nadav and Avihu did, that they have to innovate praying in ways that express their fervor. While there can be great value to pouring our hearts out to God, we must also do so in a structure that He considers legitimate. It is not our place to approach the King of Kings insisting on doing things our way because we think that the way He asks us to pray is insignificant. When women feel that they only have legitimacy when they pray like men, replete with taking over men's roles in the synagogue, wearing *tallitot* (prayer shawls), *tefillin*, and the like, they are imitating Nadav and Avihu. They are missing the humility that we need in order to stand before the Master of the Universe and broadcasting that He must have made a mistake by giving us distinctively feminine roles.

Not everything about Nadav and Avihu's prayer was negative. Like them, we should try to pray with passion and achieve closeness with our Creator. Nevertheless, we must be careful not to overstep the bounds of our egos; we must allow the Almighty's knowledge of what is in our best interests to determine how we pray.

## SAYING *KADDISH*

Women frequently ask if they can say *Kaddish* for a deceased relative. *Kaddish* is a prayer written in Aramaic that sanctifies God's Name. It may only be said in a prayer quorum of ten (or more) men, which is sometimes difficult to find. There are times when nine men assemble for prayer, but it is impossible to get a tenth man to join them. In such a case, if a woman is allowed to say *Kaddish*, may she be counted as part of a *minyan*?

For the reasons stated earlier, women are never counted as part of a *minyan*. They are however, allowed to say *Kaddish* under certain circumstances. This requires elaboration.

Saying *Kaddish* in our prayers is of relatively late origin. A *midrash*[190] says that an orphan approached Rabbi Akiva shortly after the father's death. The boy wanted to bring merit to his father's soul, so the rabbi told him to say *Kaddish*.

Sometime later, the rabbis decided that whenever a parent would die, the son should say *Kaddish* in order to bring merit to the parent's soul. If a parent passes away and leaves behind a child who cares to sanctify God to the world, it reflects well on the parent. Since the parent's death motivated the child to sanctify God's Name, the parent's soul is rewarded for this.

The rabbis specifically enacted that sons and not daughters were obligated to say *Kaddish*. They recognized the hardships that it would place on women to have to abandon their families or neglect other pursuits to search for a *minyan*. Therefore, they never required women to say *Kaddish*.

Prior to the time that sons started saying *Kaddish*, only the cantor said it, and he did so on behalf of the entire congregation.

Nowadays, if a daughter wants to say *Kaddish* for a deceased parent who left no sons, she may do so, as long as a man is also saying *Kaddish* in the same *minyan*.

If a man or woman whose parents are still alive wants to say *Kaddish* for someone, the parents must give their consent.

If a woman wants to say *Kaddish* for a parent or other relative who left no close kin, she may achieve the same results by attending a *minyan* every day and answering "Amen" when another mourner says *Kaddish*. Under these circumstances, answering "Amen" is as if she personally sanctified God's Name.

Since it is no simple matter for most women to say *Kaddish* with a *minyan* every day, it is generally recommended that they choose a different option that does the same for the deceased's soul. It is preferable that they hire a man (usually someone who has lost one or both parents himself) to say *Kaddish* in her stead. Most *yeshivot* (men's schools for higher Jewish education) and some Jewish charities can arrange for someone to do this. (It is customary to give a donation to the *yeshiva* or charity if the person does not accept payment.)

Another option instead of saying *Kaddish* is for a relative of the deceased to observe an extra religious precept that was formerly neglected, or to do it more scrupulously than before. One can also give extra money to charity or sponsor Torah learning or lectures in memory of the deceased.

## WOMEN'S PRAYER GROUPS

The Women's Movement sparked a great interest in establishing women's prayer groups. These took place mostly on Shabbat and on the holiday of Purim and were attended by traditional Jewish women starting in the 1970s. All-women groups made it possible for observant women to lead services, sing melodies and harmonize the way they liked, read the Torah (or the *Megillah* on Purim), and get called up to the Torah while still conforming to Jewish law.

During the mid-1970s, certain religious authorities permitted women's prayer groups that followed the same rules that apply to women praying individually. It is technically permitted for a woman to lead a group of women in prayer. Since women are required to learn Torah, every morning they should say the same blessing that men say before learning Torah, followed by a short selection from the Torah and Mishnah. Instead of saying these blessings at home, or in the preliminary prayers, women in these groups would say the blessings over the Torah when they got called up for an *aliyah*. When praying with a women's prayer group, some women also wrapped themselves in a *tallit* that was specifically made for a woman, since it is prohibited for women to wear men's clothing and vice versa.

With the passage of time, the rabbis saw that these innovations were mostly so that women could act like men and thereby prove their equality with them. Their desire to pray in all-women's prayer groups was often so that they could join the bandwagon of secular feminism, rather than expressing a desire to pray more sincerely as a Jew. As this became more generally apparent, the technical compliance with Jewish law (*halacha*) became subject to an overriding objection to women cantors, reading from a Torah scroll, and wearing *tallitot* publicly in these groups.

Many of the women who were involved in these groups did not know what was forbidden to pray without a *minyan* and they made many mistakes, thereby desecrating God's Name. Since women can never constitute all or part of a *minyan*, groups of women are prohibited from saying prayers such as *Kaddish*, *Kedushah*, the repetition of the *Shemoneh Esrai*, and the invitation to prayer known as *Barchu*. Likewise, the Torah is not read publicly if no *minyan* is present. The potential spiritual benefit of these groups was more than offset by the disrespect to God that they displayed.

There is a principle that Jews are not allowed to imitate gentile customs. Once women's prayer groups were viewed as a means for achieving equality by doing what men do, they became forbidden because they emulated non-Jewish ways. Imitating non-Jews includes incorporating the philosophy of secular feminism into Judaism. There were no inequalities or inadequacies in the preexisting Jewish ways of praying that logic would have required changing. Therefore, it is no longer permitted for women to pray in groups where they read the Torah from a scroll. Also, women are generally discouraged from wearing female *tallitot*, since their motivation to do this is usually to make a statement that they are on par with men. If a woman is fully observant of all of the *mitzvot* that apply to her, certain rabbis permit women to wear a *tallit* in private when her desire is to find one more avenue by which she can serve God. Since she wears it in total privacy, her motivation cannot be to impress anyone by her equality, which is something that Judaism already grants her.

Over time, interest in all-female prayer groups waned. Either women attended traditional services led by men, or went to "egalitarian" *minyans* where both men and women lead the services, usually sit together, and women are counted as part of a *minyan*. All of these are practices that *halacha* forbids.

Today, there are only a small number of women's prayer groups that conform to Jewish law. They are called groups, rather than *minyans*. Rather than stressing how women can pray like men, they make it possible for women to pray more intensely than they might otherwise. Most of these groups prohibit men from attending, obviating certain technical problems that would arise from women singing in the presence of men.

Should a woman want to stand in front of her Creator and offer heartfelt prayers, she should certainly do so. We don't need to be visible to others to talk to Him.

## STANDING IN GOD'S PRESENCE

A story is told about a rabbi who kept a slip of paper in each pocket. One slip read, "For my sake was the world created." The other slip read, "I am but dust and ashes." When we approach the One Above with the humility that comes from believing that we are but dust and ashes, we can stand in front of our Maker and be pleasing to Him. Once we have gained an audience with the King of Kings, we can have the audacity to ask Him to grant our petitions and change the world for our sake.

We can now understand why our sages viewed Chana's prayer as the model for all subsequent prayers. Her initial belief was that God was the Creator and Director of the world, and she felt humbled by this.

When some people feel very humble, they think they are too insignificant for God to hear to hear their prayers, and they can't pray. Such people feel that they have no right to ask the Master of the Universe to listen to them.

What was special about Chana was that in her humility, she realized that if God is all-powerful, she *must* ask Him for what she needs. If He won't help her, how else can she become spiritually fulfilled? Realizing that He wanted her to ask Him to provide for her, and to know that He would hear her prayers, she felt that she merited having the world change for her sake. With this insight, she was able to pour out her heartfelt prayers to have a child.

Chana's mode of praying was the ultimate. She taught us that God wants us to know that He can provide everything that we need, but we need to pour out our hearts and ask. It is not intermediaries, standing in a visible place in front of a congregation, fancy apparel, the Temple, or pyrotechnics that compel our Heavenly Parent to answer our prayers. Our prerequisite to being heard is simply having the humility of Chana in coming before Him—first as dust and ashes, and then with the audacity of, "For my sake was the world created"—that invites Him to respond to our requests.

# 8

# "Blessed Are You...Who Did Not Make Me a Woman"

Without a doubt, a blessing that men say every morning challenges many people. Soon after waking, both men and women say a series of blessings that praise God for various kindnesses that He does for us every day, which we tend to take for granted.

The fourth blessing in this series has two versions, said by men and women, respectively. Men say, "You are the source of all blessing my Lord, our God, King of the Universe, who did not make me a woman (*ishah*)." Women say, "You are the source of all blessing my Lord, our God, King of the Universe, who made me (with the qualities that exemplify) His will (*kirtzono*)."

It is easy to misinterpret the content and intent of these two blessings. As a result, there have been countless articles, books and lectures that portray traditional Jews as misogynists who thank the Almighty every morning for not having made them so unfortunate as to be female. These critics further insist that the blessing said by women demonstrates their passivity in resigning themselves to second-class citizenship.

## RECEIVING WITH DIGNITY

It has been previously mentioned that our Creator put all of us here only in order to bestow goodness on humanity. If He simply gave to us unreservedly, without our doing anything to deserve it, we would feel like freeloaders. The Talmud says that a person would rather have a smaller quantity of something that he or she personally produced than a larger amount of the same thing that came with no personal investment or toil.[191]

He created us with free will so that we could make choices that accord with His will, and thereby earn His goodness which we then receive with dignity. When we make choices that go against His will, we become unworthy of receiving many of His gifts. We also forfeit the emotional pleasures of earning God's beneficence through our efforts.

If it were our nature to only want to do what the Almighty wants of us, and we were totally clear about what that entailed, we would follow His will all of the time. However, that would not be due to our free choice. We would not be tempted by any other alternatives! In order to make sure that we truly have free will to make Godly or non-Godly choices, He created human beings with two inclinations. We each have a part of us that wants to soar higher and do what our Heavenly Parent wants us to do. We also have a competing desire that does its best to get us to act contrary to what He wants. These two inclinations are respectively known as the *yetzer hatov* and the *yetzer hara*.

## THE TWO INCLINATIONS

The *yetzer hatov* is what motivates us to draw close to and understand God and His will for us. It inspires us to do what He wants and gets great satisfaction when we strive to reach greater spiritual heights. The *yetzer hara* includes, but is not limited to, the part of our psyche that Freud termed the "id." It consists of our physical and egocentric desires that demand immediate gratification. People who want to eat whatever and whenever they please, to have sex when and how they wish, and to express their anger and aggression without restraint are motivated by their ids/*yetzer hara*. The *yetzer hara* wants us to gratify our animalistic and egocentric instincts in an unbridled manner. It wants us to think that we are the ultimate masters of our lives, the ultimate determiners of what we can and should do. It encourages us to legitimize and satisfy our drives for power, status, materialism, and the like.

The *yetzer hara* is very clever and has many modes of operating. When Adam was created, he had no internalized desire to oppose God's will. *Yetzer hara* for him was a theoretical idea, a potential force, but it was not an integral part of him. The *yetzer hara* was only internalized into people after Adam and Eve sinned in the Garden of Eden.

The biblical narrative about the serpent enticing Eve to eat the forbidden fruit was intended to be understood literally as well as allegorically. In that story, the serpent is termed a *nachash*. The Hebrew word *nachash* not only means "serpent," but also "to guess," or "to create doubt." The serpent was a representation of the *yetzer hara*. It attempted to create doubt in Eve's mind as to whether or not she should follow her Creator's will.

The machinations of the serpent and Eve were prototypical of how the *yetzer hara* operates and how it tempts the human being to succumb to its wiles.

The sole reason for the *yetzer hara*'s existence is to make us doubt whether we should follow the Almighty's will. Its job is to tempt us to disobey our Creator. Our job is to see it for what it is and refuse to succumb to it. The *yetzer hara*'s *modus operandi* were beautifully illustrated in the serpent's encounter with Eve.

## THE EVIL INCLINATION

The serpent used four arguments in its attempts to persuade Eve to sin. These four methods are paradigms for how the *yetzer hara* generally entices people to disobey God. First, it tries to convince us that the Master of the Universe has forbidden so much that it is impossible to observe His many commandments. Thus, the snake asked Eve, "Didn't God forbid you to eat of every tree in the Garden?"[192]

Since God had only told Adam not to eat from one tree, the snake wanted Eve to believe that what the Almighty had prohibited was simply too onerous for her to be capable of adhering to it all. Through this ploy, he wanted Eve to feel that if she couldn't obey everything that was expected of her, she may as well not bother with any of it. The *yetzer hara* undermines what we accomplish by focusing on, and then exaggerating, what we cannot do.

The snake then told Eve that if she would eat of the forbidden fruit, "You shall not surely die."[193] The *yetzer hara*'s second ploy was to convince her that violating God's will would have no negative consequences.

The snake's third argument was that eating the forbidden fruit would result in Eve's "eyes being opened."[194] The snake wanted Eve to believe that the sensual pleasure from tasting the forbidden fruit would justify eating it. The *yetzer hara* convinced her that if sensual pleasures felt good, that must prove that they were meant to be enjoyed. In actuality, the pleasure inherent in various acts says nothing about whether they are objectively and morally good or not (as eating an entire pint of high-fat ice cream in one sitting proves).

When we focus only on the short-term effects of our actions, we are sure they will be positive and enjoyable. By doing this, we lose sight of how bad their long-term consequences will be.

The snake's final argument to Eve was that by sinning, she "will be like God."[195] One of the traditional commentators explained this to mean that she would be able to create worlds,[196] just like the Almighty did. This argument was especially appealing because human beings were created with a strong drive to be creative and productive.

People often complain that a moral way of life is too limiting and that it interferes with their ability to be creative and productive. Sin promises to open up new vistas for us, if we only avail ourselves of its opportunities.

In general, the *yetzer hara* convinces us to fall prey to the illusions of what sin has to offer—knowledge, power, and sensual pleasure, all to be enjoyed without negative repercussions. Sometimes, it even convinces us of how important, healthy or spiritually valuable it is to go against what God really wants us to do!

## FIGHTING THE BATTLE

Our lives are likened to battlefields. The Almighty created us with the ability and desire to serve Him, yet with a very strong, competing drive that encourages us to sin. We engage in a battle between wanting to do God's will and wanting to indulge our own desires until the day we die. Our Creator wants us to overcome these continual challenges so that we can become worthy recipients of the unimaginable blessing that He wants to give us.

Had God made us with these two competing desires, with no knowledge of how to win the battle, our lives would be chaotic and meaningless. However, He gave us the Torah and guidelines from our sages so that we can know how to win our spiritual wars. Of its 613 commandments, 365 tell us what not to do and 248 tell us what we must do. Since the time of the Second Temple's destruction in 70 CE, we can only observe a fraction of these laws because many only applied when we had the Temple or when the majority of Jews live in Israel.

No single individual can personally observe all 613 *mitzvot* because many of them apply only to specific people. For example, a king must observe laws that don't apply to anyone else. The same is true for laws that are relevant only to Levites, while others apply only to priests or to non-priests. Some laws apply only to women, while others apply only to men.

Therefore, we don't only fight a spiritual battle as individuals, but we also fight a national battle. Every Jew has an important role to play in this national fight to do God's will. In this war, men are considered to be the front-line soldiers. In any war, combat soldiers have rigidly prescribed schedules of when to report for duty. In Judaism, men are the soldiers who have rigidly prescribed times when they must report for duty to the King of Kings. They partly do this by praying three times a day and saying the *Shema* within specific time frames every morning and evening.

In this analogy, men attend synagogue as part of their mustering for inspection and briefing several times a day. This constantly reminds them of their duties and charges.

In a war, soldiers are not free to exercise much personal choice as to whether or not to accept their responsibilities. Soldiers cannot make excuses and decide not to accept their missions. In this sense, *mitzvot* are neither suggestions nor personal preferences. They are requirements that, once delegated, need to be adhered to in order for the soldiers to be victorious. This is why we were given the Ten Commandments, not the Ten Suggestions.

Jewish women are like generals who are removed from the front lines in order to oversee the war away from the trenches. They cannot objectively evaluate how the soldiers are faring unless they are far enough away from the battlegrounds that they can view the war *in toto*. Women must be able to see the forest for the trees, whereas the men attend to more of the details.

This is one suggested reason as to why women are relieved from certain time-bound positive *mitzvot* and from public positions. Both of these situations might otherwise detract from their ability to oversee the total progression of the battles. Women are in charge of maintaining the troops' morale and replenishing their supplies.

## THE TWO TORAH SCROLLS

The Torah requires a king to have two Torah scrolls, one of which he must take with him whenever he goes out to war. He keeps the second one in his treasury and is supposed to read from it whenever he is home. One reason why this is necessary is because the Torah scroll that is taken into battle is likely to become worn and tattered, and in time may become illegible. Therefore, when the king returned from battle, he could read from a pristine Torah scroll in his chambers. That was an unadulterated version of what the original Torah said, without any distortions that resulted from going through a war.

Men and women have different individual and national roles through which they serve the Almighty. Men can be viewed as analogous to the Torah scroll that goes out to battle. After interacting with the outside world, they can eventually lose sight of what their true objectives should be. Jewish women can be viewed as analogous to the Torah scroll stored in the king's treasury. They are supposed to be guardians of the uncompromised, original Torah.

Today, both men and women come home from their days on the battlefield, and it is an ongoing challenge for each to keep his or her spiritual and moral compass. This is one of many reasons why it is important for both men and women to study Torah on an ongoing basis. Without enough Torah, it is easy for women to lose their spiritual focus and get overly involved with work as an end in itself, with socializing, shopping, eating, cooking, and/or with materialistic pursuits. Without daily personal prayer as well, it is easy for them to lose their ongoing connection with God.

When women are married, they are supposed to bring the Almighty into their and their family's daily lives. If they have internalized enough Torah, they can offer opinions when they think their husbands have become distorted by the pulls of the outside world. (Since many women do not have husbands who can be proper, objective spiritual mentors to guide them, a woman should consult such a person from time to time to make sure that she is on the right spiritual path.)

Women who are steeped in Torah values and who have good intuition model what God's true will is supposed to be. They were given the ability to continually draw their husbands and children back to proper standards. Through this process, women have often been the backbone of Jewish survival.

## "WHO DID NOT MAKE ME A WOMAN"

Since a woman does not have as many external "props" as men do to keep a proper perspective about what our Creator really wants of us, she has a much more difficult role staying spiritually strong than does a man. The regimentation of men's lives by assembling for daily public prayer and the requirement that they study Torah every day makes it much easier for them to successfully battle their negative inclinations.

This is one suggested reason as to why men praise God for not making them women. Men are grateful that He gave them the easier task of being foot soldiers rather than generals. Men have additional, specific commandments that help them conquer their negative drives. Women must act as officers, and they have fewer specific instructions as to how to plan their battles. They must use their intuition and intelligence in spiritual endeavors to a greater degree than do men, and their job is therefore fraught with much greater dangers.

As has been noted, Hebrew is a very precise language. A man says a blessing every morning that God did not make him an *ishah*. There is no precisely comparable word in English for this term. Had the blessing used the Hebrew word for female, *nekaivah*, he would be praising God for not making him a female. As we saw in the Garden of Eden story, *ishah* denotes a woman at the pinnacle of her spiritual greatness just as *ish* refers to a man at his spiritual finest.

One reason that has been advanced as to why the blessing is worded negatively (that the Lord "has *not* made me") rather than praising God for making man an *ish*, is because the Talmud says that it would have been easier for man had he never been born. Once people are born, they sin. However, insofar as man has been created, the Talmud concludes that He should examine his deeds and serve his Creator.[197]

Men have very mixed feelings about being born only to fight a lifelong spiritual battle. On the one hand, they are happy to have the opportunity to live a meaningful life. On the other hand, life is full of unending challenges, only some of which they will overcome successfully.

This situation can be likened to a chaplain who is drafted into a war. He can't thank the president of his country for drafting him because he would have preferred to stay out of the war altogether. Yet he is grateful that he is not fighting in a position where he may get wounded or die.

Similarly, a man can't praise God for making him a man because he doesn't know until the day he dies if he will succeed in accomplishing what he was put here to do. He can't be grateful for something he may never achieve—becoming a man of great spiritual accomplishment (*ish*). Therefore, a man doesn't praise God for making him a man.

No one can say that he was created as someone of great spiritual achievement because no one is born great. We may have tremendous potentials, but until we actualize them, they have no intrinsic value. In Judaism, our achievements are far more important than our potentials. Therefore, we try to develop our positive qualities in order to bring our potentials to fruition.

## DOING GOD'S WILL

One suggested reason as to why women praise God for making us with traits that are in sync with His will is because we were created spiritually similar to Him. His desire in creating the world was to give life to His creations, to whom He could then bestow goodness. Women resemble this ideal more than men, insofar as women can give birth, and they tend to be more nurturing than men are.

When understood in this context, it becomes quite obvious that the different blessings of the sexes do not disparage women (or men). If anything, they highlight the fact that when we get up in the morning, we have significant things to achieve in the course of the day ahead.

In fact, our saying these blessings simply continues a theme that begins when we open our eyes every morning. The first words we say are, "I thank You, living and everlasting King, that You returned my soul to me. Great is Your faith (in me)."

The first words we utter every morning are that God has faith in us. He believes that we are worthy of living another day and are indispensable agents for carrying out His plan for the universe. For this reason, He restores our souls to us every day, as a way of affirming that we have a mission. This short declaration reminds us that we can individually and collectively make a unique and indispensable contribution to the world every day.

Thus, when a man praises the Almighty every morning for not making him an *ishah*, he shows his acceptance of his mission. He simultaneously expresses his gratitude for being given many guidelines to help him become spiritually great. When a woman praises her Creator for making her according to His will, she accepts that she has a more difficult task than a man. She takes on that extra responsibility with enthusiasm because she knows that her Creator gave her the gifts to be successful in her endeavors.

## HISTORICAL BACKGROUND

Two blessings precede the present ones in the daily morning prayers. The first one says, "You are the source of all blessing my Lord, our God, King of the Universe, who did not make me a non-Jew."

The second one says, "You are the source of all blessing my Lord, our

God, King of the Universe, who did not make me a slave."

The present blessing says, "You are the source of all blessing my Lord, our God, King of the Universe, who did not make me a woman."

It seems very strange that this sequence of three blessings is all worded in the negative—what God did not make us. This unusual wording suggests to some people that we can only understand the blessing about "not making me a woman" in its historical context.

These blessings were formulated roughly 2,000 years ago, around the time that Christianity developed. Original Christianity was preached only to Jews who believed in the Torah and the necessity of observing *mitzvot*. After their leader died, Paul created an offshoot of his religion that was meant to appeal to pagans who wanted an easy road to heaven without the discomfort of observing *mitzvot*. He claimed that the laws of the Torah were anachronistic and that he got a revelation to dispense with them. This is why the New Testament states, "There is no longer Jew or gentile, slave or free person, male and female. For you are all one in (their savior)."[198]

This background helps us appreciate the theory that these three blessings were originally composed as a polemic against Christianity. One of many fundamental differences between Christianity and Judaism is that Jews believe that God meant it when He said that the Torah is immutable and irreplaceable, and that we must observe *mitzvot* in order to have a spiritually fulfilled life. He also meant it when He told the Israelites 3,300 years ago that He chose the descendants of Jacob to be His special nation forever. When He told the Jews that it is our job to be a spiritual light unto the nations by observing *mitzvot* forever, He didn't make a mistake.

The Church taught otherwise. It insisted that *mitzvot* had become irrelevant, and that God had replaced Jews with Christians as His chosen people.

Judaism teaches that deed is much more important than creed. We reinforce our belief in God by observing *mitzvot* that require us to act ethically in business, observe the weekly Sabbath and Jewish holidays, eat only kosher food, honor our parents, and love our neighbor as we love ourselves. Our character and beliefs are molded by how we behave. Creed in the absence of moral behavior is meaningless. We become Godly people because of how we live; we are not redeemed by shifting responsibility for our behavior to someone else.

The rabbis who composed our morning prayers wanted Jews to wake up every morning and appreciate the value of doing *mitzvot*, even though doing them can be difficult—especially in times of Roman and Christian persecution.

The author of the Gospel quote above wanted to erase the uniqueness of the Jews and denigrate the *mitzvot*. The Gospels claim that it doesn't do any good to observe the *mitzvot*. All one has to do is to believe in the Christian savior and he or she will get eternal reward.

According to Judaism, gentiles need to observe the Seven Laws that apply to the descendants of Noah. According to Christianity, no one need do more than simply believe and they get a free pass to heaven.

We can appreciate why doing *mitzvot* is so important by analogizing having a relationship with the One Above to being in a loving human relationship. Imagine your fiancé telling you, "I love you dearly in my heart, and I will never do anything for you." That's no relationship! A real relationship requires doing for each other—buying gifts and spending money on things that the other person needs or appreciates, communicating, learning to temper your desires and behavior for the good of the relationship, and the like.

*Mitzvot* require us to do the same. If you love someone, you get up in the morning and speak to them lovingly. We do the same when we pray. If you know your spouse enjoys a cup of coffee, you make it for him. Lying in bed and just thinking about the coffee doesn't make it appear. When you see that your spouse needs something, you do your best to make sure that he has it, and he hopefully does the same for you. And even though you might be more comfortable wearing worn and stained clothes whenever you are home, you dress nicely for him and are responsive to his feelings. Simply thinking about how you could be nicer, more attractive or more loving doesn't accomplish anything. Deeds are what count.

*Mitzvot* were designed to make us more spiritually refined, and to enable us to build bridges with the One who told us to do them. They are the tools for having a relationship with Him. Depending upon who we are, He gave us exactly those *mitzvot* that facilitate our using our life circumstances to be the best that we can be.

In the days when Jews owned slaves,[199] a slave needed to observe fewer time-bound *mitzvot* than a free Jew, because his first obligation was to use time to serve his master. As we discussed, women also need to observe somewhat fewer *mitzvot* than men. According to Christianity, everyone is the same—Jew, non-Jew, slave, free person, man, woman—no one needs to do *mitzvot*. Just believe and everyone goes to heaven.

To discourage Jews from thinking that we get a free pass in life by simply believing, the rabbis composed the three blessings mentioned above. By starting every day emphasizing what we are not, these prayers remind us that we are privileged to serve the Almighty as He has asked—by doing *mitzvot* that apply to us and that sanctify every aspect of life. We remind ourselves every morning that our Creator gave us free will as a great gift. We were meant to use it to spiritualize the world, rather than profess our helplessness. It is our job to make the world a better place using our thoughts, speech and actions. Our Creator did not put us here to live as Jews, give us a game plan for eternity, then change his mind midstream. He has the same plan for us now that He always did. It is a sacrilege to believe that a person must save us instead of believing that each of our choices has meaning.

Whichever rationale the reader prefers as to why men say the blessing "who has not made me a woman," we can know that this prayer was not meant to denigrate women. The rabbis were meticulous in making sure that we never say a blessing for nought. Every blessing they ordained is supposed to bring greater glory to God and help every Jew to become closer to Him.

# 9

# Separate Seating in the Synagogue

Perhaps no aspect of traditional Judaism is more disturbing to nonobservant Jews than the fact that men and women sit separately in traditional synagogues. Separation seems non-egalitarian and divisive, not to mention unfair to women. It is assumed that if women are seated to the side, behind or above the men with a physical barrier dividing them, the women cannot be equal participants in Judaism.

In order to discuss this topic, let's first understand how Jews prayed originally and how synagogues were a part of that.

In ancient times, pagans typically made offerings and sacrificed to their gods to convince the deities to give people what they wanted. Our forefather Abraham opposed this. He reasoned that there was no reason to worship idols, the sun, moon or other forces because there could only be one God who runs everything in the world. Abraham lived in a place where the locals believed in a moon god, yet the moon disappeared every morning and the sun seemingly replaced it. If a sun god was all-powerful, the sun should not disappear every evening. Abraham reasoned that there must be one omnipotent God who created the heavens and the earth and everything in them. Such a deity could only have put us here in order to be good to us.

When the author was young, school books credited the Jews with giving the world monotheism. But what difference does it make if there is one God or many gods? If there are many gods, none of them is perfect. Each is limited and has needs, making it possible for people to try to placate them by giving each what it lacked. In return, people believed the gods would reward them with rain, children, crops, health, and the like.

The kind of God that Abraham believed in was perfect. His only desire was for people to live by His code of ethics. If there is only one ultimate Power and Creator who made and controls everything in the world, He doesn't need us to give him food, or to sacrifice our children to Him. He also can't be manipulated by us to get what we want. His only desire must be for us to become the best we can be. Since God is perfect, becoming our best means becoming as much like Him as we can.

The imperfect gods that people created were in their image—or worse. The Greek and Roman gods engaged in the worst immoral behavior imaginable—murder, sexual immorality, theft, betrayal, and so on. The God of Abraham created man in His image. His only desire is that we become like Him—kind, just, moral, and so on—so that we can be close to Him and get pleasure from that relationship.

Our forefathers Abraham, Isaac and Jacob each found his own unique way to connect to God, and each had a special place where and time of day when he prayed. There, each could see God's works of nature, think about His interactions with them and the world, and experience the Divine Presence. Each of their wives communicated with the Almighty wherever she was in the course of her day.[200]

This kind of prayer became almost nonexistent after Jacob's descendants went into exile and were enslaved in Egypt. After the Israelites left Egypt, God told them to build a portable Sanctuary known as a Tabernacle, or *Mishkan*, where His Presence would be accessible to any Jew who wanted to find Him. This formal structure provided a central place where Jews could recreate the closeness to our Heavenly Parent that our forefathers and foremothers had once enjoyed in their daily lives.

Eventually, after the Israelites settled in the land of Israel, the *Mishkan* became a permanent structure in a town called Shilo.

Roughly 400 years later, King Solomon built a Temple on Mount Moriah in Jerusalem as the central place for Jewish worship. It stood for 410 years until the Babylonians destroyed it and killed or exiled most of the Jews who lived in Israel. Seventy years later, about 42,000 Jews returned and built the Second Temple in Jerusalem on the same site where the First Temple had stood. Around the year 20 B.C.E., King Herod flattened out Mount Moriah and built a huge platform known as the Temple Mount, surrounded by four enormous retaining walls. He renovated and beautified the Second Temple to a point where the rabbis said, "He who hasn't seen Herod's Temple has never seen a beautiful building in his life."[201] Around that time, as many as one million Jews made annual pilgrimages to the Temple on the holidays of Passover and Succot.[202]

Inside the *Mishkan* and Temples a prescribed series of daily offerings and prayers took place, plus additional ones on the New Moon and Jewish holidays.[203] These were designed to bring people close to God, on His terms. It was very important not to deviate from the prescribed rituals and ceremonies. These created a feeling of awe for God and respect for the sanctity of His "dwelling place" on earth. Anything that detracted from the sense that one was standing in the Divine Presence was forbidden or discouraged.

For example, it was forbidden to wear shoes in the Temple because the ground there was holy. While shoes give us a footing that enables us to walk, they are also a barrier between our feet and the ground. In the Temple, people wanted to connect to the holy ground, so they went barefoot.

It was also forbidden for people to take a purse or wallet with them onto the Temple Mount because we don't conduct business when we should be focusing on intimacy with the Creator.

Men and women had to immerse in a ritual bath prior to entering the Temple. That put them in a state of ritual preparedness for the awesome encounter with the divine that they were about to have. Barging into the Almighty's house without proper preparation and without regard for His rules had serious consequences.

It was during the Second Temple era that the first synagogues were built.[204] These were local, centralized places where Jews prayed and learned Torah[205] publicly instead of individually. During this time, prayer services paralleled the times of the Temple offerings and included some of the same prayers that were said in the Temple. The goal of the synagogue was to facilitate each person making his or her personal connection with the Almighty and create an atmosphere that was conducive for God's Presence to join them. Although the prayers were said in public, what each person achieved was intensely private.

In our lives, the fewer distractions we have, the easier it is to achieve intimacy with someone we love. Likewise, there are certain ways we should behave if we want to create an atmosphere of respect and awe for our King. The structure and rules of traditional synagogues are responsive to both of these needs.

## CONDUCT IN A SYNAGOGUE

In order to focus all of our attention and love toward our Heavenly Parent, we are not supposed to kiss people in the synagogue. Kissing our spouse, children, or friends shows that we love others when all of our affection is supposed to be directed to God.

Synagogues are not meant to be social halls with prayer services that help us feel content and happy. They are meant to give us a space to withdraw from the world in order to introspect, work on our relationship with the Master of the Universe, and feel love and awe for Him. One suggested reason as to why He gave us the ability to love is so that we could experience some part of how He "feels" about us and know how we should feel toward Him. We should feel grateful for having families and feel love for others in the synagogue; however, instead of expressing those feelings directly there, we channel our feelings in God's home to Him.

It is important to experience and develop meaningful human relationships outside the synagogue. We should experience a relationship with God everywhere, but we do it to the exclusion of everything else in the synagogue. Just as a married couple can relate most intimately to each other when they remove any distractions, we do the same in the synagogue by focusing our attention exclusively on our Maker.

The synagogue is God's home and we are welcome to sit in His Presence as invited guests. Just as there are rules about how guests should conduct themselves in any host's home, the same is true about how we behave in the synagogue. The Almighty has set rules about how He wants us to pray and gave us detailed plans as to how we should build our houses of prayer. Our Scriptures and prophets gave our ancestors precise instructions as to how to build the Tabernacle and both Temples. Today, even though there are many things that we may do to make our synagogues beautiful, awe-inspiring, and conducive to prayer, we are still not at liberty to design them completely according to our personal preferences. Our modern houses of prayer are still the Almighty's "home," and we build them to His taste, not ours.

Thus, we have divine rules about how we can encourage God's Presence to dwell on earth. Our synagogues need a specific design to make our prayers acceptable. We also need to be in a frame of mind that is conducive to meaningful communication with Him.

Humility is a prerequisite for prayer, and we must combine it with reverence for the synagogue. We are forbidden to do anything in a synagogue that detracts from our sense of awe at being in the Almighty's presence. For instance, it is normally forbidden to talk in a synagogue, with the occasional exception of asking for something we need in order to pray properly (as when asking where the prayer books are, or what page the Torah reading is on). We are likewise forbidden to eat or drink in a synagogue, to use it as a social hall, or to walk through a synagogue as a shortcut to get somewhere else. Nothing that transpires in a synagogue should distract us from feeling that we are humbly standing in the palace of the King of Kings. All of our thoughts, emotions, and speech there should be directed toward building closeness with, and reverence for, the Master of the World.

The Torah commands all Jews "to love the Lord your God and to serve Him with all your hearts and with all your souls."[206] The sages interpret this to mean that all of our powers and feelings should be used to serve God in prayer.[207] These feelings include our desire to do His will, as well as the desire we have *not* to do His will. These latter feelings include wanting to serve our own egos instead of using those feelings to serve our Creator.

We all have egocentric desires. We don't want to share what we have with others; we want others to honor us and give us attention, even when we don't deserve it. We may keep or take undeserved money from insurance companies or that a cashier wrongfully gave us, or take items from work that don't belong to us. If we acknowledge that these are immoral desires, we can change the way we direct them so that we use them to serve God. For example, we can get honor and attention by helping others or by giving charity to an organization that will put our name on a plaque. If it is hard for us to share material things with others, we can start by sharing our time and talents. In these and other ways, we integrate our feelings that want to serve God together with those desires that want to serve our egos, eventually worshiping our Creator fully.

One of the Torah's main functions is to teach us how to be holy. There is a specific *mitzvah* to be holy because God is holy. This is interpreted to mean that we must avoid inappropriate sexual relationships. Wherever the Torah mentions restraint against immorality, it is preceded or followed by a reference to holiness. "Whoever fences himself away from immorality is called 'holy'."[208] This teaches that any time we want to be in a holy place, or think holy thoughts we must first "fence" ourselves away from immoral thoughts and actions.

Part of being a holy people involves guarding ourselves against mingling with the opposite sex when it can lead to immodest behavior or inappropriate sexual thoughts. Even though many modern synagogues also serve as social or community centers, their true function is to be a place where we can draw down the Divine Presence and allow it to infuse us with sanctity. We must be especially careful to comport ourselves properly in such venues.

The Torah says, "My sanctuary you shall revere."[209] The Talmud adds that synagogues are to be regarded as miniature Temples.[210] Many of the laws that govern the synagogue's sanctity and the sense of propriety necessary there are derived from the laws that applied to the Temples.

## STRUCTURE OF THE TEMPLES

Each Temple was a rectangular building with several sections. The Western section included an area known as the Holy of Holies. In the First Temple,[211] it housed the Holy Ark that contained the tablets of the Ten Commandments and the original Torah scroll that Moses wrote. Only the High Priest was allowed to enter the Holy of Holies, and only when he performed a special ceremony there on the Day of Atonement (*Yom Kippur*). It was a capital offense for anyone else to enter there, or for the High Priest to enter there under any other circumstances.

The middle section of the Temple, known as the Holy, housed the *menorah* (seven-branched candelabra), the incense altar, and a golden table on which showbread was displayed. The eastern section was outdoors and had two parts: the Israelite Court had an altar for animal offerings and a laver used to ritually wash the priests' hands and feet before they performed their divine service.

At the far eastern section was a courtyard enclosed by a wall. This area was known as the "Women's Court." It was separated from the Israelite Court by a wall with a door in the center, with fifteen steps leading up to the Israelite Court. Women who wanted to pray at the Temple did so in the Women's Court. If they came with an offering, they brought it into the Israelite Court. The separate courts made it possible for both sexes to pray and offer sacrifices, but with a minimum of mingling.

## INTERMINGLING

There were ten miracles that took place every day in the Temple.[212] Its enormous sanctity and God's manifest Presence through these miracles were obvious to every Jew at the time. Even so, worshipers still had inappropriate thoughts and exhibited immodest behavior with the opposite sex when large crowds congregated in Herod's Temple. For this reason, special separations between men and women were added during mass celebrations there. At such times, women normally stood outside the courtyard and men stood inside.[213]

A tremendous celebration was held at the Temple every *Succot* (holiday of Tabernacles) known as the "Joyful Ceremony of Water Drawing" (*Simchat Bet Hasho'eva*). When it originally took place, the women stood inside the Women's Court and the men stayed outside on the Temple Mount. These two areas were separated by a physical divider (*mechitzah*) that the sages anticipated would allow the men to see into the Women's Court. What they didn't expect was the excess frivolity (*kalut rosh*), prohibited physical contact and immodest behavior that resulted[214] when men stood near one of the open gates to see the ceremony and rejoicing.

Subsequently, the sages arranged for the women to sit outside the Temple and for the men to sit inside. The sexes still mingled inappropriately. Finally, when the rabbis saw that a physical divider alone was not sufficient to prevent inappropriate mingling, they made an "innovation" for the holiday. They constructed a balcony where the women stood above while the men stood below.

It was prohibited to make engineering or architectural innovations in the structure of the *Mishkan* or Temples since they were built to exact specifications based on divine instructions. For example, King David told his son Solomon regarding building the First Temple:

> "Take heed now, for the Lord has chosen you to build a house for the Sanctuary. Be strong and do it." Then David gave Solomon his son the pattern of the porch, and its houses, and its treasuries, and the upper chambers, and the inner rooms, and the place (of the ark with its) covering....[David said,] "All this is written by the hand of the Lord who made me wise, even all of the works of this pattern."[215]

The sages understood from these verses that they were not allowed to alter the Temple plans that were prophetically revealed to King David. Therefore, they made sure that there was a scriptural basis for adding a temporary balcony.

## SCRIPTURAL BASIS FOR *MECHITZAH*

The scriptural basis for requiring the sexes to be separated during public prayer says, "The land shall mourn, every family apart—the family of David by itself, and their wives by themselves, the family of the house of

Natan by itself, and their wives by themselves..."[216] One interpretation of this mourning is that it refers to the eulogy for the Messiah, the son of Joseph.[217] He will be a man who will help the Jews materially and militarily. He will be killed in the cataclysmic War of Gog and Magog that will immediately precede the coming of the Messiah who is a descendant of King David.

We might think that when people are plunged into such deep mourning they will be too sad to act frivolously. Yet, it was prophesied that men and women should mourn separately at that time.

A Talmudic interpretation of the above verse from Zechariah says that the people will be mourning at a time when they no longer have a desire to do what is morally wrong. If the sexes must mourn separately under such circumstances, how much more is separation required when we have a desire to behave inappropriately! Thus, the rabbis reasoned that the sexes should be separated in the Temple when they will be distracted by the opposite sex from behaving with the proper decorum.

Some rabbis opine that the only reasons for the *mechitzah* and balcony in the Temple were to prevent the sexes from inappropriate conversation and touching. For example, Rabbi Moshe Feinstein, *z"tl*, a modern expert on Jewish law, concluded that the sages were not concerned about men in the Temple seeing modestly dressed women. The divider was needed only to prevent intermingling of the sexes.

However, Maimonides (a brilliant medieval rabbi) believed that the balcony was put in the Temple to keep the sexes from mingling[218] as well as to prevent the men from looking at the women.[219] Since a physical divider didn't achieve the latter goal, a women's balcony was built above where the men stood.

## SYNAGOGUE *MECHITZAHS*

Rabbi J. B. Soloveitchik, a contemporary of Rabbi Feinstein, ruled that a synagogue without a *mechitzah* forfeits its status as a miniature Temple, even if the men and women sit separately. Since its holiness derives from its similarity to a Temple, a synagogue can only be holy when it has discrete sections for men and women that are separated by a barrier.

According to Jewish law, a synagogue where both men and women pray must have a physical structure that separates the sexes.[220] This is preferably achieved with a balcony where the women sit above the men, as was done in the Temple. If this is not feasible, and men and women must sit on the same plane, there must be a physical divider that precludes interpersonal contact or conversation. Even if men sit on one side of the synagogue and women on the other, biblical law requires them to be separated by a barrier. Ideally, it should extend at least five feet from the floor and be approximately shoulder height. Lower than this will not prevent men from conversing with the women.

If women sitting in the balcony are modestly dressed according to Jewish law, Rabbi Feinstein opined that they need not be screened from the men's view, as seeing them will not lead to frivolity. However, if the women's upper arms, thighs, chests or hair on married women's heads are exposed, a curtain or screen must be put up so that the men can't see those body parts. This is because men are not allowed to say the *Shemoneh Esrai* or the *Shema* in a place where women's bodies are overly exposed.

When Reform Judaism began in the nineteenth century, it dispensed with most Jewish laws and rituals, yet men and women still sat separately for prayer services. The abrogation of separate seating for prayer had its roots in Christianity.[221] Isaac Mayer Wise decided to dispense with separate seating when he used a Baptist church to house his Reform prayer services for the High Holidays in Albany, New York. He liked the fact that Baptist men and women prayed together, and he initiated such seating in his own synagogue.[222] That paved the way for Reform temples, as a matter of course, to have mixed seating.

## ARGUMENTS AGAINST *MECHITZAH*

People who object to a *mechitzah* often maintain that no one gets distracted or has sexual thoughts when sitting next to someone of the opposite sex in a synagogue. Experience, though, tells us otherwise. If our minds and hearts are supposed to be totally focused on God when we pray, we would expect that attractive people of the opposite sex sitting near us will be more distracting than when we sit among the same sex. Whether or not the biblical law requiring separation of the sexes in the synagogue makes sense to us, it stands on its own merit. Nevertheless, many people want an intellectual understanding of why God commanded such a law.

One explanation could be that the Almighty intended it to be exciting when men and women interact, as this encourages couples to get married and enjoy staying married. It is often women, more than men, who believe that it is normal for relationships not to be sexually charged or stimulating when we interact with the opposite sex. Therapists (and people who listen to locker room talk) know how uncensored men and women fantasize about the opposite sex in "nonsexual" situations.

Healthy human beings were created to be sexually responsive to their environments. It is hard enough to temporarily banish sexual thoughts when no objects of our fantasies are in view. It is much more difficult when they are within reach.

All normal people have sexual thoughts and feelings. The Jewish laws that seem so restrictive about sexual expression and intermingling preserve the excitement, sensuality, and meaning of physical intimacy for married couples. They also help channel these wonderful feelings within the framework of marriage.

Unfortunately, the media constantly bombard us with sexually provocative images. We are further desensitized to the excitement of touching thanks to social hugs and kisses and the casualness with which unmarried couples have sex. While sex seems to be ubiquitous, real intimacy seems to be an endangered species.

For someone who is sensitive, the brush of a hand against the skin, the press of someone's knee against their leg, the sensuousness of a woman's hair accidentally skimming a man's face can and should be exciting. It is a sad comment on current times that contact that should be suggestive or arousing is often meaningless. Even though many people have been desensitized to what should be intimate behavior, this does not justify creating situations to degrade it even further. If someone has lost his or her appreciation for the sexual excitement of sitting next to the opposite sex, this is not a reason to institutionalize such "numbing" by sanctioning mixed seating in the synagogue.

When someone who has not lost this sensitivity prays in a synagogue without a physical barrier between the sexes, the setting usually detracts from his or her worship of God.

## SEPARATE BUT BETTER

The necessity for a physical division between men and women in the synagogue was never meant to be discriminatory to women. Certain problems that result from *mechitzahs* not being esthetically appealing or being user unfriendly to women are unfortunate side effects that have nothing to do with Jewish law.

Although some people view the separation of the sexes in the synagogue as derogatory to women, there is no mention in any scriptural, Talmudic or rabbinic sources of anything in this regard that denigrates females. If anything, it is men who are more likely than women to be distracted, and they who need greater protection than women in this area. Women are generally considered to be less distracted by men's bodies than men are by women's looks.

One criticism of certain *mechitzahs* is that they make it difficult for women to see or hear the services. As women have participated more and more in synagogue life over the past few decades, *mechitzahs* in many places have become more user-friendly. When that is not the case, there is nothing wrong with women suggesting architectural or design changes that eliminate these practical obstacles while conforming to the letter and spirit of Jewish law. Sometimes the men have no idea how it feels to be a woman praying behind an opaque curtain or wall. If there is something that can be done to make women feel more welcome, many men are happy to do so.

One reason why certain *mechitzahs* relegate women to small and unattractive prayer areas is because men tend to attend the synagogue more often, and in greater numbers, than women do. Women are not required to pray in the presence of ten men, and for many reasons, are often unable or uninterested in coming to the synagogue on weekdays. It is even difficult for many women to attend regularly on Shabbat and Jewish holidays. Thus, women are usually a minority of the congregants at most synagogues. The majority of the limited space is then allocated to men, who tend to be the regular worshipers.

If a woman has no concurrent obligations, such as taking care of her children, elderly parents, a need to be at work, or tending to domestic responsibilities, it is preferable for her to pray with a *minyan* rather than alone if she is able to do so. However, many women do have concurrent obligations that take precedence over the preference to pray with a *minyan*.

In schools such as Stern College for Women in Manhattan, the women's section occupies the majority of the synagogue. Synagogues and college *minyans* have altered the size and designs of their women's sections when significant numbers of women started to attend services regularly and there was enough space and money to make changes. Since synagogues usually have limited space and money, and their facilities are used 365 days a year, the planners usually allocate the most resources to those who will use it the most.

One purpose of the *mechitzah* is that men should not be distracted by the women, but that doesn't mean that women shouldn't be able to see what is going on during the services. Some *mechitzah* have an upper part made of lattice-work or special fabric that allows the women to see the goings-on in the men's section while preventing the men from seeing the women. A number of synagogues have one-way glass *mechitzahs*. From the men's side, the glass reflects like a mirror, but is completely transparent from the women's side, allowing the women an unobstructed view of the services.

## OUR AVERSION TO RESTRICTIONS

There is one additional, typically unstated reason why many people oppose having a *mechitzah*. We like to feel that we have ultimate control over our lives. We learn from the story of Adam and Eve that as soon as God limits what we can have or do, that which is forbidden becomes irresistibly desirable. Forbidden fruits are always the sweetest.

The Midrash says that when God gave the Jews laws governing sexual morality, they wept. The Talmud says that the ancient Israelites engaged in idolatry only to have an excuse to engage in illicit sex. (Idolatrous rites were notorious for including sex.) In the twentieth century, a number of American Orthodox congregations moved to the suburbs where many of the no-longer-observant members vehemently opposed erecting *mechitzahs*. It was as if God once again commanded us to physically separate the sexes, and people wept.

Perhaps the great opposition to *mechitzah* is that it is an irrefutable reminder that we are not supposed to be the ultimate determiners of how we should behave. The idea that we should sit the way we want in God's house of prayer is our way of saying that we don't want to live with divine rules. We want to control our lives and let God in where and when we decide He fits in with our lifestyles and perspectives.

Many Jews are willing to practice rituals that make rational sense, or that feel emotionally fulfilling. Yet, many of us recoil at the notion that we are supposed to observe commandments simply because our Creator told us that is His will. If they make sense to us, and fit in with our sense of what is politically correct and egalitarian, we feel in control.

The *mechitzah* reminds us that some things are absolutely prohibited, regardless of whether we like or understand them. Many people resist that idea because we don't want to turn control over the most intimate parts of our lives to our Creator. *Mechitzah* reminds us that He gives us little say over how flexibly we can interact with members of the opposite sex. He has set down rules about which relationships are permitted and which are not, and has given boundaries in these areas that are as absolute as the walls of the *mechitzah*. Whether we like it or not, we are not supposed to let our feelings be the final arbiter of how much, and under what circumstances, we can enjoy being with the opposite sex. God has already given us those guidelines, and we are reminded of them every time we enter a synagogue.

The *mechitzah* represents a major confrontation between our desire to chart our own course and our need to be humble in allowing the Almighty to guide our behavior. We must let Him tell us what pleases Him. If we really want Him to "be One, and His Name One,"[223] we have to accept His authority to tell us how to live, and trust His judgment as to what is best for us. Worshiping the Almighty in the presence of a *mechitzah* ratifies that He is the King who makes the rules, rather than our telling the Master of the Universe how we will allow Him to enter His palace.

# 10

# The Jewish Marriage Document and Jewish Marital Obligations

**M**arriage is important for Jewish men and women. The Talmud states, "Any man who has no wife lives without joy, without blessing, and without goodness...without Torah, without a protecting wall...and without peace....Any man who has no wife is not a proper man.[224]

The Talmud waxes eloquent about a couple's first marriage. It says, "A man finds happiness only with his first wife, for it is said, 'Let your fountain be blessed and joy with the wife of your youth.'...As soon as a man takes a wife, his sins are buried, for it is said, 'Whoever finds a wife finds a great good and finds favor with God.'"[225]

In the secular world, the starry-eyed, Hollywood view of marriage is that two people fall in love, have sex, live together (not necessarily in that order), get married, and live happily ever after. There is rarely any portrayal of the actual work that is needed to make marriage happy and fulfilling, such as compromise, communication, and caring. In the real world, civil marriage has some legal consequences, but it requires almost no responsibilities. In fact, if one goes to a suburban municipal office to get a marriage license, she might find the dog license window next to the bureau for marriage licenses. The only difference between being fit to own a dog and fit to be married is paying a few dollars!

In Judaism, marriage is far more than a legal entity that legitimizes sex. Among other things, it creates a lifelong opportunity for people to become givers to one another in a sanctified relationship. As such, they can draw the Divine Presence into their home and become Godlike by creating and raising children. Having a successful marriage requires much more than good chemistry, having fun together, and falling in love. Each must fulfill certain obligations and roles that create a framework within which their emotional connection and spiritual growth will blossom and stay vibrant.

The Torah prescribes certain laws that enable a man and woman to create a holy relationship where two very different individuals can live in harmony. To this end, husband and wife each have a different practical and spiritual role, as we will see.

Real and lasting relationships require each partner to do some very specific things. Relationships can be great when a couple enjoys skiing together and eating out, but too often they fall apart when it comes to doing the housework, raising the children, and paying bills. Jewish marriage is much more than two people pledging to honor and cherish each other "'til death do us part." It is not enough to tell someone that you love them on the day that you marry them and do only what pleases you from then on. Marriage requires nurturing, communication, dealing with differences, quality time, intimacy, and practical ways of building a life together. To this end, Judaism has laws that tell husbands how they must treat their wives and vice versa that go back 3,300 years.[226]

Some of these laws are spelled out in the Jewish marriage document known as the *ketubah* (Hebrew for "that which is written.") The groom gives it to his bride under the wedding canopy right after he marries her to make sure that they both know what he obligated himself to do for her. By understanding what this document says, we can appreciate how concerned the Torah and ancient rabbis were with protecting women financially, emotionally, and socially. The laws are very biased in favor of women, and were revolutionary in the societies where Jews lived until modern times.

## JEWISH MARRIAGE

In the Western world, most people think of marriage as an egalitarian venture where two people decide to spend the rest of their lives together. Although Judaism requires both parties to make an absolute commitment to each other, marriage is legally a unilateral, not a bilateral contract. Marriage is effected by a man deciding that he wants to take care of a woman for the rest of his life, and then obligating himself in various ways to make that happen. If a woman agrees to this, they are married.

A contemporary Jewish marriage requires three things: The man must give his wife a marriage contract (the *ketubah*), a ring, and afterwards have sexual relations with her. During the marriage ceremony, the groom gives the bride a ring. When she accepts it, they implicitly agree to have an exclusive relationship with each other from that point onward. Once the couple has pledged to have this kind of exclusivity, the obligations of marriage (some of which are spelled out for the man in the *ketubah*) begin.

## WHAT IS A *KETUBAH?*

The *ketubah* is a legal document written in Aramaic[227] that spells out the husband's obligations to his wife. It also delineates a lump sum that he will pay her if they get divorced or he dies. That amount consists of a pre-established amount of money, whatever capital and personal possessions she brings with her when she marries, and the amount that she or her family paid for the wedding. The *ketubah* is signed by two witnesses[228] and by Sephardic grooms as well.

In ancient times, the amount of a divorce settlement was sufficient for the woman to invest and derive a steady income from it.[229] Although the actual sum could vary, it was at least enough to support herself for a year. This was especially important in societies where women could not support themselves through paid employment. This amount gave them the ability to raise children without having to work outside the home.

It may have been customary for men to give their wives a *ketubah* even before the Torah was given.[230] In those days, until about 2,000 years ago, a man had to give his father-in-law or the father-in-law's agent a certain sum of money when he got married as an escrow payment in case the husband died or divorced his wife. The Jewish Supreme Court (Sanhedrin) then changed this arrangement and required giving a *ketubah* as a promissory note in lieu of the money.[231] The rabbis determined that from then on, a man would mortgage his estate to his wife's *ketubah*. This allowed her to collect her *ketubah* payment when her husband divorced her or died. This same legislation may also have required the *ketubah* to be a written document,[232] even though a binding oral agreement had originally been sufficient.[233]

The *ketubah* was considered so important that the Sanhedrin forbade a husband and wife from living together if she (or her agent) did not have one in her possession.[234] It was designed to make it expensive for a man to divorce his wife,[235] thereby protecting women from many of the disastrous financial, emotional, and social consequences of divorce.[236]

A standard *ketubah* for a first marriage reads as follows:

> On the [...] day of the week, the [...] day of the [Hebrew] month of [...], the year [...] from the creation of the world, according to the way that we count here in [...], the groom [...] son of [...] said to this virgin, Miss [...] daughter   of [...], "Be my wife according to the law of Moses and Israel. I will work, honor, feed and support you in the manner of Jewish men, who work, honor, feed, and support their wives faithfully. I will give you the settlement (*mohar*) of virgins, 200 silver *zuzim*, which is due you according to Torah law, as well as your food, clothing, necessities of life, and conjugal needs, according to the custom of the world."

> Ms. [...], this virgin, agreed, and became his wife. This dowry (*nedunya*) that she brought from her father's house, whether in silver, gold, jewelry, clothes, home furnishings, or bedding, Mr. [...], our groom, accepts as being worth 100 silver *zekukim* altogether.

> Our groom, Mr. [...] agreed, and added to hers, from his (money) an addition-al 100 silver *zekukim* to match hers. The entire amount is 200 silver *zekukim*.

> And thus declared Mr. [...], our groom: "The obligation of this *ketubah*, this dowry, and this additional amount, I accept upon myself, and upon my heirs. It can be paid from the best part of the property and possessions that I own under the heavens that I (already) own or will own in the future. (It includes) what can be mortgaged and what cannot be mortgaged. All (of it) shall be mortgaged and secured to pay this marriage document, this dowry, and this additional amount from me, even (taking) the shirt from my back, during my lifetime, and after my lifetime, from this day and forever."

> And the obligation of this *ketubah*, this dowry and this additional amount was accepted by Mr. [...], our groom, in the strictest (manner) of all marriage documents and additional amounts that daughters in Israel are accustomed to, that are made according to the enactments of our sages, of blessed memory. (This is) neither a speculation nor a sample document.

> We have made an acquisition from Mr.[...], son of [...], our groom, to

Ms. [...], daughter of [...], this virgin, about everything which is written and spelled out above, with something that is appropriate to make this acquisition. And everything is proper and established.

(Signed) [...] son of [...] Witness

(Signed) [...] son of [...] Witness

## MARITAL OBLIGATIONS

The Talmud details a husband's marital obligations, but not in one place. These laws differ somewhat from current practice, but they give an excellent idea of how the rabbis regarded Jewish women thousands of years ago. Maimonides, in the twelfth century, organized Jewish laws that are dispersed throughout the Talmud into chapters in his book, *Mishnah Torah*. Many of the man's marital obligations appear in his *Hilchot Ishut* there. Following is a free translation of excerpts from chapters 12-14:

### Laws of Marriage[237]

When a man marries a woman...he is responsible for providing her with ten things, and he is entitled to ten....Three are obligations based in Torah law—to provide her with *sheirah, kesutah,* and *onah.* These respectively mean that he must provide her with food, he must clothe her, and he must have sexual relations with her.

He has seven rabbinic obligations. The first...is he must pay her if he divorces her. The remaining six obligations...are to pay for her medical care...; to redeem her if she is taken captive; to bury her if she dies; to provide for her needs from his estate; and to allow her to remain in his house after he dies for as long as she is a widow. Also, he must provide for their daughters from his estate after he dies until they are betrothed. Their sons inherit the money promised in her marriage document....

His... rabbinic benefits are: whatever she makes, earns, or finds belongs to him; he can enjoy use of the interest on her capital while she is alive;... and he inherits her estate, having precedence over everyone else, if she predeceases him.

The woman gives up what she makes and earns in exchange for her husband providing her with food. He redeems her...in exchange for him getting the interest on her capital...He buries her in exchange for inheriting her prenuptial possessions...

If a woman says, "I don't want you to provide me with food and I won't give you what I earn or make," we listen to her...

(A Jewish woman does not have to work outside the home and her husband must still feed her. If she chooses not to work outside, she must do certain domestic chores. If she decides to work outside and keep what she earns, her husband is not required to feed her.) But if the husband says, "I don't want to support you, and I will not take what you earn or make," we don't listen to him as her earnings may not provide enough food for her.

(Thus, women had the choice to waive many of their husbands' obligations in order to waive the women's corresponding responsibilities; however, the husband could not waive his obligations to her without her consent.)

When a couple gets married, a woman is automatically entitled to her ten rights and a man to his four enumerated above, whether or not they are stipulated in the *ketubah*.

A woman can agree to waive a man's usual obligations with three exceptions: he must fulfill his wife's sexual needs, he must agree to pay her at least the usual amount stipulated in the marriage contract if he dies or divorces her, and he has the right to inherit her if she predeceases him.

### Clothing, Shelter and Household Necessities

He is required to give his wife warm clothes in the winter and lightweight clothes in the hot season...plus a belt, a head covering, and shoes for each of the Jewish festivals. These should be appropriate for the way that women dress in the country where they live. He must also give her household objects such as a bed and mattress, eating and cooking utensils, and a place for her to live.[238] Plus, he must give her adornments, such as colored scarves...and makeup. The clothing, a place to live and household objects he provides are according to his financial means. If he is wealthy, a court can even force him to buy his wife silk, embroidered clothes, and gold vessels if he does not do so of his own accord. He must buy her clothing that is comparable to that of women of her social standing so that she can feel comfortable in social situations.

### Sexual Obligations

Men who are healthy and who don't do exhausting work have sex with their wives every night. Those who work in the city where they live are supposed to be sexually intimate with their wives twice a week. If they work in another city, they have relations once a week. Torah scholars have sex with their wives once a week, on Friday nights, because Torah learning diminishes their strength.

A woman may prevent her husband from taking a job in a city that isn't close by so that he won't reduce his sexual relations with her. He may not go away without her permission. Thus, she can prevent him from leaving work that requires him to be with her frequently in order to work where he has sex with her less often.

There is probably no other society where the wife's sexual needs determine her husband's obligations to be with her. All of the above frequencies are predicated on her desire to have sex. The man's sexual needs are considered to be of lesser importance, and he is required to regulate his sexual relationship with his wife according to her desires, not his. This is, and always has been, a revolutionary idea!

From the above excerpts, one can appreciate how concerned Judaism was with the physical, emotional, financial and sexual needs of women for the past 3,300 years!

Now that the man's obligations to provide "food, clothing and conjugal needs" have been partially explained, the financial obligations of marriage can be addressed.

## JEWISH INHERITANCE LAWS

According to Jewish law, sons inherit their father. Daughters inherited only if there were no sons. Widows retained use of their husbands' houses and lived there until they remarried or died, supported from the estate in the manner to which they had been accustomed. Unmarried daughters could do the same. Sons only inherited whatever was left of the estate after their unmarried sisters and mother were provided for, even if this meant that the sons had to beg for a living. (It was considered beneath a woman's dignity to have to beg.)

When a woman married, her husband was responsible for housing, clothing, and feeding her, and Jewish courts could make him do so if he shirked his obligations. By requiring men to support their wives (unless the wives waived this), and by depriving women of certain property and inheritance rights, Jewish law tried to assure women's financial well-being. Effectively, this system was designed to prevent women from becoming impoverished if a man died and left only a small estate that would otherwise be shared with sons. It also freed women to concentrate their energies on raising families without the need to, albeit with the option of, working outside of the home.

## MONEY AND THE *KETUBAH*

When a daughter was betrothed, her father customarily gave her some type of gift. This capital, money, and/or other gifts were known as *nedunya*. Shimon ben Shetach instituted the husband's right to use all of the premarital gifts that his wife's father had given her. However, if the husband sold or disposed of these gifts, or if they were damaged or lost, he had to pay her their original value if they got divorced.[239] If the wife waived her husband's obligation to redeem her if she were taken captive, she could use her premarital possessions herself, and any losses she incurred were hers.

Thus, if a father gave his daughter an apartment and money as *nedunya*, the husband could rent out the apartment and invest the money if he so chose. The rental income, accrued capital and interest from the investment then belonged to him. As portfolio manager, rental agent, and safekeeper of his wife's property and money, he was liable for any losses or damage that occurred during his proprietorship.

For example, if at the time the couple got divorced the stocks that he had bought with her money had lost half of their value, he had to give her the stocks as well as repay her the missing money. If she owned property that became damaged or destroyed, he was liable for all of the losses and had to replace the worth of what was lost. In the event of the husband's death or divorce, all of the *nedunya* capital reverted back to the woman.

If a wife died, her husband inherited her estate. When he died, her *nedunya* passed to her sons, even if he had other children by another wife.

A standard *ketubah* states that a woman brings *nedunya* worth 100 silver *zekukim* into marriage, or half that amount for a widow or divorcee. When silver costs around $15 an ounce, 100 *zekukim* is estimated to be worth around $12,000.[240]

### The Marriage Settlement

In biblical times, when a woman got married, she got *nedunya* from her father, and the groom paid her father a sum of money known as *mohar*. This was essentially the woman's money that was left in safekeeping with her father.[241] (If the groom were to give her the money, it would revert back to him once they were married.)

In the time of Shimon ben Shetach, men became reluctant to marry and to stay married due to the financial obligations of so doing. Prior to this time, a groom gave his father-in-law money to keep for his bride at the beginning of their marriage. It was difficult for many poor young men to acquire this sum of money. On the other hand, once men gave this money to their fathers-in-law at the start of marriage, they lost subsequent use of it. Thus, they had no financial incentive not to divorce their wives at whim. Once they had paid their initial marriage settlement, divorce incurred no monetary penalty or financial obligations to their former wives. This was because divorced men didn't have to support ex-wives or pay them alimony.

Shimon ben Shetach began the current custom of having the *ketubah* specify that the marriage settlement would be directly payable to the wife in the event of divorce or his death. This replaced the former system of having the money paid up front to the father-in-law. This made the current *ketubah* a promissory note that the groom gives to his bride that is only payable if their marriage dissolves. This removes some of the previous financial discouragement for men to marry, but applies it if they want a divorce, thereby protecting women from being divorced against their will. It also strengthens the institution of marriage and family stability.

## Tosefta

The *ketubah* specifies that the groom gives his wife a marriage settlement, *nedunya*, plus an additional sum should she ever collect her *ketubah* money. This additional sum parallels her dowry and is called *tosefta*.[242] It shows his love for his bride[243] and equals the amount of the *nedunya* that the bride brings into marriage.

Thus, three elements comprise the *ekar ketubah*—the financial obligations of the marriage contract. (1) The *mohar* is the marriage settlement that the groom pays, and equals 200 *zuz*. Its exact value is the subject of great rabbinic debate. Some authorities maintain that it is however much a woman needs to support herself for a year, while others say that it is a specific monetary amount. (2) The *nedunya* is what the bride brings into marriage and the groom agrees to repay her if the marriage ends. (3) Finally, the groom adds his *tosefta*,[244] which he or his heirs pay in the event of divorce or his death.

The actual worth of the *ketubah* is ambiguous because it is rarely relevant to current Jewish divorce settlements. Almost all divorcing couples elect to dissolve their marriages according to considerations other than the *ketubah's* monetary stipulations.

The *ketubah* was designed to accomplish several goals: It encouraged men to get married and stay married, while providing for women's financial security during and after marriage. It also allowed women to receive risk-free management of their capital by their husbands.

Overall, a *ketubah* is a husband's pledge to be financially, emotionally and physically caring to his wife. Women do not give their husbands corresponding documents stipulating their responsibilities, nor do they sign a *ketubah*. One reason for this may be because Jewish law assumes that women know how to act as proper wives without a written document stipulating their obligations.

## Modern Prenuptial Agreements

In order to reduce recalcitrance (usually on the man's part) in granting a divorce when one spouse wants it, Jewish couples are advised to sign prenuptial agreements. Standard ones obligate both spouses to attend a rabbinical court for binding arbitration when one or both parties want a divorce. A spouse who fails to do so pays $150 (or some other specified amount) per day to the spouse who wants the divorce until the divorce is granted. More about this can be found at http://theprenup.org/pdf/Prenup_Standard.pdf.

# 11

# Sexual Intimacy and Mikvah

**M**any Westerners view sex as the ultimate pleasure, and relate to others as objects that fulfill their drives and fantasies, disconnecting intimacy and love from sexual pleasure. Other couples share a deep bond and express their emotional closeness and intimacy through their physical relationship. Judaism, however, makes it possible to have an even deeper connection than simply physical plus emotional. The laws that govern sex sanctify a couple's physical relationship by making God a partner to their intimacy.

In Judaism, marriage is termed *"kiddushin"*—sanctification. Many people feel that their wedding day is one of the happiest days of their lives. Yet for a Jewish couple, the wedding day is not only a time of great happiness, but also one of holiness. It is sometimes referred to as a mini-Day of Atonement for the couple. Unless the wedding takes place on a Jewish New Moon, or non-festival holiday such as Chanuka, the couple customarily says the confessional from Yom Kippur and fasts.[245] They wear white, to symbolize being free of sin just like on Yom Kippur. They pray to have a happy and meaningful life together, to build a lasting Jewish home, and for their loved ones to get what they need. Their prayers are considered to be very powerful. It is said that God forgives all of the sins of a bride and groom on their wedding day.[246]

The Jewish laws that govern marital intimacy are known as "family purity." Modern people might prefer to translate this as "family holiness." These laws remind us to treat the opposite sex as people, not as objects, and they enable us to sanctify what would otherwise be animalistic drives.

Jews sanctify sex by abstaining from physical contact before marriage.

146

Couples only engage in sex after they commit to an exclusive and holy relationship as marriage partners, and after the woman has properly immersed in a ritual bath known as a "*mikvah*." The Creator intended physical intimacy to be an ennobling experience where a man and woman bring His Presence into the world when they join together physically. The intensity of sexual pleasure is heightened by the fact that it is reserved for one special person with whom we plan to spend the rest of our lives.

The *Song of Songs* is a book in the Jewish canon (*Tanach*) that describes a love relationship between a man and a woman. One of the greatest Jewish sages, Rabbi Akiva,[247] said that all of the books in the Jewish canon are holy, but the Song of Songs is "holy of holies."[248] While marital relations can be emotionally and physically fulfilling, such intimacy should not be disconnected from the God who made it possible. Sex was not only meant to strengthen the love bonds between husband and wife. It also lets them extrapolate from the intensity of their love how deeply God must love us, and how deeply we can love Him. Sexual relations occurring in the proper way allow human beings to feel the deepest intimacy, giving and merging possible.

As was mentioned, the Temples had a Holy of Holies where the High Priest went and experienced an intimate closeness with the Divine Presence every Yom Kippur. The Holy of Holies was termed "the bedroom" of the Jewish people because the Divine Presence was experienced there, just as He is in the loving, joyful, intimate union of a husband and wife.

Judaism asks us to become holy by separating ourselves from what can't be sanctified, and by elevating what can. The Almighty created a physical world so that we would sanctify its permitted pleasures, abstain from pleasures that we can't make holy, and relate to the divine image in others instead of their superficial aspects. This attitude helps us appreciate why sex is supposed to be much more than a way to simply get physical and some emotional pleasure.

Sex itself is morally and emotionally neutral. When we enjoy it in ways that our Creator forbade, we damage ourselves and our partner—no matter how good it feels. When we enjoy it with His blessing, He becomes a partner to our intimacy. This happens when we become givers who connect to the divine image in our partner and have relations in a state of holiness. Such an act integrates a couple's emotions, souls, and bodies, while the Divine Presence hovers above them.[249]

Some other religions denigrate marriage and sex as concessions to the flesh, or to man's degenerate passions. For example, the Church professed that people should preferably be celibate, or if they can't exercise self-control, "it is better to marry than to burn with passion."[250] In Catholic thirteenth-century Spain, Nachmanides wrote, "God did not create anything that is inherently shameful...He is pure of spirit, and nothing that comes from Him is intrinsically bad....Whatever ugliness there is comes from people misusing what God gave them."[251] His writings reflect the Jewish belief that the Almighty wants people to get married and experience sexual intimacy. That gives them a sense of how the Almighty wants to be close to us, and how deeply we should want to be close to Him.

We feel a strong yearning to unite with a mate because of the way God made humanity. Adam and Eve once shared one body and one soul, but they were separated. By reuniting sexually, they reunited their souls.

Since our soul was once one with our life partner's before coming into the physical world, we feel incomplete until we reunite with our soul mate. Our sex drive is fueled by our soul's yearning to find completion with a spouse. Our bodies are vehicles that allow us to reunite two halves of one soul.

All too often, a person's sex drive becomes disconnected from its spiritual source, allowing him or her to pursue sexual pleasure as an end in itself. Sex was intended to be an act of spiritual elevation, not one of self-service or hedonistic, animalistic couplings.

Sanctified sex unites our physical desires with our spiritual yearnings. One reason the sex drive is so powerful is because of its inherent potential for sanctity. The more potential for holiness something has, the greater is our potential to debase it. How we channel our sexuality has a far stronger spiritual effect than most people realize. The amount of holiness we create during marital intimacy even affects the quality of the soul that the Almighty puts into a resulting child.

A couple who wants to conceive should concentrate on bringing a child into this world who will make it a better place and fulfill his or her Godly mission here. The holier the intimacy that a couple creates during marital relations that leads to conception, the less limited their child will feel about what he or she can accomplish.

God wants us to invite Him into the most private part of our lives. Sanctifying sex is as important as observing the Sabbath and the Day of Atonement and eating kosher food. We make the Almighty our partner in every aspect of our lives, including in the bedroom.

# KNOWLEDGE

The Torah terms sex "*yediah*," which means "knowledge." This is because marital relations were meant to be an outgrowth of a total understanding between a husband and wife. *Yediah* means intellectual knowledge, integrated with emotional understanding that culminates in actions. When the Torah says that a man "knew" his wife,[252] it means that he expressed his love and understanding of her by nurturing her emotionally and physically. This reflects the idea that a couple should know and understand each other emotionally, intellectually and spiritually before physically celebrating their closeness. Such total unity helps promote the kind of spiritual and emotional development that our Creator wanted us to have.

As we saw earlier, husbands are required to temper their sex drives according to what will give their wives physical and emotional pleasure.[253] This includes their having relations whenever their wives show interest, provided they are allowed to be intimate. Depriving a wife of relations for a prolonged period of time is grounds for divorce.

## Time

The Torah uses the term *onah* to describe a man's obligation to fulfill his wife's sexual needs. *Onah* means "time." A couple has to devote time, on a regular basis, to creating and sustaining their friendship, companionship and closeness. Women who are in touch with their emotional/spiritual side will not find sex intimate if it is devoid of deep emotional connection and long-term commitment. Spending time together on a regular basis is usually necessary for women to feel such bonding.

Jewish men actually owe their wives as much time after marriage as they led them to believe before marriage they would spend together. The first year of marriage husbands may not stay out of town overnight without their wives' permission, and men are required to be especially attentive to their wives during those twelve months.[254]

## Real Intimacy

Using sex primarily for fun or our own pleasure divorces our souls and minds from our bodies and emotions. Judaism wants us to be integrated, and to use sex to bond us with our mate. To that end, it prohibits couples from having relations when they are not getting along, or when either is contemplating divorce, is drunk, is asleep, or does not want it.[255] This is because sex cannot be intimate or holy if a couple doesn't feel lovingly towards one another and focus on the other. Jewish marital relations are based on taking care of a partner whom we love and appreciate, not using a partner to gratify our lusts. Sex was meant to be shared by two people who love and are fully committed to each other. It is an experience of being fully aware of, and connected to, one's partner. Having sex while fantasizing about someone other than a spouse, being drunk, and so forth, are ways of pleasuring only ourselves and cannot unite two divine souls.

Nachmanides wrote how a man is supposed to have relations with his wife: "He should initiate sexual intimacy by first talking to her lovingly, making her feel tranquil and happy to be with him, then arousing her with words that make her feel desire, emotional attachment, love and passion. When he is ready for intimacy, he must make sure that she feels the same. He should not try to arouse her too quickly. He should be patient, try to please her, and make sure that she is sexually satisfied before he achieves his satisfaction."[256]

Part of what makes sex holy is the husband's sensitivity to his wife's emotional and physical needs. His desire to provide for her needs, rather than his own, sets the stage for a relationship where he is primarily a giver—like God—rather than a taker.

## *MIKVAH* AND RITUAL IMPURITY

Jewish law forbids a husband and wife from touching each other when the woman has or expects her period, or has hormonally caused uterine bleeding, and has not yet properly immersed in a ritual bath (*mikvah*). This is based on the Torah verses, "When a woman has a flow of blood, where blood flows from her body, she shall be separated ("*niddah*") for seven days...."[257] "And to a woman who is separated, [a man] should not approach to uncover her nakedness [i.e., to have sex]."[258] This verse bars all loving touch that could lead a man and woman to intimacy, such as holding hands, hugging, kissing, and so on. Practically speaking, this means that once a young woman gets her first period, she remains a *niddah* until she properly immerses in a ritual bath just prior to her wedding.

The rabbis forbade unmarried women from ritually immersing to remove their *niddah* status because non-marital sex is forbidden. Jewish dating, then, is very different than secular dating. It is only done to find one's marriage partner. The process involves a couple getting to know each other as potential marriage partners without the distractions or benefits of a physical relationship. While chemistry in marriage is important, sharing one's body with multiple partners or in a non-sanctified way even with one person before marriage can be emotionally dulling and/or spiritually damaging. At the very least, when couples don't have premarital physical relationships, the excitement and intensity of marrying one's first love and sharing intimacy with only one person can be directed into their marriage.

For technical reasons, modern married Jewish couples typically abstain from physical contact from the time that a woman anticipates her period until seven days after it ends.[259] After these twelve or more days have passed, she immerses in a *mikvah*, after which the couple may resume their physical relationship.

Some people misinterpret the above biblical verses that discuss women becoming *niddah* and immersing in a ritual bath. They think that this disparages women, and that ancient Jewish men thought that women who had their periods were dirty and degraded. Such misconceptions came about due to mistranslations of biblical Hebrew and a spotty knowledge of Jewish law. When we had the Tabernacle and Temples in Jerusalem, the Torah required both men and women to immerse in a *mikvah* under certain circumstances[260] having nothing to do with hygiene. That ritual immersion is unrelated to being physically clean is quite obvious from the fact that women must be scrupulously clean before immersing. The effect of the immersion is to create spiritual purity, although there are often emotional benefits as well.

Some people who have little understanding of the spiritual basis of Jewish laws think that the laws of family holiness, and many others, are outdated. For example, since people who eat undercooked pork rarely get trichinosis, some think that the Torah forbade eating pig so that people wouldn't get sick. They assume that since we now know the importance of fully cooking pork, there is no longer a reason to avoid eating bacon. Similarly, they misunderstand that the purpose of a woman's immersing is to cleanse the body, thereby making immersion in a *mikvah* irrelevant for women who keep clean.

Such Jewish laws are not for hygienic reasons, although observing them sometimes yields beneficial medical results.[261]

Although Jews no longer observe the complex laws of ritual purity and impurity because we don't have a Temple in Jerusalem, it is helpful to understand the concept. This allows us to better appreciate the wisdom of the laws of family holiness in maximizing the physical relationship of husband and wife.

The words "ritual purity" and "impurity" are actually poor translations of the Hebrew terms *taharah* and *tumah*. Spiritual purity and impurity are not states where a person is wholesome versus degraded. The word *tumah* cannot be exactly translated into English, yet we have some idea of what it implies.

Ritual impurity exists on seven different levels, only several of which apply specifically to women. In Temple times, both sexes went to the *mikvah* in order to regain spiritual purity.

For example, a man who had a seminal emission became ritually impure, as did a couple who had sexual relations. A woman who experienced a flow of blood from her uterus, even when not menstruating, became ritually impure. A person who was in the same room with a corpse also became impure. Such ritual impurity referred to a form of spiritual blockage. It did not mean being taboo, evil, or corrupted.

The most serious source of ritual impurity is a dead person. A corpse is totally unable to express its soul's potentials. Death completely disrupts the body's ability to utilize and express the soul's power.

When Jews observed the laws of ritual purity, someone who had been in close contact with a corpse became ritually impure for a week. Such people were forbidden to enter the Temple and could transfer spiritual impurity to other people and to objects until they reinstated their spiritual purity.

Although corpses, or Jews who touched them, contracted or transferred ritual impurity, there was no stigma attached to this. For example, Jewish law requires treating a corpse with the utmost respect. We must act with dignity when near it, doing nothing that would cause grief to the soul that was once in it. Since it is pained by no longer being able to reach greater spiritual heights through the body, we are not allowed to study Torah near a corpse. We may not leave a corpse unattended for even a moment between the time of death and burial, even though being in the same room with a corpse makes one ritually impure. We also normally require burial within 24 hours of death because it is considered denigrating for a corpse to remain unburied any longer than is absolutely necessary. The importance of burial is so great that if there is no one else available to bury a Jew, a Jewish priest, who is normally forbidden to willingly contract such impurity, is required to attend to the burial.

## SPIRITUAL BLOCK

Perhaps Judaism views death as the ultimate source of impurity because it renders the soul completely unable to influence the body to serve God. When the soul's potential influence is partially disrupted, it creates lesser levels of ritual impurity. For example, there was once a form of skin disease known as *tzaraat*.[262] It was similar in appearance to psoriasis, yet was caused by certain sins, including slandering another person. It has been suggested that *tzaraat* was the body's way of expressing that its soul's influence on it was blocked.

Judaism theorizes[263] that over the millennia, people have become more technologically advanced but less spiritually aware. In our world, people develop psychosomatic illnesses; their emotional states can manifest as stomach pains, headaches, neck stiffness, and the like. In biblical times, people's bodies manifested both spiritual and emotional states. Over time, people's sensitivity to the body-soul connections diminished, so that physical symptoms no longer invariably reflected disruptions to the soul's ability to affect the body.

During our lives, we invariably encounter many situations that we would prefer not to experience. The Torah gives us guidelines to help us react constructively when these undesired situations arise. The Jewish laws of *tumah* (literally, blockage) and *taharah* (literally, spiritual free flow) allow us to take potential spiritual blockage and use it to eventually come to greater spirituality.

### Ritual Impurity Due to Contact with Death

The primary source of ritual impurity, *tumah*, is a dead person. Seeing a dead person is disturbing. It can, at least momentarily, cause us to question whether there are really a God and an afterlife.

Since priests minister to the Almighty, there is no room for them to have even a shadow of a doubt about His existence and Providence over the world. Thus, it is not surprising that Jewish priests (*cohanim*) are prohibited from going to cemeteries or being in proximity to a corpse. This is especially true of the High Priest, who was never allowed to have any personal doubts intrude on his divine service on behalf of the entire Jewish nation. Perhaps this is why he was not even allowed to defile himself for a close relative, as other priests were permitted to do.

Thus, it has been theorized that the state of *tumah* has an element of spiritual doubt attached to it. When we confront death, and our own mortality, we can succumb to despair and lose our faith. When we have close contact with a corpse, especially if it is that of a loved one, we might feel that life has lost its purpose, since everyone eventually dies. This sense of futility can result in our blocking access to our soul.

Judaism offers an alternative. Confronting death can stimulate us to think about the true purpose of life and to draw ourselves away from that which is only ephemeral. It can motivate us to accomplish more, and give our soul greater influence over our body and physical life. The laws of ritual impurity can encourage us to respond appropriately when we confront mortality and death.

## Tzaraat

When Jews were punished with *tzaraat* for abusing their power of speech, they were isolated from others for a week or more. This helped them experience the effect that their misuse of speech had on those they had slandered. Just as their slander caused others to be shunned by the community, the slanderers themselves experienced this same isolation. When the isolated people stopped misusing their speech, the *tzaraat* disappeared. They could then rejoin the rest of the Jewish community.

It is interesting that if someone did not stop badmouthing others, the *tzaraat* might spread on his or her body. As long as it continued to spread, the person was banished from the community. But, if the *tzaraat* covered the entire body, the person went home. It has been suggested that this indicated that the person was unwilling to learn the message that the *tzaraat* was supposed to teach, so further isolation would serve no purpose. God can do His best to encourage us to live meaningfully. We have to be willing to learn the lessons.

## POTENTIALS OF SEX

As is the case with death and *tzaraat*, sex has the potential to block spiritual influences on us if it is not used properly. Our Creator gave men and women powerful sex drives as vehicles for holiness. When properly directed, sex can result in the creation of a child and the drawing down of a divine soul. Some describe marital intimacy as the ultimate ratification of God's belief that we can unify the most diametrically opposed forces within ourselves—the most intensely physical act with the greatest spirituality.

All aspects of the physical world, including our physical desires, can create infinite good and holiness if they are used properly. However, since sex has so much potential to be misused, its spiritual accomplishment when used properly is correspondingly profound. Sex must either enhance or detract from a couple's spiritual and emotional bonds and growth. It can't leave a couple spiritually untouched. It can reinforce someone's animalistic tendencies and disconnection from real closeness, or help us realize our greatest potentials as emotionally developed, spiritual seekers. When sex occurs under the right circumstances, it enables a couple to celebrate their knowledge of, and love for one another. In the process, they become unified with their Creator as their partner.

## RITUAL IMPURITY TODAY

When the Temples stood, any Jew who was ritually impure was forbidden to enter it. However, being ritually impure under any other circumstances was permitted. Nowadays, all Jews are ritually impure because of coming into direct or indirect contact with a corpse. This is so because the means for removing this specific type of impurity was lost when the Second Temple was destroyed. Everyone today is presumed to have been in a room with a corpse, or to have had contact with someone else who was, thus becoming ritually impure.

The sole implication of ritual impurity for modern Jews is that we are all forbidden to enter the area on the Temple Mount in Jerusalem where the Temple once stood. There is no implication that Jews are sullied or bad because they are ritually impure.

Apart from avoiding part of the Temple Mount, Jews have not concerned themselves with various types of ritual impurity since the Temple was destroyed. For more than 1,900 years, *tumah* (ritual impurity) and *taharah* (ritual purity) have been inoperative in daily life. When women immerse today, it is primarily to change their status from being sexually forbidden to their husbands to being sexually permitted.

There is a misconception that a *niddah* may not have sex with her husband because she will make him "unclean." Women who immerse in a *mikvah* still retain the ritual impurity that disqualifies every Jew from entering the Temple. A *niddah* remains sexually off-limits to every man since this prohibition derives from the verse that tells men not to approach such a woman to have sex. The prohibition of physical contact between a *niddah* and a man is independent of whether such contact could make him ritually impure.

For example, a modern woman who is *niddah* may touch her father,

her male children, or other women. If transferring *tumah* was what made contact between a *niddah* and her husband prohibited, a *niddah* could not touch anyone!

## SEXUAL INTIMACY

It has been theorized that the Jewish laws regarding sexuality are more rigorous than laws restricting many other areas of life because sexuality is such a powerful gateway for either holiness or the opposite. Expressing sexual feelings should affect us. Perhaps Judaism only permits it in the framework of marriage because it is only there that one can totally commit oneself to a partner. This framework of sanctified exclusivity allows sexual relations to be a conduit for the Divine Presence to join the couple.

Physical intimacy between a husband and wife is metaphysically understood to parallel the male and female attributes of God. There is an aspect of men that parallels the divine attribute that gives by acting upon the world, and an aspect of women that allows the world to be receptive to divine providence. The Almighty gave some part of these attributes to us so that we can imitate Him by our actions. Through sexual intimacy, a husband and wife can become like God in creating life.

The Talmud says, "There are three partners in the creation of a child—the father, the mother, and God."[264] In the most physical, potentially animalistic acts, a couple can reach a pinnacle of spirituality by creating a child who is imbued with a divine soul. The more harmonious, loving, and holy is the relationship between a husband and wife, the greater is the spiritual contribution to the child who can be conceived through their union.

Sex can only be positive and holy if it involves giving, especially on the man's part. The laws that govern sexual expression reflect the Creator's concern that the body and soul form an integrated and balanced unit. Thus, when one spouse responds to the other's desire for sexual intimacy, this act of sensitivity forms the foundation for the sanctification of their subsequent union. In Judaism, sensitivity to one's spouse is a cornerstone for true intimacy.

In order for sex to be holy, a man and woman must be married according to Jewish law. The woman must have properly immersed in a *mikvah* and not subsequently had uterine bleeding that would require them to separate.[265] The couple must also be in states of mind where they lovingly concentrate on their spouse.

The communion of hearts and minds alone does not legitimize two consenting adults having a physical relationship. Certain relationships (incest, adultery, premarital sex) are so distracting that they make it impossible for two people to integrate their physical and spiritual selves. No matter how positive a couple's intentions, they cannot create true fulfillment if their physical union takes precedence over their spiritual union.

The sexual discipline of Judaism helps preserve the proper balance and unity between body and soul that our Creator wanted us to have. When sex cannot be sanctified, such as when two people aren't married, or when a wife is *niddah*, relations are forbidden.

## LAWS OF FAMILY PURITY

A Jewish ritual bath is one of the most important institutions of any Jewish community. Building it takes precedence over building a synagogue or school for Jewish studies, or buying a Torah scroll. This is because of the central importance that observing the laws of physical intimacy has in Jewish communal and family life.

The basics of what is termed "family purity" are as follows: A woman becomes *niddah* whenever she has non-traumatic bleeding that emanates from her uterus. This normally occurs when she has a menstrual period, but it can also occur for other reasons, such as mid-cycle bleeding. At that point, she and her husband must refrain from physical contact with one another. They may also not do things that might lead to such contact, so they sleep in separate beds, don't sit close enough that their bodies touch, and don't hand things to one another.

A *niddah* is also prohibited from doing certain "wifely" tasks for her husband, such as serving him food in her usual manner, or pouring him a drink. An outgrowth of this is that the husband appreciates the many kindnesses that his wife normally does for him that he might otherwise take for granted.

### Ending the Niddah Status

The laws of how to end a woman's *niddah* status are more comprehensive than can be detailed here. It is customary for women who are about to get married, or who want to go to the *mikvah* for the first time during marriage, to take an 8-12 hour course of instruction in these laws. They are usually given one-on-one, although group classes are available in some large religious communities. A short summary follows:

A woman becomes *niddah* once her menstrual period begins. She then waits a minimum of five days, or until her period ends, whichever is longer. To definitively determine that her period has ended, she gently inserts into her vagina a small piece of soft, white cloth wrapped around a finger.[266] She does this during daylight hours, prior to sunset. If the cloth shows no blood when it is withdrawn, her period is considered to have ended. (She may repeat this as many times as is necessary to obtain a white specimen when she withdraws the cloth.)

It is customary for the woman to leave a small white cloth inside her until nightfall to ascertain more definitively that her bleeding has ceased. If this cloth is unstained when she removes it that evening, she begins counting seven "preparatory" or "white" days. She wears white underpants during that week so that if she stains, showing that her period has not really ended, it will be easy to discern given the white background.

A woman normally does an internal examination with a white cloth every morning and late afternoon of these seven white days to be sure that no bleeding occurred. If there are no signs of bleeding that week, she prepares herself to immerse in a *mikvah* at its completion. She preferably starts these preparations before sunset on the seventh white day, finishing after dark. She can then immerse.[267]

She prepares for the *mikvah* by removing all jewelry including earrings, and bandages. She brushes and flosses her teeth, shampoos her hair without conditioner, and combs it free of tangles. She removes any nail polish and makeup, cuts her fingernails and toenails, and makes sure there is no dirt underneath. She takes a bath and cleans her entire body, removes any dirt or loose pieces of skin on her body, as well as secretions in the ears, eyes and nose.

When a woman immerses, she is not allowed to have even a speck of dirt on her. This is because immersing is a way of renewing our spiritual connection with God. Nothing is supposed to intervene between the body and the water when we seek to resume intimacy with the One Above via this process.

A woman may prepare for her immersion at home, or in rooms provided for this purpose at the *mikvah*. If she prepares at home, it is customary to shower at the *mikvah* just prior to immersing to ensure that she is totally clean. After nightfall (approximately 45 minutes after sunset), she may immerse.

## Privacy

*Mikvahs* are usually in unmarked buildings, set away from the main street. This is due to the absolute privacy that is supposed to surround a woman's immersion. No one except her husband and the *mikvah* attendant are supposed to know when she is *niddah*, or when she immerses. This is why all preparation rooms at a *mikvah* are private, and the immersion itself is not discussed with anyone. If men drive their wives to or from the *mikvah*, they are not allowed to stay near the building, to ensure that they not see any women coming to immerse or leaving.

Most *mikvah* buildings have a waiting area for women, and many have the feel of a spa. The preparation rooms typically are furnished with a bathrobe, towels, disposable slippers, combs, nail clippers, shampoo, soap, and whatever else might be needed to properly prepare for immersion. Normally, each room opens directly into the *mikvah* room so that no one besides the *mikvah* attendant can see the woman about to immerse.

## A Personal Prayer

Many women like to say a personal prayer as a preparation for the beautiful act that they are about to do. Here is one favorite:

> May it be Your will, Lord our God, that Your Divine Presence rest between my husband and me. And may Your holy Name be unified through us, and cause a spirit of purity and holiness to enter our hearts. Distance me from all bad thoughts and fantasies, and give my husband and me a pure and clean soul. Let neither of us look at anyone else in the world, but let my eyes be on my husband, and let his eyes be on me. And let it seem to me that there is no man in the world who is better, more handsome, and more gracious than my husband....And so should I seem to him, that there is no woman in the world who is more beautiful, gracious, and appropriate for him than me. All of his thoughts should be directed toward me, and not toward anyone else....As it is said, "Therefore shall a man leave his father and his mother and cleave unto his wife."
>
> And may it be Your will, Lord our God, that our union be beautiful, a proper union of love, unity, peace, and friendship; a union that is proper according to the law of Moses and Judaism; a union with proper fear of Heaven and fear of sin; a union that will result in deserving children who are righteous, perfect, and upright. A union that will result in healthy children, full of blessing...through which will be fulfilled the verse, "Your

wife should be like a fruitful vine in your house, your children like planted olive trees around your table."

Our union should be one in which my husband is happier with me than with all of the good things that he has in the world....Our union should never be one of anger, quarreling, contention, or jealousy. Rather, it should be one of love, unity, peace, friendship, humility, modesty, and patience. It should be a union of love, righteousness, doing charitable deeds, and doing good to (God's) creatures. It should result in a healthy and good child, whose body will not be damaged or lacking, who will have no affliction, plague, sickness, disease, pain, trouble, weakness, or failing, and who will not lack goodness all the days of his life.

We should form a union that will allow holiness and purity to flow in thought, speech, and action as befits proper Jews, in our souls, spirits, and bodies. Our union should be according to the Jewish laws of holiness, with success and blessing, the blessings of heaven above and of the deep below, blessings of the breasts and the womb. A union of holy and pure seed, good and beautiful, sweet and acceptable.

Therefore, in order to unify the Holy One, blessed is He, with His

Divine Presence...I am prepared and ready to immerse myself according to the law of Moses and Israel. May it be Your will, Lord God, that You purify us, and sanctify us with Your holiness, and cause to flow down to us from You a spirit of purity and holiness. And be pleased with us, and with our deeds, and let us be worthy of doing Your will forever, all the days of our lives. And bless us from Your blessing, because You are the Source of all blessing, forever.[268]

### The Immersion

After completing her preparations at the *mikvah*, the woman presses a button that summons the *mikvah* attendant. The woman wears the bathrobe and slippers provided, then enters the *mikvah* area. The attendant checks the woman's body to make sure there are no stray hairs on her, or that she hasn't forgotten to remove her earrings, rings, nail polish, bandages, and the like. The attendant may also ask the woman if she has done all of the appropriate preparations. The woman then disrobes and takes off her slippers and walks down a few steps into the *mikvah* itself.

A *mikvah* looks like a tiny swimming pool, usually about 5 feet by 8 feet, and three-and-a-half to four feet deep. It contains comfortably warm, usually chlorinated water. The dimensions of *mikvahs* are similar around the world. In fact, when Masada was excavated in the 1960s, a number of *mikvahs* were found there that the Jews had built and used there during and after the Great Revolt. When modern rabbis inspected them 1,900 years later, they were found to have the same specifications as do our modern *mikvahs*.

More than 100 *mikvahs* have been found near the Temple Mount in Jerusalem which Jews used before going up to the Second Temple. The main differences between ancient and modern *mikvahs* are the amenities that are offered today: toilets, comfortable preparation rooms, tiled surfaces, and heated water that is changed regularly to keep it very clean.

When she is ready to immerse, the woman stands on the floor of the *mikvah* with her feet apart, her arms away from her body, and her fingers spread. This makes sure that the water reaches every part of her body. When she stands, the water usually reaches her chest, so she quickly bends her knees and dunks her head under water to entirely submerge herself. She keeps her eyes and lips gently closed, and allows the life-affirming water that symbolizes the pristine waters of the Garden of Eden to touch every part of her.

When she immerses, she symbolically shows that she has no existence independent of God. She submerges underwater in an almost fetal position, and emerges spiritually newly born. She is unencumbered by any spiritual barriers between herself and her Creator. She is now ready to connect physically and spiritually in a holy and spiritual union with her husband.

When she stands up, the attendant says, "Kosher" if she properly immersed. If she is married rather than a bride-to-be, she puts a dry washcloth or other covering on her head and says the blessing, "You are the Source of all blessing, Lord our God, King of the Universe, who has sanctified us with Your commandments and commanded us concerning the immersion."

If she covered her head, she hands the cloth to the attendant and immerses another two (or more) times, depending on her custom. When she walks up the steps to leave the *mikvah*, the attendant holds up her robe in a way that the attendant can't see her naked body. The woman covers herself and goes back to her room to get dressed.

Many couples find it very moving to meet each other as soon as the woman leaves the *mikvah* building.[269] Now that they are permitted to touch each other, it is like seeing each other at the wedding canopy and getting married all over again. In fact, the Talmud asks, "Why did the Torah decree that the ritual impurity of a woman's period would last for seven days?[270] Because (when a husband) is continuously with his wife, he might come to loathe her. Therefore, the Torah said that she should be in a state of *niddah* for seven days, in order that she be as beloved to her husband as the time when she first came into the bridal chamber."[271]

This is how observing the laws of family holiness renews a woman's bonds with God and her husband every month.

## EFFECTS OF FAMILY PURITY

We can never know God's precise reasons for commanding any of the Torah's laws. Nevertheless, there are obvious outgrowths of the laws that govern sexual relationships. Not the least of these are instilling in both sexes an appreciation for the beauty of sanctifying our bodies rather than using them for egocentric or animalistic pleasures. When we are raised with a consciousness that our bodies can be holy, we treat them with great respect—whether they are ours or someone else's. One of the many things that sets Jews apart from every other group on Earth is that the Almighty told us, "Be holy, because I, the Lord Your God, am holy."[272] This requires us to set boundaries on our physical relationships so that we don't get involved in forbidden sexual relations that can't be spiritualized.[273]

Most of the world's religions make God small, giving Him human qualities, and bringing Him down to man's level. Judaism believes in man's potential greatness, and in our ability to go up to God's level. When we fence ourselves away from degrading, self-indulgent behavior, and reject using the physical world as an end in itself, we elevate ourselves and create a dwelling-place for the Almighty on earth. By asking, "What does He want me to do in this situation?" His will for us becomes central to our lives, and we raise ourselves up to His level.

The divorce rate in the Western world has been alarmingly high for decades. There are many reasons for this, part of which can be ameliorated by continually refreshing and deepening one's marriage. We can do this by infusing spirituality into the sensual and material.

The 12-14-day monthly interval of physical abstinence that Jewish couples observe provides an ongoing framework to work out their differences, put "emotional deposits" into their "relationship account," and continually create meaningful goals that bond them as a couple. Each time they resume having a physical relationship, they have built a stronger foundation for it.

The laws of family holiness help prevent men from viewing their wives as objects to serve them domestically or sexually. During the period of separation, the abstinence helps each appreciate how much they enjoy closeness with each other. As well, the prohibition against the wife doing "wifely" tasks for her husband in the usual way underscore to him how much she normally does for him, which he should not take for granted. This is a time to develop their friendship and appreciation for each other using words and actions that continually renew their marriage.

During this time, wives should make sure not to neglect their appearance. If they look attractive, but not attracting, it can activate their sex drives in a low-key manner. As the period of abstinence continues, this creates some sexual tension that contributes to the sense of having a honeymoon every month when the wife returns from her immersion.

## TIMES FOR SPIRITUAL EVALUATION

Jewish women have many opportunities for spiritual evaluation. Every Sabbath and holiday, they light candles, say the blessing(s), followed by personal prayers. At these precious moments, many women feel very close to their Creator. These special times give them a chance to introspect and evaluate what has happened during the past week. They can also contemplate what they want the week ahead to be like.

When a woman lights Shabbat candles, she can ask herself, "Am I happy with the way I spent this past week? Are there things that I need to improve going forward? What has the Almighty given me that I should count my blessings for at this moment?" She humbly requests additional gifts that she wants from God in order to actualize her spiritual potentials and be a better Jewess, wife, and/or mother. These are times of intimate communion with her Creator, an opportunity to evaluate where she is coming from and where she is going.

Every time that a woman goes to the *mikvah*, she has a similar opportunity for introspection and evaluation. She can ask herself, "What has happened between my husband and me these past two weeks? Am I satisfied with how things went? Did we spend enough quality time together and make the most of our opportunities together? Do I need to be less critical and more appreciative? Do I need to express my desires and tell him what I want instead of complaining? Do I need to be more positive, be a better listener, and offer less advice about how he needs to do things? Do we need to communicate better, put more spirituality into our lives, and/or be careful not to gossip about others? Have we centered our Shabbat and holiday meals around God and the children, instead of just having fancy meals with mundane conversation?"

She then visualizes what she would like the next two weeks to look like, and prepares for it mentally, emotionally and spiritually. In this way, women can use their *mikvah* night as an opportunity to review their marriages and make sure that they are going in the direction that they should.

## BONDING THROUGH FAMILY HOLINESS

Couples can differ greatly in how they observe *mitzvot*. For example, a husband may be more stringent than his wife in how he keeps kosher, or she may be more stringent in how carefully she observes the Sabbath. Their attitudes about keeping *mitzvot* may also differ. The one area in which a couple must be totally on the same wavelength is in how they keep the laws of family purity. This need to be equal gives the couple a wonderful opportunity for bonding in their relationship.

The process by which a couple adjusts to an identical commitment to these laws has at least two effects: First, it brings about a true union and parity between husband and wife. Second, they bring God into their marriage in the most intimate way possible. They realize that whatever feelings they have toward one another, they are both limited by the constraints of Jewish law. When our Creator oversees and is a partner to their relationship, a couple cannot relate to each other in terms of, "What's good for me?" Rather, the relationship becomes one of, "What's best for us, in God's eyes?" Developing the self-restraint to be absolutely congruent in this area sets the stage for resolving other differences and for mutual respect in all other areas of marriage.

After some years of marriage, many couples feel bored with one another. Observing the laws that govern marital relations adds a special significance to life. Every time a married woman returns home from the *mikvah*, she and her husband experience the tremendous power that they wield. They literally have the power to create or to destroy worlds, both physically and spiritually. They can come as close to being God-like as it is possible for mortals to be. Every month, a fertile couple must decide if they wish to take on the challenge of creating life or of preventing it.[274]

This idea of creation applies to their relationship as well. Will they use the opportunity for renewed physical bonding to bring life to their marriage, or will it stunt their growth? Will they get so caught up in the physical pleasure that they stop appreciating their partner's needs, sensitivities and uniqueness?

A couple may be physically intimate on many levels. If it occurs without emotional and spiritual preparation, it is like a check that is drawn on an empty bank account. Its depth and potential meaning stay unappreciated and untapped.

The process of separation that precedes even holding hands or kissing can be used to make emotional contributions to a couple's relationship. When their physical contact is backed up by verbal expressions and by shared communication, a much deeper bond cements them, and their subsequent physical intimacy reflects that.

## SIGNIFICANCE OF A WOMAN'S CYCLE

Biologists and anthropologists have tried to explain away the significance of menstruation and menopause as artifacts of evolution. Their ideas have nothing in common with the Jewish perspective about women's physiology.

Judaism teaches that everything in the physical world was designed to reflect how it was meant to be used. By understanding the meanings of physical creations, we can use them as vehicles to draw down greater spirituality. Women's menstrual cycles were designed to teach us about the physical world's limitations, and the need to elevate it toward spiritual goals.

A couple is required to abstain from sex when a woman has her period. The Almighty created the menstrual cycle, starting with Eve, as a result of her sin in the Garden of Eden. It has been theorized that this cycle was to be a means by which she could partially rectify her failure to communicate properly with Adam. It was passed down to her female descendants so that subsequent generations could collectively rectify her initial failures of communication in Paradise.

People often misunderstand or deny that the menstrual cycle is anything more than a biological fact. Many ancient societies thought that menstruating women were dirty and taboo, and should be shunned. Modern societies go to the opposite extreme and tell women that they should not let their periods affect them in any way, including having intercourse at those times.

Judaism says that when a married woman has her period, she should use this as an opportunity to communicate constructively with her husband in non-physical ways. She should use their separation as a recurring reminder to contemplate how to spiritually enhance her own life, as well as that of each member of her family.

When a woman gets her period, an egg (potential life) and the lining of her uterus both die and leave her body. This loss of potential life, along with its nurturing environment, reminds a woman every month that physical life is finite. Her body gives her this message at exactly the time that the Torah says that she and her husband should separate. Just as she becomes aware that physical life is limited, the couple becomes aware that their physical relationship should be limited. Those weeks are times to develop the spiritual aspects of their marriage, in order to enhance and make it enduring.

In addition, when a woman is trying to conceive, she typically feels a sense of loss and sadness when she gets her period. Her body tells her, in no uncertain terms, that her chance to create a new life has slipped away. The blood reminds her of the potentials that were lost. Her immersion in a *mikvah* can help her emerge from her mourning and feel hopeful once again. When she does this, she experiences the essence of the Garden of Eden, with its affirmation of the soul's immortality and her connection to the Infinite.

## SEVEN WHITE DAYS

Women are required women to count seven days after their menstrual flow has stopped before they can immerse in a *mikvah*. The number seven has mystical significance in Judaism, and symbolizes perfection in the physical world. This is because the universe was created in seven days, with the physical world being created during the first six days. The Almighty created the Sabbath on the seventh day. The universe was not complete until the physical world culminated in a day of total receptivity to its Creator. The Sabbath is a day that transcends the physical world, yet enables mortals to see the physical world in its proper perspective—as an integration of physical that is revealed with spiritual that is hidden.

The Torah requires certain people who are spiritually blocked, such as those who came in contact with a corpse, or who had *tzaraat*, or who were *niddah*, to count seven days prior to reinstating a spiritual free flow. This symbolized that people who are spiritually blocked and who are not fully in touch with what is hidden (spiritual) need seven days to reconnect fully to their spiritual Source. At the end of an entire week, they can transcend the physical world and fully reconnect with the spiritual.

## CHANGES DUE TO WOMEN

Married women currently count seven days after their hormonally-induced uterine bleeding stops. They may only immerse in a *mikvah* after this week passes without their discharging any blood.

In ancient times, women could have a flow of blood that did not require waiting an entire week after it stopped before they could immerse. The number of days that they counted after each term of bleeding depended upon when in their cycle each flow began. The number of days ranged from none to seven, depending on timing factors too complex to discuss here.

Approximately 2,000 years ago, Jewish women were concerned that the laws were so complex that they might count too few days. Were this to occur, couples would be intimate when sex was forbidden, and they would violate a serious Torah prohibition.

For this reason, our female ancestors collectively decided that they would always wait one week after their bleeding stopped before immersing in a *mikvah*, and our rabbinic sages affirmed that decision. These women determined how the law would be practiced by adding their stringencies to what was required.[275]

It should be noted that rabbinic enactments always take into consideration the needs and limitations of Jews who will be affected by them. Our sages did not give legal decisions ensconced in ivory towers, unaware of the ramifications of that their decrees would have on people's daily lives. They were well aware of how imposing legal safeguards and stringencies would affect individuals, and they never did this if the results were expected to be too onerous for the Jewish people to bear.

## THE RITUAL BATH

A woman ends the seven white days by readying herself for, then immersing in a *mikvah*. At least part of a *mikvah*'s water comes from a natural source, such as a spring or rain water. One reason why a Jacuzzi, bathtub or swimming pool cannot serve as a *mikvah* is because their water comes via pipes, and is not directly connected to their natural source.

As was mentioned earlier, all ritual impurity represents a barrier to our ability to connect fully to our spiritual Source. When God put Adam and Eve in the Garden of Eden, they were intended to live forever. He placed them in a paradise where death didn't exist. Death can only occur when a body disconnects from its spiritual Source. Thus, death is a result of severing ties with the Infinite and Eternal God. When the first couple sinned and were banished from the Garden of Eden, the Almighty loved them and their descendants so much that He wanted them never to despair of reconnecting with Him.

As part of His tremendous compassion, He infused some of the essence of the Garden of Eden into our world. He delineated places where we can dissolve the shackles of our mortality and regain the pristine spiritual connection with Him that existed in Paradise. One such place is the *mikvah*; another, natural bodies of water.

The Torah says that four rivers flowed out of the Garden of Eden.[276] All natural earthly waters are fed by them. This is why a *mikvah* must contain natural water, not water that is channeled by human effort. Just as the waters in which we immerse are connected to their source, so do we reconnect to our Source when we immerse in them.

Before immersing, we can take a few moments to introspect and meditate. What is the true function of our body, and how were we meant to integrate it with the spiritual? When we immerse, we can think about releasing the spiritual blockages that were part of us, and becoming spiritually pristine as we connect to our Source, facilitated by the womb-like natural water.

Even though Jewish men sometimes immerse in a *mikvah*, it is the Jewish woman who has the primary ability to bring the influence of Paradise into her body, her home and her family. Hence, the laws governing sexual intimacy are not called "laws of personal purity" but rather "laws of family purity."

During Temple times, anyone who experienced *tumah* was reminded what was lost when the first couple was expelled from the Garden of Eden. A person who was *tamei* (spiritually blocked) was barred from entering the Temple, just as Adam and Eve were barred from the Garden of Eden.

When a woman observes the laws of family holiness, she creates a temple inside her body. Just as it was forbidden to enter the Temple in a state of *tumah*, it is forbidden for a man to enter his wife's body when she is in that state. Once she has properly immersed in the waters of Eden, she leaves her *tumah* behind. In this state of spiritual free flow, couples can again aspire to the state of perfection that existed in the Garden of Eden and in the Temple. They can enjoy a taste of that when they join their bodies with the Divine Presence.

When a woman immerses in the *mikvah* and sanctifies her sex life, she reconnects herself, her husband, and any resulting children with the Source of all life. She gives her entire family spiritual equilibrium by linking them with the Creator of the Universe.

## BACK TO THE SOURCE

A *mikvah* must contain at least 40 *seah* (about 200 gallons) of water. The number 40 symbolizes the number of days that it takes for an embryo to attain human form. It also symbolizes the number of days needed to make a new spiritual or physical creation. The *mikvah* itself represents the womb.[277]

The Hebrew words *mayim* (water) and *mikvah* both start with the Hebrew letter *mem*. *Mem* is the exact middle letter of the Hebrew alphabet. It symbolizes the transition point between the beginning of life (rebirth) and its end (death). The *mikvah* and its water help us make the journey between tasting death (being in a state of spiritual blockage) to birth and renewal.

Immersing in a *mikvah* reminds us that we can always get past our past and change our lives for the better. We are helped to regain our spiritual purity and reconnect with God by submerging our ego to His will. Since water can always change its form, it represents our ability to change and transform our identity. The laws of *mikvah* symbolize that constructive change and spiritual rebirth are always possible.

## IT'S NEVER TOO LATE

As is the case with many other rituals in Judaism, the *mikvah* has to be experienced to be truly appreciated. At the same time, no one should be deterred from observing the laws of family holiness if she does not feel the emotional and spiritual benefits of doing so. While there are always spiritual benefits to doing any *mitzvah*, not everyone is emotionally sensitive enough to appreciate them. We can strive to develop that sensitivity over time.

If a married woman has never properly immersed, she remains a *niddah* from the time that she got her first period. This is true even if she can no longer have children, is infertile, or is postmenopausal. She can give herself a wonderful gift by trying out the *mikvah*! When she does, she will be connecting herself to more than 3,000 years of Jewish women who have sanctified their home lives and bodies through the rituals and perspectives of family holiness.

# 12

# *Birth Control*

The Creator's first commandment to humanity was to be fruitful and multiply.[278] People did have children, yet instead of making the world a place that was moral and good, they became totally corrupt. The Almighty responded by wiping them out in the Great Flood, except for Noah and his family, who survived by staying in a special ark. When Noah and his sons emerged from the ark to a world that was totally devastated, God blessed them and said, "Be fruitful, and multiply, and bring forth abundantly in the earth, and multiply in it."[279]

According to one Torah commentator,[280] our Creator had to command human beings to procreate. This was because man was created in the divine image, and as such, he might think that he should only engage in spiritual and intellectual pursuits. The commandment to reproduce was a divine reminder that man needed to be involved in, and to preserve, the material world.

This Noahide commandment to reproduce was transferred from Noah's descendants to the Jews. This occurred when God appointed them to fulfill the spiritual potentials that all of humanity should have brought to fruition, but didn't. The commandment to procreate is fundamental for Jews because it makes it possible for future generations to observe the rest of the Torah.[281] The Talmud even goes so far as to say that "he who does not try to procreate is as if he committed murder."[282]

## MEN SHOULD BE FATHERS

Jewish men are required to procreate. The Mishnah defines what this biblical commandment entails:[283]

> "A man should not abstain from the obligation to propagate the race unless he already has two children. Bet Shammai ruled (that a man must father) two males and Bet Hillel ruled (that he must father) a male and a female."

This Mishnah is based on the Torah verse, "male and female He created them."[284] This refers to humanity's original creation with both genders.

However, there are two additional rabbinic *mitzvot* regarding fathering children that Jewish men are supposed to fulfill:[285] The first is based on a scriptural verse, "For thus says the Lord, Creator of the heavens: He is the God who formed the earth and made it, He established it, He didn't create it void—He formed it to be inhabited."[286] This is interpreted to mean that men are supposed to reproduce so that the world will be populated.

The Talmud discusses the second rabbinic commandment, which is based on the verse, "In the morning sow your seed, and in the evening don't withhold your hand (from sowing), because you don't know which will prosper, this or that, or if they both will be equally good."[287] In the Talmud, Rabbi Joshua used this verse to support his belief that "if a man had children in his youth, he should also have children in his old age."[288]

A man's *mitzvah* to procreate requires him to father at least two children who will grow to maturity and who will in turn have children of their own. Since no one ever knows if his children will later reproduce and contribute to the world's habitation, a man should father more than the minimal number of children to ensure that he has fulfilled his obligation.

Practically speaking, Jewish legal writings do not distinguish between the biblical and rabbinic commandments to procreate. As a result, Jewish law never assumed that a couple could automatically use birth control once a man had fathered two children. In fact, Maimonides wrote, "Although a man has fulfilled the *mitzvah* to procreate, he is still commanded by the rabbis not to refrain from procreation as long as he has strength."[289]

## Marriage and Procreation for Women

A woman is neither obligated to marry[290] nor to procreate. Maimonides wrote that women should marry lest they be suspected of immoral behavior.[291] Since people usually want to express their sexual feelings, if a woman stays single, she might be motivated to find non-marital sexual outlets, or at least be assumed to be doing this.

The Talmud says that women are not required to procreate because the *mitzvah* to "be fruitful and multiply, and fill the earth, and subdue it" applies only to people whose nature it is to subdue—i.e., to men.[292] A different opinion states that women are not obligated to have children because giving birth can endanger their lives.[293]

A Talmudic commentary notes that even though a woman is not personally obligated to procreate, she does a *mitzvah* by getting married.[294] This is because marrying enables her husband to fulfill his obligation to be fruitful and multiply. Moreover, when she helps her husband to bear and raise children, her reward for doing this is greater than his.[295] The Talmud adds, "The enabler of an act is greater than the one who does (the act)."[296] In other words, even though women are not commanded to marry nor to have children, their reward for doing so is great.

## Mystical Perspectives about Procreation

The Talmud not only discusses Jewish legal aspects of procreation, it also mentions a mystical perspective that underscores the importance of having children.[297] It says that the Messiah will not come until enough people have been born to allow all of the souls that are waiting to come into this world to be put into bodies. The extent to which Jewish parents prevent themselves from bearing children is the extent to which our ultimate redemption may be delayed.

This same idea is part of the reason why Jewish couples should have children even when Jewish law does not require them to do so.[298] No couple can predetermine that the children whom they are destined to bear and raise will not make vital contributions to the world. Every person has a unique contribution to make in furthering the goals that God has for humanity. If a soul is prevented from coming into this world, its intended contributions will be held back.

More than 2,500 years ago, King Hezekiah was punished with a nearly fatal illness for deliberately not having children.[299] The Talmud relates that the Almighty sent the prophet Isaiah to inform the king that he would die and not have any share in the World-to-Come.[300]

Hezekiah tried to defend his actions by saying, "I didn't marry (or have children) because I saw through divine inspiration that my children would not be righteous." (This turned out to be correct.)

Isaiah replied, "Of what concern are God's secrets to you? You should have done what you were commanded to do and let the Holy One, blessed is He, do what pleases Him."

After being reproved, Hezekiah married and had children.[301] He lived fifteen additional healthy years.

## MODERN BIRTH CONTROL

The main leniencies for which rabbis allow using birth control tend to be medical considerations for the mother, or hazards that having more children might present to the health of already existing children.

Many Jews feel that we should do all we can to replenish the millions of Jews who were annihilated during the Holocaust, and the millions subsequently who have been lost to our people through assimilation and intermarriage. Having many children would help to replenish the spiritual contributions and large numbers of souls that were eradicated during and after World War II.

Since Judaism only permits sex between two people who are married according to Jewish law, it is obviously not permitted for unmarried couples to practice contraception as a means of avoiding pregnancy. Rather, they should sublimate their sex drives in a way that fuels their personal and spiritual growth, rather than diminishing it.

Married people have many rationales for using contraception. Even though observant Jews tend to have a higher birth rate than other Jews, non-observant Jews often have the lowest birth rate of any group in the Western world.[302] There are many reasons for this.

Some couples don't want to bring children into a world that is polluted, violent, and filled with problems. Yet, from the time that the Jews were enslaved in Egypt until modern times, Jewish history has been replete with oppression, slavery, pogroms, persecution and genocide. Nevertheless, observant Jews never abstained from having children who would live in a hostile or immoral world. We are here to make the world a better place, not to avoid playing a role in it.

Many people use birth control so that they won't be encumbered by children, whom they see as hampering their freedom and draining their personal and financial resources. This is often based in selfishness. Our lives were not given to us so that we could party and be as comfortable as possible. One of the greatest ways of developing ourselves and becoming less self-centered is by deciding to be good parents, then doing what it takes to make that happen.

Some use birth control to avoid financial hardship. These issues, though, have rarely motivated observant Jews to use contraception. There is an idea that the Almighty sends each child into the world with a financial package that his parents will use to raise him. Sometimes this happens in obvious ways, where someone gets a better job when a new child is born, or a parent gets an inheritance or gift from the child's grandparent. Expecting to have a number of children may mean that fathers will have to get better job skills or a better education, actively seek a better job, or work harder to make enough money to support his family.

Some proponents of birth control insist that it is irresponsible to have children in an already overpopulated world that doesn't have enough resources to go around. Since Judaism puts a premium on providing for existing life, it agrees that parents who cannot feed their children should not have more. However, that is rare for most Jews in the Western world. Unless such dire circumstances exist, the Almighty wants us to continually populate and replenish the world.

The difference between impoverished nations and the reality for most Westerners, who enjoy a level of unprecedented affluence in the history of the world, is illustrated by a comical story:

A grandmother chides her beleaguered grandson for playing with his food, "Why don't you eat all of the food on your plate? Don't you know how many children are starving in China?"

The precocious boy quips back, "And if I eat all of my vegetables, name three children who will be less hungry!"

It is not automatic that when (relatively) affluent people use birth control it benefits poor people. The poor will always need help from those who are wealthier, better educated, and more powerful. Issues that are usually attributed to overpopulation such as destruction of natural resources, pollution, and starvation are usually related to how resources are distributed and used, as well as due to political and economic policies. Countries such as the United States produce more than enough food to supply their own citizens, as well as many others. As the world's population has grown, so has the ingenuity to provide people with necessities such as clean water and food. Small family size in Western countries, though, does not reduce use of resources.

For example, a child born in the United States will create thirteen times more ecological damage during his or her lifetime than a child born in Brazil. The average American will drain as many resources as 35 natives of India and consume 53 times more goods and services than someone from China. From 1900-1989, the U.S. population tripled while its use of raw materials grew by a factor of 17. The U.S. has less than 5 percent of the world's population, yet uses one-third of the world's paper, a quarter of the world's oil, 23 percent of the coal, 27 percent of the aluminum, and 19 percent of the copper. Their per capita use of energy, metals, minerals, forest products, fish, grains, meat, and even fresh water dwarfs that of people living in the developing world. American fossil fuel consumption is also double that of the average resident of Great Britain and two and a half times that of the average Japanese. Americans also create half of the world's waste.[303] Ironically, American consumers rank last of 17 countries surveyed in regard to sustainable behavior. They are also among the least likely to feel guilty about the impact they have on the environment, yet they are near the top of the list in believing that individual choices could make a difference.[304]

Instilling respect for the value of others' lives, nature, and taking care of God's world can do a lot more for the environment than simply limiting family size.

The Torah is replete with stories that teach the importance of giving of ourselves and helping others, instead of focusing on taking and amassing ever greater material comforts. Jewish law recommends that we give a tenth of our after-tax income to charity.[305] If we give our proper share to those who are needy, that helps solve problems of distribution of resources much more than Jews limiting their family size.

Our giving also encourages the Almighty to give us more. This is based on a verse that can be homiletically understood to mean, "Give ten percent so that you will become rich." We are promised that the more charity we give, the more blessing God will bestow on us, causing us to have greater and greater wealth. If everyone who had more than basic necessities gave 10% of their incomes to the needy in ways that encouraged them to make moral choices, helped them to create a healthy environment, and prepared them to get good jobs, poverty would lessen faster than if Jews had fewer offspring.

## FINANCIAL CONSIDERATIONS

Many rabbinic authorities oppose Jews limiting their family size by marital abstinence or using contraception when there is no justifiable medical reason or extreme financial need.[306] Poverty that threatens a family's physical or spiritual welfare may be a reason to delay marriage until their financial situation improves, or it may allow them to use acceptable forms of birth control.[307]

Birth control is often permitted when a family subsists at poverty level and having additional children will unbearably strain the family. However, when such is the case, they should consult with a rabbinic authority before deciding to use contraception.

Obviously, the definition of lacking financial wherewithal can be very subjective. American parents may define it as meaning that they will have to give up their spring vacations to the Caribbean or forego certain materialistic dreams. These are generally not valid justifications for limiting family size.

One consequence of marriage is that a couple's life is supposed to change. We are supposed to grow through the process of having children and raising a family. Part of that requires us to reassess what is really important in life and what should be secondary considerations.

A story is told about a man who wished to see heaven and hell. An angel acceded to his request and showed him hell. The man saw people sitting around long banquet tables overflowing with delicacies of every description. Unfortunately, the residents were all emaciated and anguished. Their hands were tied in such a way that each could reach the food in front of him but not bring his hands close to his mouth. They were eternally tortured by the tantalizing food that they could see, smell, and touch, but never taste.

Then, the angel took the man to heaven. Much to his surprise, he saw the same scene of tables laden with delectable foods. Yet the residents who sat around the tables had their hands tied in exactly the same way as the poor souls he had just seen in hell. Here, however, everyone was happy and well-fed.

The puzzled man asked the angel, "How is it that in both places, everyone's hands are tied, yet in hell each person is starving, and here they are well-nourished?"

The angel smiled. "It's quite simple. In hell, everyone is concerned with feeding himself, but that is impossible. As long as they try to put food into their own mouths, they starve.

"In heaven, everyone feeds the person next to him."

When people are mostly concerned with what feels best to them, there's never enough time, money, or emotional energy to give to others. When people have the attitude that every child is a blessing and a gift from the Almighty, they often discover ways to raise a larger family than they previously thought was possible.

## PERMISSIBILITY

Some rabbinic authorities permit women to use birth control in order to space having children if the parents would not be able to raise several young children at the same time, and/or if their domestic peace would otherwise be disrupted.[308] The same is true for a couple who is having serious marital problems and risks getting divorced. In general, though, women are mostly allowed to use contraception for medical reasons. For example, if a pregnancy might endanger her life, modern authorities permit her to use birth control. Contraception may also be used where the woman wants to avoid the extreme pain of childbirth, or where pregnancy would cause her serious medical problems, such as blindness or psychiatric illness.[309]

Couples who get a rabbinic decision to allow them to use birth control for other than ongoing health reasons generally get a reevaluation every year or two. Women who already have a son and a daughter usually get more leniency to use birth control than does a couple who has not yet fulfilled the obligation to procreate.[310]

In general, using birth control is prohibited for financial considerations that are not pressing, for social reasons, for general convenience, or because a child may be born retarded, unless the child's problems will prove a serious detriment to the mother's psychiatric well-being.

## *ONAH*

One of a Jewish man's marital obligations is to regularly provide sexual pleasure to his wife.[311] This *onah* is a *mitzvah* separate from the *mitzvot* of marriage and procreation. Even when it is biologically impossible for his wife to become pregnant, a husband is required to fulfill his obligation of *onah* with her. Sexual relations under these circumstances should occur in a procreative manner (i.e., he climaxes inside her).

Part of *onah* requires a man to have intercourse with his wife when she desires it, whether or not she is capable of becoming pregnant. *Onah* involves giving joy to his wife during marital relations[312] and responding to her desire to be intimate with him. A couple is supposed to have mutual, pleasurable bodily contact during intercourse.

According to certain opinions, *onah* also requires the complete union of the couple's bodies.[313] The necessity for this is derived from the verse, "Therefore shall a man leave his father and his mother and cleave unto his wife, and they shall be one flesh."[314] They can only be "one flesh" if the couple's bodies make unimpeded contact with each other, with ejaculation occurring inside the woman's reproductive tract. Anything that precludes such contact, or that prevents ejaculation from occurring in the normal fashion is considered to interfere with proper sexual relations.

## FEMALE CONTRACEPTION

The rationale for allowing birth control when the mother's or other children's health are at risk derives from the following Talmudic selection:[315]

> Three women may (or must) use a contraceptive tampon (*moch*) in their marital intercourse: a minor, a pregnant woman, and a nursing woman. The minor because (otherwise) she might become pregnant and die as a result. A pregnant woman because (otherwise) she might cause her fetus to become a sandal (a fishlike fetus that will be aborted). A nursing woman because (otherwise) she might wean her child prematurely, resulting in his death....This is the opinion of Rabbi Meir. But the sages say that the one and the other have marital intercourse in the usual way, and mercy will come from Heaven (to save them from danger), for the Bible says, "The Lord guards the simple."[316]

The question of whether the above three women *may* or *must* use contraception is a matter of dispute. Rabbenu Tam, a medieval Talmudic commentator, understood Rabbi Meir to mean that the above three women *must* use a *moch*, whereas the sages say that these women don't have to use a *moch*, but they *may*. According to the commentator Rashi, Rabbi Meir meant that the above women *may* use a *moch*, while the sages say they *may not*. These differences in opinion result in differing views as to when contraception is permitted. For instance, authorities differ as to whether the above-mentioned three women are paradigms of the types of women who may use birth control, or are the only categories of women who may do so. Thus, certain authorities allow any woman whose life might be threatened by pregnancy to use contraception,[317] while others maintain that only the above-mentioned three women may use it.[318]

## PREFERENCES

When women may use contraception, there is hierarchy of most-preferred to least-preferred means. This is based on understanding what a *moch* is, the degree to which birth control interferes with the woman's *onah*, and what different kinds of birth control do to sperm.

Judaism strongly prohibits improperly discharging or destroying a man's seed (*hashchatat zera levatalah*). This includes discharging semen without normal intercourse (such as by masturbating or by *coitus interruptus*) and a man's destroying his sperm after it is emitted. Thus, birth control that prevents intercourse from proceeding in a normal manner (which will be defined below) or destroys sperm is often prohibited.

A rabbinic authority, Rabbi Chaim Sofer, wrote that when contraception impedes total contact between the man's and woman's bodies, it violates the prohibition against destroying seed.[319] This is because sex in this manner does not have a man "cleaving" to his wife while becoming "one flesh" with her. In addition, the free flow of the ejaculate inside the woman's body is considered to add to her pleasure, and is normally required for sex to be considered "proper." Rabbi Sofer did not consider birth control using a condom as allowing proper intercourse, since it separates the man's and woman's flesh. Such relations result in the man "casting his seed as if on wood and stones."[320]

Rabbi Sofer added that using a diaphragm allows the bodies to have unimpeded contact with each other, and the ejaculate follows its normal course "in full physical pleasure" and in the "flaming ardor of passion."[321] Even though the sperm can't enter the uterus, a diaphragm doesn't diminish the pleasure of having sex, and so the act is permitted. In general, the more a contraceptive interferes with sexual pleasure, the less acceptable it is.

Thus, even when medical reasons necessitate using birth control, making it impossible to fulfill the *mitzvah* of procreation, the *mitzvah* of giving a wife full sexual pleasure is still important. Birth control should not interfere with a wife's *onah* any more than is necessary. The permissibility of the type of birth control depends upon the degree to which it permits the satisfactions of *onah* and whether or not sperm are destroyed once they are emitted.

Many modern halachic (Jewish legal) authorities do not emphasize a differentiation between the *mitzvahs* of *onah* and of procreation. They opine that having intercourse using a diaphragm is considered to be "casting upon wood and stones" because it creates a mechanical barrier to the sperm entering the uterus, and is therefore not a valid form of contraception.[322] Other authorities allow it when contraception is medically indicated.[323]

Most rabbinic authorities agree that if contraception is permitted, a woman is permitted to destroy her husband's sperm once intercourse has proceeded normally. The man, however, may not do this.

Thus, birth control is preferred that doesn't interfere with the viability or passage of sperm in the woman's body, but such forms of contraception are not always medically acceptable or otherwise feasible. Rabbinic experts may recommend less-preferred types of contraception for such women. Couples are not required to abstain from sex when pregnancy can be hazardous to the woman.[324]

When birth control is permitted, temporary methods such as birth control pills, hormonal implants, diaphragms, spermicides, and the like are preferable to permanent means, such as tubal ligation and female sterilization. (There is a separate prohibition against female sterilization.) Women who use temporary forms of birth control due to medical or psychiatric problems typically have their situations reassessed every year to see if they have changed.[325]

Jewish law prefers that women use birth control pills, vaginal rings, patches or hormonal implants because they don't interfere with normal intercourse, and they don't destroy sperm. However, many rabbis prohibit their use due to their medical complications. Next preferred are IUDs (intrauterine devices) and spermicides. Yet, here, too, some rabbinic authorities prohibit using IUDs because of their medical complications. Diaphragms are next on the hierarchy of preference, followed by condoms. Finally, tubal ligation is the least preferred method, but may be necessary when permanent birth control is required.

Two problems with hormonal forms of birth control are long-term medical problems, and breakthrough bleeding and spotting. The latter may prevent women from going to the *mikvah* after the usual 12-14 days of separation. When that happens, the hormone dose may need to be adjusted so that non-menstrual bleeding stops.

Current IUDs are not preferred by many authorities because the devices either kill sperm or make it impossible for a fertilized egg to implant in the uterine lining. The medical complications of infection or a perforated uterus make them less preferred by some rabbis who otherwise accept them as a means of birth control.

Some authorities prohibit using spermicides because they destroy the sperm as soon as they are discharged, and men are forbidden to discharge sperm in a way that they can't have any reproductive potential.[326] Nevertheless, many authorities consider chemical methods of birth control preferable to mechanical methods.[327]

If getting pregnant will endanger a woman's life, and she can't use birth control, surgical sterilization (such as tubal ligation) is permitted, especially if she and her husband already have two or more children.[328] Since a woman is not required to "be fruitful and multiply," the prohibition against her undergoing sterilization is very different than for a man.

The Torah specifically prohibits a man sterilizing himself[329] but not a woman sterilizing herself.[330] Even though women are urged to help the world become inhabited, they are not required to build the world by destroying themselves.[331] Thus, if pregnancy threatens their lives, they are not obliged to have children.

## MALE CONTRACEPTION

There are presently five main types of male birth control: *coitus interruptus*, condoms, abstinence, the rhythm method, and sterilization.

The Torah strictly prohibits *coitus interruptus*,[332] which begins as normal sex, but ends with the man ejaculating outside the woman's body. It is generally forbidden for a man to ejaculate outside his wife's body. An exception is made if fertility testing requires the semen to be examined and it cannot be collected from the wife's reproductive tract after having intercourse.

Using condoms is forbidden because they cause sperm to be destroyed and also prevent the man and woman's flesh from fully touching. Only when no other form of birth control is possible, and the couple's domestic peace will be disrupted, can leniencies allow condom use.[333]

Abstinence is forbidden because a man is not allowed to "reduce his wife's conjugal rights"[334] unless she agrees not to have sex. Abstinence prevents a man from fulfilling both *onah* and the *mitzvah* of procreation. Nevertheless, when a couple may use birth control for other than medical reasons, abstinence has occasionally been condoned.[335]

The rhythm method involves a couple abstaining from sex when the woman is fertile—usually around the middle of her cycle. Although it can be preferred *halachically* if it is agreeable to both spouses, rhythm is often unreliable.[336] If there are medical reasons why a woman must not get pregnant, doctors usually recommend that more trustworthy methods of contraception be used. There is also an emotional and physical toll for observant couples who already abstain for the first 12-14 days of a woman's menstrual cycle each month. Separating even longer after she immerses in a *mikvah* can be difficult.

Sterilization, such as vasectomy, is categorically prohibited due to a specific injunction that forbids castration.[337] In some circumstances, a castrated man is even prohibited from having intercourse.

In sum, this chapter has presented an overview of Jewish attitudes about birth control that is neither comprehensive nor applicable to a specific couple. Any couple considering using birth control should not rely on the opinions cited above to determine if their particular circumstances warrant using contraception. It is best if they consult a knowledgeable rabbi who can assess their circumstances and give a response that is tailor-made for them.

# 13

# *Abortion*

Judaism teaches that each person has a unique role and mission that no one else can ever fulfill. God custom designs each of us with strengths and gives us challenges throughout our lives that enable us to bring our unique purpose to fruition.

The importance of each person's uniqueness is underscored by Him making all forms of life *en masse* when He put them on earth. Insects, birds, fish, mammals, trees and grasses were all created in "swarms." Man and woman were the only creations that were brought into being individually. This informs us that it was worthwhile for the Almighty to create the entire universe for the sake of one person. Moreover, each individual is so precious that the Talmud declares, "Someone who saves a life is (viewed) as if (he or she) saved an entire world. Someone who destroys a life is as if (he or she) destroyed an entire world."[338]

## SCRIPTURAL SOURCES

The topic of abortion appears early in the Torah. It says, "Whoever sheds the blood of man in man, his blood shall be shed, for in the image of God He made man."[339] This commandment was addressed to Noah and his descendants, and is one of the seven laws that gentiles are required to observe.[340]

The Talmud asks, "Who is a man in man?" Rabbi Yishmael interprets this to mean a fetus, since a developing child is a person within a person.[341] The rabbis derived from this verse that a gentile is prohibited from murdering anyone, including a fetus. Several rabbinic authorities assert that a gentile who aborts a fetus for purposes others than saving the life of the mother has not technically committed murder, although it is a capital crime. This is because the fetus is not considered to be a person until it is born.[342]

There are additional textual sources that prohibit Jews from causing abortions. The laws that govern intentional abortions by Jews are derived from laws pertaining to accidental abortions. The Torah says about those, "When men fight, and one of them pushes a pregnant woman and a miscarriage results, but no other misfortune ensues, the one responsible shall be fined as the woman's husband may demand of him, the payment to be based upon the judges' reckoning."[343]

When an accidental abortion occurs, Jewish law requires the person who caused it to pay monetary damages to the parents for the loss of their fetus.

Aborting a Jewish fetus is generally forbidden, yet Jewish law does not regard it as manslaughter.[344] This is because the fetus is not considered to be a person until it emerges from its mother's body. The Talmud says that the punishment for murder applies to a "man," but not to a fetus.[345]

Even though a Jew's aborting a fetus is not punishable by a human court as murder, it does not mean that Jews may abort fetuses at will. Only the One who gives life is allowed to reclaim it. Therefore, abortion for or by a Jew is prohibited, unless the mother's life is threatened by the pregnancy.

Judaism requires us to preserve existing life to the best of our ability (unless someone has been judged guilty of a capital crime and has received a death sentence). Euthanasia, suicide, and maiming or mutilating a person's body are normally prohibited because they desecrate the image of God that is housed in us. In addition, we are only allowed to use medical interventions such as amputation or therapeutic disfiguring when we have an overriding requirement to heal ourselves from illness or disease.

Since Judaism values life so much, when a pregnancy endangers the mother's life, and it is not possible to remove that threat without aborting the fetus, we are required to save her life rather than that of her potential child. In such circumstances, the fetus is viewed as a potential murderer. Jewish law allows us to kill someone in self-defense if that person is planning to kill us. When we have no alternative, abortion is allowed or even mandated in the above situation.[346]

Rabbinic authorities who take this perspective accord a fetus the same status as a live person. When it is the fetus whose life is endangered, we desecrate the Sabbath or Yom Kippur when doing so is necessary to save the fetus' life.

## WHY NOT ABORT?

Even though Jewish law does not view intentionally aborting a Jewish fetus as a capital crime, unwarranted abortion is prohibited and is viewed as a serious sin. Several reasons for this are:

1. A man whose wife is capable of conceiving may only emit sperm in a potentially procreative manner. Abortion causes the sperm that fertilized her egg to be destroyed.[347]
2. Even though a fetus is not a "person," it has to be treated as if it is a partial person. This means that its life cannot be terminated without serious justification (such as when continuing the pregnancy might threaten the mother's health or life).[348]
3. According to many authorities, abortion is murder, even though it is not punishable as such by a human court. God may punish the act to the same extent as He does murder.[349]

Some minor considerations also prohibit abortion.[350]

## WHO OWNS OUR BODIES?

Many secular people believe that our body belongs to us, and therefore each individual should have ultimate say over what happens to it. It then follows that only the woman whose body is affected by pregnancy should decide if she will abort her unborn baby.

Judaism takes issue with this premise. The Torah says that men and women were created in the divine image and no one owns his or her body. We are merely its proprietor. The Almighty loaned us our body to use in His service until such time as He decides to revoke our life. It therefore follows that we are supposed to take care of our body as best we can.

Jews do this by following the laws of the Torah, and gentiles do this by observing the seven Noahide laws. We are supposed to do whatever we can to preserve and maintain our physical health, as well as our inner image of God.

This philosophy means that no one whose wishes violate the Torah has ultimate say about what happens to him or her. Life does not belong to any individual, nor is it anyone's right to decide when to end it. This is why Judaism prohibits suicide and euthanasia. Life—potential and actual—is a gift that only the Almighty can grant. It is solely up to Him to decide when it should begin and when it should end.

Life is sacrosanct. We are not allowed to forfeit it willingly unless we are forced to transgress one of the three cardinal sins of Judaism: murder, idolatry, and incest or adultery. In any other circumstances, we must do everything in our power to sustain and protect life.

The Zohar, a Jewish book of mysticism, says that three types of people chase the Divine Presence out of the world. They make it impossible for Him to dwell here and cause prayers to go unanswered. One of these people is someone who performs abortions, because he or she destroys God's handiwork.[351]

Although Judaism puts a premium on preserving life, it also puts a premium on morality. If people abstained from premarital sex, relatively few abortions in Western countries would take place. For example, in 2013, an estimated 984,000 pregnancies were aborted in the United States.[352] Twenty-one percent of all US pregnancies that do not end in miscarriage are aborted.[353] In 2012, 85% of all US abortions were for unmarried women.

By comparison, Israeli women had approximately 20,000 abortions in 2012, a drop of 21% since 1990.[354] They had 117 abortions per 1,000 live births in 2010, as compared to 228 per 1,000 live births that same year in the US.[355] About half of Israeli abortions in 2012 were for pregnant women who were unmarried.

American women who aborted gave three main reasons for doing so: Three-quarters said that having a baby would interfere with work, school or other responsibilities; the same number said they cannot afford a child; and half said they do not want to be a single parent or are having problems with their husband or partner.[356] Only twelve percent gave physical or health reasons as a factor in having an abortion.[357] And although it was often cited decades ago as an important reason to legalize abortion, only one percent of abortions were for women who had been raped.[358]

By comparison, 19% of Israeli women who aborted their fetus cited the reason as health risks to themselves, and 18% did so due to congenital physical or mental defects in the fetus.[359]

Judaism does not view abortion as an alternative form of birth control, nor as a solution for people who wish to be sexually active without being responsible for the consequences of their behavior.

People often seek validation of their needs and rights. In Judaism, people who have rights also have corresponding responsibilities. Judaism does not believe that everyone has the right to be sexually active. It does believe that if people are married, they are granted the gift of enjoying sexual pleasure with their spouses. In allowing themselves this privilege, they accept the responsibilities that are an integral part of sexual intimacy. Unless there are valid reasons for a woman to use birth control, one of the responsibilities of sex is the possibility of creating a new life.

## THE FETUS

Until it is born, an unborn child is considered to be a limb of its mother and a potential life.[360] Before an embryo is 40 days old, it is considered to be "mere water" (*maya d'alma*).[361] From 40 days after conception until birth, the fetus has more status. This is reflected in a law that applied when the Temple stood. When a fetus was spontaneously aborted 40 or more days after conception, its mother brought an offering to the Temple, just as if she had given birth to a live baby.[362] This supports the idea that an unborn child was considered to be a person.

## WHEN IS ABORTION PERMITTED?

The rabbinic opinions that allow or prohibit abortions in various circumstances are complex and often differ from each other. The discussion here about the permissibility of abortion is merely illustrative and should not be considered comprehensive or definitive.

Abortion is generally allowed, or even required, when the mother's life is at risk.[363] Whether abortion is allowed when the mother's health is at stake is a matter of contemporary debate.[364] Examples of conditions that threaten a woman's health and could justify having an abortion include a worsening of cancer, deafness,[365] and severe pain.[366] Life-threatening psychiatric illness caused by pregnancy is also considered a valid reason for an abortion.[367]

In order to justify having an abortion for psychiatric reasons, rabbis require that a mental health expert determine that a woman's pregnancy or giving birth will pose a risk to herself or others. Such risks include her becoming suicidal, homicidal or having an emotional breakdown. A therapist would take into account the woman's prior psychiatric history when discussing such a situation with a rabbi.

Although it is usually forbidden to abort a fetus that was conceived through rape, some rabbis permit it when the mother's physical or emotional health may be harmed by her shame, anguish, or embarrassment.[368] It is usually forbidden to abort a baby conceived through adultery.[369] As with rape, however, it would be permitted if the mother's mental health would be seriously threatened.[370]

## FINANCIAL CONCERNS

Many American women cite financial problems as their motivation to have an abortion, yet Jewish law does not consider poverty a sufficient reason to abort a potential human being.

Although bearing a child and giving it up for adoption is not emotionally palatable to some women, it is spiritually preferable to aborting. At the present time, ten percent of American couples are infertile.[371] The infertility rates among Jewish couples are higher, in part because Jewish women tend to be highly educated. Many of them delay marriage until they have finished their education or are vocationally established, by which time their fertility has declined.

There are thousands of Jewish couples and millions of American couples who would be delighted to adopt a baby. Many of them are hampered by the availability of healthy, adoptable babies. If women chose to give birth when they have unwanted pregnancies, millions of babies could be placed in good homes.

It is especially sad that many Jewish women choose to abort for elective reasons. Jews have one of the lowest birth rates in the Western world. Also, 75% of Jewish couples in the US who want to adopt must do so via overseas adoption.[372] The situation is even more daunting for Jews in Israel, where there is currently a five-year waiting list to adopt.[373]

Some women who would otherwise abort their babies mostly need support to get through their pregnancies. An Israeli organization (EFRAT–C.R.I.B.) helps women to get accurate medical information, financial and/or emotional support to continue their pregnancy. To date, they have saved 64,000 Jewish babies.[374]

## HANDICAPPED FETUSES

It is common for doctors to evaluate the test results of pregnant women and advocate abortion when they believe that the baby will have birth defects. However, tests and doctors' interpretation of them are not always accurate. Many women decide to abort when they are told that their child is likely or certainly going to be born physically or intellectually handicapped. Yet some women choose not to abort when they are advised to terminate their pregnancies. Some of these women prepare to raise a handicapped child. Others get a second expert opinion which is sometimes more encouraging. Some women keep the pregnancy against their primary obstetrician's advice and things turn out very differently than the doctor predicted.

The author was about to give a lecture when a woman, Bethany, came over to her and insisted on speaking to her. Bethany had bought the present book a year earlier, shortly before she got a phone call from her dear friend Elise.

Bethany was surprised to hear Elise sobbing. "What's the matter?" Bethany asked.

"I just came back from my obstetrician," Elise choked. "He did some tests on me and told me that the baby that I'm expecting will be defective. He told me that I should abort it. When I told my mother, she told me that I should listen to the doctor and abort as well. Bethany, I want this baby. I don't want to abort it."

Bethany told her, "Wait! I just read about abortion in this book I got. It says that you shouldn't abort." (That is not what this book says, that was Bethany's interpretation.)

Elise stopped crying. "I'm so happy you said that, Bethany. I really want to keep this baby. I'm not going to end its life."

Bethany ended her story. "That was six months ago. Dr. Aiken, you should know that Elise gave birth to a perfectly healthy child a few weeks ago, thanks to your chapter on abortion."

Almost all rabbinic authorities forbid aborting abnormal fetuses,[375] although one authority allows it.[376] In general, abortion is not even allowed when the pregnant mother contracts rubella,[377] has taken drugs that can cause chromosomal damage,[378] or will be born with physical or intellectual defects.[379] Children with physical deformities and mental retardation are also God's creations and have a right to live. Since the value of human life is infinite, any part of it is also infinite. One is not allowed to abort a baby solely because it will be born with a physical or mental defect.

The Chazon Ish, a renowned rabbi, used to stand up as a sign of respect when a mentally retarded young man entered his study. When questioned about his behavior, he explained, "If the Almighty saw fit to limit this person's free choices so much by creating him mentally retarded, he must have such a spiritually great soul that it does not require a great deal of refinement. Therefore, I stand in his presence, just as I would stand in the presence of anyone who has great spiritual stature."

Judaism's view on abortion is consistent with the premium that it places on the value of life, plus our faith that God will help us to grow through the challenges that He gives us. When the Master of the World determines that life should begin, we have no right to decide that we know better than He does how and when to terminate it. Even when doctors accurately diagnose fetal defects, they don't necessarily know how those will affect a child's life.

## TIME FRAME

When an abortion is permitted, it is preferable to do it before the embryo is 40 days old[380] because some rabbinic authorities do not yet consider the embryo to have the status of an unborn person.

This chapter is not meant to be a guide for women actually considering whether or not to have an abortion. Such women should consult with a rabbi who is expert in these matters and/or with a support organization such as EFRAT.

# 14

# *Divorce*

While Judaism prefers adults to be married, it recognizes that not every couple will be compatible. When a husband and wife cannot live together harmoniously, Judaism allows them to get divorced. Nevertheless, divorce is not to be taken lightly. A broken marriage is considered such a tragedy that the Talmud says,[381] "When a man divorces his first wife, even the altar sheds tears for him, [as it is written[382]:] 'You cover God's altar with tears, and with weeping, and with crying out...because the Lord witnessed between you and the wife of your youth, with whom you acted treacherously.'"

## MARRIAGE AND DIVORCE AS CONTRACTS

Jewish marriage and divorce are each effected via a contract. Unlike civil contracts, all Jewish contracts are unilaterally executed, even though they require the consent of both parties. This means that one person initiates a contract and the other one accepts it. In order for a Jewish marriage to be valid, the man must initiate it, and the woman must accept its terms. (This does not imply that she cannot have any say in those terms. She may negotiate financial and practical terms as she sees fit, as was discussed in Chapter 10.) Once the man initiates the marriage contract and the woman accepts it, they are married.

The Talmud says that men initiate marriage contracts because it is they who actively pursue wives, rather than women actively pursuing husbands.[383] One reason that has been theorized for this is that single men feel more incomplete than do single women. This derives from Eve's having been formed from Adam's body, thus causing him to lose a part of himself. As a result, his male descendants forever feel that some part of them is missing as long as they are without their female "half." In the eyes of Jewish law, men also have a stronger emotional and spiritual need for marriage than do women.[384] A Jewish marriage provides a living laboratory where men can change from being mostly takers who live for themselves to total givers to a wife and children.

## THE DIVORCE PROCESS

Since marriage is a unilateral contract that the man initiates, he must be the one to initiate its dissolution. The Torah describes how it is done:

> If a man takes a woman and marries her, and it comes to pass that she is displeasing to him because he finds some immodesty in her, he shall write her a bill of divorce, and place it in her hand, and send her from his house. When she (then) leaves his house, she may go and marry another man.[385]

This scriptural verse is the source for Jewish laws of divorce. It requires husbands to be the active agents in any divorce proceedings. This means that a divorce is only valid if the husband gives his wife a bill of divorce, known as a *get*. Even though he must give it, he cannot divorce her without her consent. The rabbis made this decree approximately 1,000 years ago in order to protect women from being divorced at whim.

Although a woman cannot technically initiate a divorce, she may ask her husband to divorce her, or she may ask a Jewish court of law to convince or order her husband to do so.[386]

A husband, or his agent, gives his wife, or her agent, a written divorce document, in order to effect the divorce. This must be attended by two *bona fide* Jewish witnesses, just as two witnesses attended the initiation of the marriage. Once the man gives his wife a *get*, even if they are not civilly divorced, it totally severs their relationship as a married couple. From that point on, they may no longer live together.

## THE *GET*

A Jewish divorce document, the *get*, is normally written in Aramaic, the vernacular of the Jews in Israel 2,000 years ago. Ashkenazic and Sefardic *gittin* (plural of *get*) differ in how the names are written but otherwise state the following:

> On the ____ day of the week, the ____ day of the month ____ in the year ____ from the creation of the world, according to the reckoning of the calendar that we are accustomed to count here, in the city of ____, by the river ____, and near wells of water, I ____ son of ____, who am present today in the city of ____, which is located on the river ____, and situated near wells of water, do willingly consent, being under no restraint, to release, set free, and put aside, you, my wife ____ , daughter of ____, who is today in the city of ____, which is located on the river ____, and situated near wells of water, who has been my wife from before. Thus I do set free, release you, and put you aside, in order that you may have permission and authority over yourself to go and marry any man you desire. No person may hinder you from this day forth. And you are permitted to every man. This shall be for you from me a bill of dismissal, a letter of release, and a document of freedom, according to the law of Moses and Israel.
>
> ____ son of ____ Witness
>
> ____ son of ____ Witness

Due to the complexities of how a *get* must be written, a Jewish divorce must be conducted by experts in such matters. This is why the writing and giving of a *get* should be done under the auspices of three men who constitute a Jewish court of law, known as a *bet din*.

The *get* itself is written on a blank piece of paper by a Jewish scribe, using a quill pen and ink. He writes the text on twelve lines, and the document is then notarized by two valid witnesses. Even though the rules governing how to write a *get* are very precise, the process of writing and giving it can take less than an hour.

Before writing a *get*, the scribe must ascertain the precise Hebrew and English names of the divorcing parties, as well as any nicknames by which they and their parents are known.

If there is no chance of reconciliation, the husband and wife are discouraged from speaking to each other from the time the scribe (known as a *sofer*) begins to write the *get* until the husband gives it to his wife. This is to ensure that the husband says nothing that invalidates his intentions to divorce his wife before the proceedings are completed.

After the *get* is written, the husband, or his agent, hands the *get* to his wife, or to her agent. When he does this, he recites a formula that states that from that moment on she is no longer his wife and is henceforth free to remarry. She demonstrates her acquisition of the *get* by carrying it with her as she walks several feet away. She then gives the document to the *bet din* who cut it with a knife or scissors. This precludes anyone else with the same names from using it. This is an added precaution against the remote possibility that someone else would use a *get* that was not specifically written for them.

The torn *get* is then filed away. The woman and her ex-husband receive documents a short time later attesting to the fact that they were divorced according to Jewish law.

Unlike in most civil courts, the entire process of initiating and getting a Jewish divorce can be extremely brief. It can be accomplished in one day if both parties consent and there are no unusual circumstances during the divorce proceedings.

Once divorced, a man may immediately marry another woman if he so desires. A divorced woman must wait approximately 90 days before she can marry another man. This is to ensure that the paternity of her child will be known if she is pregnant at the time of her divorce. If a husband and wife wish to remarry each other and he is not a *cohen* (Jewish priest), they do not have to wait at all.

Once a couple divorces, certain restrictions apply to their remarriage. They may not remarry each other once the woman has subsequently married another man. In addition, men of priestly descent may marry widows but not divorcees. Thus, a *cohen* may never remarry his wife if he divorces her, even if she has not married anyone else in the interim.

## CIVIL DIVORCE

A civil divorce has no religious validity in severing a Jewish couple's marital ties. A civilly divorced Jewish couple is still married in the eyes of Jewish law until they obtain a Jewish divorce. This distinction affects the status of a couple's subsequent sexual relations with people other than their spouse. As long as a Jewish woman is married according to Jewish law, sex with any man besides her husband is adulterous for both parties. That is, as long as a married woman has not received a proper *get*, any men with whom she is sexually intimate are adulterers, and she is an adulteress. Technically, if a married man has not given his wife a *get*, he is prohibited from having sex with any other women. However, if he does so anyway, neither he nor any unmarried women with whom he is intimate violate the prohibition against adultery, although they violate other laws.

As long as a married woman has not received a *get*, her status also affects any children that she conceives with men other than her husband. Secular law defines a bastard or illegitimate child as one who is born out-of-wedlock. By contrast, Jewish law defines an illegitimate child as one who is born from an adulterous or incestuous relationship. Thus, a child resulting from the sexual union of a woman who is married according to Jewish law with a man other than her husband is illegitimate, and is called a *mamzer*. A *mamzer* may not marry a Jew who was born from a legitimate marriage or from an out-of-wedlock relationship that would have been permitted had the couple married according to Jewish law.

The laws that define adulterous relationships and *mamzerut* apply even if women have been civilly divorced. Therefore, it is crucial for Jewish couples to obtain proper religious divorces, for themselves and for the sake of any subsequent children they may have.

## POLYGAMY AND POLYANDRY

Biblical law allows a man to be married to more than one wife simultaneously, provided his wives are not sisters and that he can support them. Approximately 1,000 years ago, Rabbenu Gershom made an edict that forbade a husband from divorcing his wife against her will. He also forbade Ashkenazic men (of German and Eastern European descent) from having more than one wife at the same time. Nevertheless, his restriction included certain provisions allowing married men to marry a second wife if 100 rabbis in three countries permitted them to do so. This might occur if the man's wife were mentally incompetent, in which case the rabbis forbade him to divorce her. He could also marry a second wife when his first wife committed adultery and refused to accept a *get*. This same leniency could be used when a wife repeatedly refused to accept a legitimate *get*.

Whenever a man uses this leniency, he must deposit his first wife's *get* with a *bet din* prior to obtaining rabbinical consent to take a second wife. This ensures that his first wife will be free to remarry whenever she is able or willing to accept the divorce.

Biblical law never allowed women to marry more than one husband, and this law cannot be changed. Once a woman is married, she can only have additional husbands if her original marriage ends due to her spouse's death or his granting her a *get*.

Because married Jewish men and women need a proper divorce in order to remarry, various difficulties ensue when this does not occur. One major problem is women becoming *agunot* (see below). Another is spouses using emotional and financial blackmail against each other.

## AGUNAH

*Agunah* means "a chained woman." This refers to any married woman whose husband does not give her a *get* after she appeals to an appropriate *bet din* for help. An *agunah* may not remarry until her husband either gives her a *get* or dies. Some women become *agunot* for reasons beyond the husband's control, such as his being abducted to an unknown location, his disappearing on a trip, or going missing in a war.

After World War II, many women whose husbands had disappeared during the war questioned whether or not they were *agunot*. This question was also raised when El Al flight 402 was shot down by the Bulgarian Air Force near Sofia in 1955, and when the Israeli submarine, Dakar, disappeared in the Mediterranean in 1965.

In biblical times, the most common reason that women became *agunot* was because their husbands went to war and did not return. Unless a husband's corpse was found, or eyewitnesses testified that he had indeed died, his wife could not assume that she was a widow. Until his death was proven, a wife remained an *agunah* and could not remarry.

During the reign of the Davidic dynasty in the First Temple era, women were better protected from becoming *agunot*. This was because any man who went to war gave his wife a specially worded *get* just prior to leaving for battle. These conditional divorces took effect only if a husband did not return by a certain date. At that time, the wife was free to remarry, even without proof of the spouse's demise. If the husband did return as planned, the divorce never took effect.[387]

During Mishnaic times (approximately 1,800 years ago), women sometimes became *agunot* when their husbands went on sea journeys and never returned. At that time, sea travel was dangerous, and it was not unusual for ship crews and passengers to drown.[388] Still, the husband's death had to be definitively proven or the wife could not remarry.

## RECALCITRANT HUSBANDS

In modern times, some husbands refuse to give a *get* to a wife who wants a divorce. Such recalcitrant husbands cause their wives to become *agunot*, a situation that rarely happened before the French Revolution. Until that time, Jewish communities usually had their own judicial authority, both in the Diaspora and in Israel. Jewish courts were empowered to use a variety of means, including physical force, to convince a recalcitrant husband to grant his wife a *get* if she wanted one.

Since a wife never gives a *get*, she can be at a husband's mercy if she wants a divorce. Some men refuse to give a *get* so that they can inflict emotional pain on, control, or extort money from a wife. They may withhold a *get* in order to punish her, avoid paying the *ketuba* money, or even blackmail her for money or child custody. (It should be noted that some women also blackmail their husbands by temporarily or permanently refusing to accept a *get* from them.)

## THE *BET DIN*

Although it seems that biblical law puts women who want a divorce at a disadvantage, their relative lack of power was offset by the *bet din's* power in these situations. These courts were allowed to use almost any type of psychological or physical "convincing" to motivate a man to divorce his wife. The *bet din* even had the authority to beat a man until he said, "I want to give my wife a *get*." If the husband died from such a beating rather than divorce his wife, she became a widow, and she didn't need a *get*!

Since Jewish law requires a husband to give a *get* of his own free will, it seems puzzling that a court can beat him until he acquiesces. The reason this is possible is because Judaism assumes that every Jew's deepest desire is to do what is religiously required of him. If a man's wife wants a divorce, Jewish law usually requires him to give it. If he refuses to do so, even after the *bet din* tells him that he must, he is considered to be confused about what his true will is. He may be afraid, he may be angry, he may feel hurt, he may have many feelings that get in the way of his most basic desire, which is to do God's will. Left to his own devices, he can't see his way clear to do what is right, so the court applies force to help remove his confusing feelings and clarify what his deepest desire really is.

Practically speaking, Jewish courts can only "convince" recalcitrant husbands to divorce their wives in countries where such means can be legally applied. There are no such countries today, including Israel, that allow Jewish courts to use such force. Thus, Jewish law empowers its courts to use means that effectively give husbands and wives equal ability to get divorced. Unfortunately, the prevailing laws of secular society and the fragmentation of Jewish legal authority often neutralize the *bet din's* power.

## THE FRENCH REVOLUTION

Even though the *bet din* was empowered to make *agunot* a rarity, recent historical developments have diluted their control. Prior to the French Revolution, divorce was considered a religious matter that was handled by the respective religious authorities in Christian and Moslem countries. Jews usually lived in their own communities, where they were geographically, socially, and legally separate from the gentiles. Due to this separation, the Jewish courts had a great deal of juridical authority over Jews.

The French Revolution changed this. It resulted in the Jews' gaining civil liberties, which ultimately led to their assimilating into French society at large. This had several ramifications: social intercourse and intermarriage with gentiles increased, the centralized authority of Jewish courts was diluted, and Jews adjudicated matters in civil courts that were formerly handled by Jewish courts. This meant that for the first time in history, secular society allowed Jews to obtain civil divorces.

Had all Jews continued to obtain only religious divorces, civil divorces would have been irrelevant to them. However, when secular Jews began obtaining civil divorces, they felt free to remarry, even without a religious divorce. Thus, secular Jews who were forbidden to marry according to Jewish law did so anyway in civil ceremonies.

## INSURING JEWISH DIVORCE AFTER CIVIL DIVORCE

Secular divorce was introduced in France in 1884. Shortly thereafter, Rabbi Michael Weil of Paris made the first attempt to deal with the problem of recalcitrant husbands creating *agunot*. He suggested that when Jewish women got civil divorces they should automatically be considered divorced according to Jewish law. This proposal was unanimously rejected by all rabbinic authorities, citing the lack of precedent in Jewish law for such an idea.

Rabbi Weil then made a second proposal. He suggested that all marriages be initiated only on condition that the husband would grant his wife a Jewish divorce if they got a civil one. Were the *get* not given by a certain time after the civil divorce occurred, the marriage would be retroactively annulled. This proposal was also rejected by all rabbinic authorities when it was first suggested, and it has been rejected every time that it has resurfaced. Judaism does not recognize such a conditional marriage because Jewish marriage and sexual intimacy require unconditional commitment by both spouses.

Judaism only permits sex between Jews who are legally married to one another. It is presumed that any married couple who has been sexually intimate has demonstrated by their behavior that they waive most conditions that modify a permanent relationship. Some rare situations can retroactively annul a marriage, but only when a man or woman withheld specific information from their intended mates before marriage. The three basic categories that constitute such information include: (1) concealing that one has a terminal illness, (2) known inability to have children, or (3) emotional problems that preclude a man's earning a living, a woman's maintaining a household, or either party's raising children. A man concealing that he is homosexual or impotent also falls within this rubric. In the absence of these, once a couple has sex, their marriage can no longer be retroactively invalidated by either spouse. It can only end through death or divorce.

## ANNULLING MARRIAGE

In 1930, Louis Epstein proposed that once a husband married, he should appoint his wife as an agent to divorce herself. That way, if he later disappeared or refused to give her a *get*, she could obtain a divorce. Unfortunately, this type of conditional divorce is untenable in Judaism because once a couple has sex, it automatically invalidates any prior divorce proceedings.

The conditional divorce given in biblical times was very different from that proposed by Louis Epstein. The ancient divorces were automatically nullified once the husband returned from his military service and the couple had sex.

Another reason why contemporary proposals for conditional marriages or divorces are untenable is because biblical law allows sexual relations to be one of the means that makes marriage legally binding. (Centuries ago, the rabbis forbade men to effect marriage by having sex, lest it resemble fornication. Giving a wedding ring is the generally accepted alternative.)

This has two implications: If a marriage is retroactively annulled, it makes every sex act within that marriage out-of-wedlock. Such fornication is forbidden by Jewish law, as well as any contract that created such a situation. Secondly, Jewish law presumes that people do not do forbidden acts if they can do the same things permissibly. This means that if the same act of intercourse could be legitimate, there is no reason to create a situation that delegitimatizes it. Since the first sexual union after a marriage ceremony can theoretically be one way of creating marriage, there is no reason to retroactively nullify it, thereby making all subsequent sexual relations illegitimate.

## HOW TO OBTAIN A *GET*

It is terrible when one spouse tortures the other by withholding or refusing to accept a *get*. At any given time, thousands of Jews, mostly women, are in this predicament.

People who are victimized by a recalcitrant spouse sometimes get friends, family, or synagogue members to boycott or picket their places of work, to socially ostracize them, and bar them from their social and religious affairs. One teacher who refused to give his wife a *get* was refused employment by every Jewish school in his town and was refused entrance by every synagogue. He gave his wife a *get* several months later.

When such situations come to our awareness, it behooves us to do whatever is in our power to persuade or pressure recalcitrant husbands to release their wives from their marital bonds.

It is recommended that Jewish women who want a divorce should first go to a Jewish court of law or to an expert in Jewish law. Many *agunot* could have avoided their situation had they gone to a *bet din* prior to negotiating a civil divorce. Once a civil divorce is granted, the leverage needed to convince a recalcitrant husband to give a *get* is often lost.

Second, property settlement should generally not be concluded until a *get* has been arranged. Unfortunately, many attorneys who are familiar with civil divorce proceedings are unfamiliar with Jewish divorce protocol and are not skilled in ensuring that a *get* is obtained along with the civil divorce. It is crucial for most women who want a *get* to consult with an attorney who is well versed in the details of Jewish divorce.

Third, an ounce of prevention is worth a pound of cure. Some rabbis will only marry a Jewish couple if they first sign a prenuptial document concerning a *get*. It obligates a recalcitrant spouse to pay the other a specified sum of money every day until a *get* is given or received. Once a spouse has asked the other to give or accept a *get*, the monetary pressure often persuades the spouse to finish the divorce rather than pay. There are several versions of such prenuptial agreements on the internet, although rabbis who conduct weddings may have their preferred wording. What is important is that the wording be legally binding in a civil court.

It should be noted that if a secular court forces a man to give his wife a *get* it could invalidate the Jewish divorce. This is because a man should not be coerced to give a *get* without a Jewish court ordering him to do so. On the other hand, if a Jewish court orders a man to give his wife a *get*, it is valid for a secular court to enforce the *bet din*'s decision.

Fourth, a woman who has questions about how to obtain a *get*, or needs support or legal advice about the process, can contact one of the following organizations:

Agunah International, 498 E 18th St., Brooklyn, NY, 11226. 212-249-4523. http://www.AgunahInternational.com . Its *bet din* is highly proactive in procuring *gets* for *agunot* when other rabbinical courts have failed to do so. They also provide counseling and financial assistance to *agunot* in need.

GET Assistance Project of the New York Legal Assistance Group (NYLAG). This is a not-for-profit law firm in New York City. It provides free civil legal assistance to people who live with domestic violence and seek a divorce. 212-750-0800 x613. http://www.nylag.org

G.E.T.; Getting Equitable Treatment, Box 131, Brooklyn, NY, 11230. 718-677-1033. Helps women to obtain a *get*. Gives information about Jewish divorce, refers to rabbinical courts and agencies. G.E.T. assigns an impartial agent who can help mobilize community members to apply social pressure on a recalcitrant spouse.

The Jewish Orthodox Feminist Alliance (JOFA), 520 8th Ave., 4th Floor, New York, NY, 10018. 212-679-8500 or 1-888-550-JOFA. http://www.jofa.org. Guides women through the process of getting a *get*, and has extensive reference material about Jewish law and the problems of *agunot*.

Kayama, 1202 Ave J, Brooklyn, NY, 11230.  712-692-1876 or 800-932-8589. http://www.kayama.org. This not-for-profit organiza-tion helps women obtain a *get* and doesn't charge for their services.

Beth Din of America, 305 Seventh Ave, 12th Floor, New York, NY, 10001. 212-807-9042. Offers rabbinical court services for Jews, including issuing a *get* and adjudicating financial and other disputes related to divorce.

# 15

# Sarah's Contribution to the Jewish People

Seven special individuals founded the Jewish nation. The first couple was Abraham and Sarah. Their son, Isaac, married Rebekah, who in turn gave birth to Jacob. He married two sisters—Leah and Rachel[389] (and subsequently their maids Bilhah and Zilpah as well). These forefathers and foremothers each contributed something unique to the collective consciousness of the Jewish people. We still benefit from these gifts today.

Abraham was a renowned intellectual. Because he used his lgic to fathom what was right and wrong, God tested him with ten trials that required him to do things that didn't make sense to him. This helped Abraham to learn that God's will, and not his intellect, should be the ultimate master of his choices and beliefs. We can only become morally perfect if we master our traits in a way that they serve the Almighty, rather than having them master us.

Abraham was able to perfect his intellect by learning to subjugate his ways of understanding how best to live to total belief in the ways of One Above. Yet he initially discovered and believed in God due to his use of logic. He saw a complex world and understood that just as a house doesn't simply materialize from nothing, the world must also have had a Creator. His logical belief in God allowed him to transmit a clear belief in God to all of his Jewish descendants. One of his main contributions to us was that any Jew can now believe in God by using his or her intellect.

This means that we can view the world, see its order, beauty and intricacy, and realize that it must have been brought into existence by a Creator.

## PROPHECY

From the time that she was a child, Sarah possessed divine inspiration (*ruach hakodesh*).[390] After she married Abraham and he became a great prophet, she surpassed him in her prophetic abilities.[391]

Prophecy is the highest level of human access to God, and it represents the highest level of human perfection. Only someone who had perfected him- or herself spiritually could attain it.[392] Both men and women have always had equal opportunities to achieve prophecy, and at some times in Jewish history it was quite common. For example, the millions of Jews who left Egypt during the Exodus were all granted prophetic visions. There were also many other Jews throughout biblical history who were prophets or who were occasionally granted prophetic visions. At the start of the Second Temple era, though, prophecy ceased.

We know little about most prophets because their prophecies related mostly to themselves. On the other hand, there were forty-eight men and seven women who were specifically charged with transmitting their prophecies to the Jewish people.[393] These female prophets were: Sarah,[394] Miriam,[395] Devorah,[396] Huldah,[397] Chana,[398] Abigail,[399] and Queen Esther.[400] Their prophecies were relevant to the people of their time, as well as for future generations. That is why they were mentioned in the Bible.

## PURITY

One reason why Sarah reached prophetic heights was because she purified her body to a point that she only used it to serve God. She dedicated every aspect of her life to fulfilling the divine will. By evaluating every event in her life, she accurately discerned which parts were good and which were bad, and then chose to do only what was good.

At one point in Abraham and Sarah's lives, there was a famine in the land of Canaan. This led them to temporarily move to Egypt, where food was plentiful. No sooner had they arrived there than Sarah was abducted and was brought to Pharaoh's palace so that he could use her sexually.[401] She had no interest in being the favorite consort of the most powerful man in the world. God miraculously protected her from his advances because she had already purified her body to such a degree that the Almighty would not let anyone defile her.

Almost anyone else in the same situation would have succumbed to the temptations that Sarah faced. Egypt was considered to be the most cultured country in the world at the time. Pharaoh's palace was an especially appealing place, and he was a world leader. In modern times, many women were thrilled to have opportunities to engage in intimate liaisons with married American presidents. Yet, despite Pharaoh's allure to many women, and the thrill that they might feel at being a First Lady in the lap of luxury, none of this held any appeal for Sarah. The palace's atmosphere left her unmoved because nothing was important to her except serving her Creator.

Sarah and our other foremothers spent their lives discriminating what could and could not be made holy. To this end, Sarah had many difficult choices to make. When she thought that she would never be able to bear children, she gave her handmaid Hagar to her husband as a concubine.

Hagar quickly became pregnant by Abraham and gave birth to a son Ishmael. It was not until 13 years later that Sarah finally had a child with her husband. As their son Isaac grew, Sarah recognized that Ishmael was a bad influence on Isaac. Her son's development required that Ishmael's influence on him not continue. For this reason, she advised Abraham to send Ishmael out of their house, and the Almighty ratified her advice.[402]

God gave Sarah and the other foremothers supernatural intuition and prophecy because they directed all of their potentials to fulfilling their divine roles. He sometimes gives people miraculous abilities when a person totally rejects what is bad and completely dedicates him- or herself to actualizing what is good.

## HER EULOGY

When Sarah died, Abraham eulogized her with the beautiful poem that Jewish husbands sing to their wives every Friday night—"A Woman of Valor" ("*Aishet Chayil*"):[403]

> Who can find a virtuous woman? She is worth much more than rubies. Her husband's heart trusts her and his wealth will not be lacking. She will do him good and not bad all the days of her life. She will ask for wool and flax, and willingly work with her hands. She is like a merchant's ships, bringing her bread from afar. She rises while it is still night, and she gives food to her household and a portion to her staff. She considers a field and buys it; from the fruits of her labors she plants a vineyard.

She girds herself with strength, and makes her arms strong. She senses that her merchandise is good; her light does not go out at night. She stretches out her hand to the spindle, and her palms take hold of the distaff. Her palm is stretched forth to the poor and her hand is given out to the destitute. She is not afraid of snow for her household because her entire household is clothed in scarlet. She makes tapestries for herself; she dresses in silk and purple. Her husband is known in the gates, where he sits with the elders of the land. She makes linen and sells it; she supplies the merchant with sashes. She is robed in strength and honor and will rejoice in the future. She opens her mouth with wisdom and the teaching of kindness is on her tongue. She looks after the conduct of her household and never eats the bread of laziness. Her children arise and make her happy; her husband praises her: "Many daughters have done virtuously, but you have excelled them all!" Grace is false and beauty is vain, (but) a woman who fears God is to be praised. Give her from the fruit of her labors, and let her deeds praise her in the gates.[404]

Although the words of *Aishet Chayil* are beautiful in and of themselves, they also allude to deeper ideas that reflect many of Sarah's deeds. Here is a homiletical interpretation of some of the verses:[405]

"Her husband's heart trusts her" alludes to what happened when Sarah and Abraham went into Egypt. He asked her to tell people that she was his sister rather than that she was his wife.[406] He did this because he was afraid the Egyptians would kill him and abduct her if they knew that he was her husband. Abraham totally trusted that she would comply with his request, and she did.

"She will ask for wool and flax" is homiletically understood to refer to her decision to separate Isaac from Ishmael by sending Ishmael and his mother out of her house. Wool alludes to Isaac, and flax alludes to Ishmael. Sarah initially gave her servant Hagar to get pregnant by her husband Abraham with the understanding that Hagar would bear Sarah a surrogate child. When Hagar became pregnant from her first intimacy with Abraham, she started disrespecting Sarah. When Hagar gave birth, she abrogated the understanding that she had with Sarah and Abraham about being a surrogate mother. She raised Ishmael her own way rather than with Sarah's values and beliefs.

When he was thirteen years old and Isaac was born, Ishmael suddenly lost his place in the family as the only child. Feeling threatened that Abraham's new baby was going to be his father's spiritual and legal heir, Ishmael began playing games with baby Isaac that endangered Isaac's life. Ishmael also became very immoral. When the situation became intolerable, Sarah had no choice but to expel Ishmael and his mother from her home, with the Almighty ratifying her choice.[407]

"She is like a merchant's ships" alludes to the incident where she was abducted by Pharaoh. Pharaoh paid Abraham 1,000 pieces of silver as part of his apology when he returned Sarah to her husband.

"She rises while it is still night" alludes to her getting up early with Abraham on the morning that he planned to offer Isaac to God on Mount Moriah.[408]

"She considers a field and buys it" refers to her having discovered the field of Machpelah, where Abraham later buried her. He, their son Isaac, Isaac's wife Rebekah, their grandson Jacob, and his wife Leah were all buried there.

"From the fruits of her labors she plants a vineyard" alludes to her being the foremother of the entire Jewish nation, which is likened to a vineyard. She created the potential for every Jew to feel close to God.

"She girds herself with strength" alludes to the time that three angels appearing as men visited Abraham, and he told her to help him prepare food these guests. The angels later told Abraham and Sarah that they would have a child together the following year at their respective ages of 100 and 90.

"She senses that her merchandise is good" alludes to the time when Abraham went to war against four powerful kings and their armies to rescue his kidnapped nephew, Lot. People warned Sarah that her husband would be killed in battle. Nevertheless, her faith didn't falter, and she trusted the Almighty's promise that not only would Abraham come home alive, but they would soon have a child together.

"She stretches out her hand to the spindle" alludes to Sarah's giving food to passersby and guests.

"Her palm is stretched forth to the poor" refers to her giving charity and clothes to the destitute.

"She is not afraid of snow for her household" alludes to the idea that her children will never go to hell (gehinnom) "because her entire house is clothed in scarlet." The Hebrew word for scarlet alludes to two commandments that the members of her household kept: observing the Sabbath and male circumcision. Both of these are signs of the divine covenant with the Jewish people. Keeping the Sabbath testifies that God created the world, and circumcision testifies that we accept responsibility for observing His commandments.

"She makes tapestries for herself; she dresses in silk and purple" foretold that Sarah's descendants would wear priestly garments of silk and purple when serving their Creator in the Tabernacle and the Temples.

"She is robed in strength and honor" alludes to the divine clouds of glory that surrounded Sarah's tent.

"Her children arise and make her happy" alludes to her joy when she gave birth to Isaac at the age of 90.

At one level of understanding, *Aishet Chayil* indicates Sarah's accomplishments during her lifetime. At a deeper level it conveys what she contributed to every successive generation of Jews. It is significant that we say these words every Friday night. The Sabbath is the time when we are supposed to elevate our bodies to the level of our souls, without allowing the external world to intrude on our spiritual equilibrium. The Sabbath's essence is precisely what Sarah achieved, insofar as she devoted herself to making peace between her body and soul. This is the same process that we hopefully undergo every Sabbath. *Aishet Chayil* can be interpreted as referring to how Sarah and those who followed in her footsteps overcame the body's desires using the influence of the soul.

## THREE ACCOMPLISHMENTS

The *Midrash* says that Sarah lit Sabbath candles every Friday evening and that they burned until the following Sabbath eve.[409] This symbolized that her spiritual enlightenment and excitement, which reached its peak on the Sabbath, didn't wane when the Sabbath ended.

Even though most Sabbath-observers feel very inspired by its holiness, this feeling tends to wane and then disappear shortly after the Sabbath ends. This was not the case for Sarah. Her sense of spiritual inspiration was no different on the Sabbath than it was on the six weekdays, since every day presented an equal opportunity for her to serve her Creator. The *Midrash* says, "Her candles burned from one Sabbath to the next."[410] This implies that the Sabbath's spirituality extended throughout the week for her.

The same *Midrash* also says that the bread that Sarah baked every Sabbath eve remained fresh from that day until the following Sabbath eve. This symbolized how Sarah created an ongoing spiritual vitality that infused all of her deeds. Nothing she did grew stale.

Most of us feel excited when we do a spiritually positive act for the first time. Unfortunately, as happens with many things, the novelty and exhilaration we once felt tends to wane as we get used to these new behaviors or rituals. In time, we may do things by rote, and our deeds grow stale. When we stop feeling inspired and lose our enthusiasm, we may do the same deeds without any emotion, or even discontinue them altogether.

This did not happen with Sarah. She retained the same feelings of excitement after doing an act day after day as she did when doing it for the first time. She never lost her joy or sense of novelty doing God's will. Her enthusiasm with serving Him never diminished.

The words of the *Shema* prayer emphasize this idea. When we say the *Shema* every morning and evening, it tells us what will happen if we keep the Almighty's commandments that He commands us "today." This is interpreted to mean that we should view every *mitzvah* as if God had just given it to us that very same day. If we do that, we will have a corresponding sense of novelty and zeal.[411]

The above *Midrash* tells us that the cloud of the Divine Presence (*Shechina*) always hovered over Sarah's tent. This is because the way she lived always invited God's holy Presence to attach itself to her. Whenever we dedicate ourselves to doing the divine will, He may respond by allowing us to experience His immanence.

Thus, Sarah merited three miracles happening throughout every week: Her candles burned, her bread stayed fresh, and the Divine Presence hovered over her tent. These miracles disappeared when she passed away, but were reinstated by her daughter-in-law Rebekah. This is because Rebekah dedicated herself to serving the Almighty in the same way that Sarah did.[412]

## SUBSEQUENT GENERATIONS

Our foremothers' and forefathers' level of spiritual awareness and dedication is considered to be the epitome of accomplishment for Jews. Nachmanides said that when the Jews left Egypt during the Exodus, and later accepted the Torah, they were still not totally redeemed. That was only fully accomplished when they built the Tabernacle in the wilderness. The Tabernacle was a divinely-given opportunity for the Israelites to show that they had unified their bodies with their souls.

After the Israelites left Egypt, they expressed to the One Above that they wanted to live in a way that He could dwell among them. In response to their request, He told them how they could live the exemplary lives that our foremothers and forefathers lived.

These spiritual guidelines were expressed in the design of the Tabernacle. Its sanctuary had a candelabrum with an everlasting light that symbolically reinstated Sarah's Sabbath candles. Just as she brought continual spiritual illumination into her tent, and from there into the world, so did the priests by lighting the candelabrum every day in the Tabernacle.

The Tabernacle also contained showbread. This consisted of twelve loaves of bread that the priests baked every Sabbath eve and placed on a special table in the Sanctuary. Like Sarah's bread, it stayed fresh from Friday until the Sabbath a week later, when the priests ate it. It stayed warm and fresh, and a small piece was so spiritually vital that it felt totally satiating.

Finally, the Divine Presence hovered over the Tabernacle just as it did over Sarah's tent. The manifestation of God's Presence over the Tabernacle symbolized that He wished to dwell, as it were, among the Jewish people. He did this most obviously in the place where the Jews showed that their main concern as a nation was with doing the divine will.

## HER DEATH

The Torah reports that Sarah died immediately after Abraham showed his readiness to offer Isaac to God on Mount Moriah.[413] God did not want Abraham to kill his son, only to show his readiness to put his love for God above all human concerns.

The commentator Rashi explains why the Torah records Sarah's death immediately after this episode.[414] She seems to have died from the shock of hearing that her husband slaughtered their son who was born in their old age. However, the reality was that Abraham didn't harm Isaac. Therefore, it is suggested that when Sarah heard that she had raised her son with a willingness to give up his life for God, she expired. She felt that her life's work in raising him had been completed, and he was ready to carry her legacy to the next generation. Her soul was so attached to her Maker that it simply left her body having fulfilled its last mission on earth.

It is unusual that the Torah describes her burial in such detail.[415] The Five Books of Moses describe many people who died, but the most attention is paid to Sarah's burial. Normally, the Torah does not focus on burial and death because a person's soul lives on after death. The soul is also much more significant than the body that housed it during its sojourn on earth.

In Sarah's case, her body was as holy as her soul, because her physicality perfectly served the essence of God within her. Therefore, her body deserved having a great deal of attention paid to it at her burial. She required a special place in which to be buried, since she had used her body in a way that unified it with her soul.

People commonly split the physical, material, egocentric, and sensual facets of their lives from the spiritual. They eat because they are hungry (or bored, or lonely) and/or because the food tastes good. They go through life striving to achieve goals that make themselves feel good. Men may treat women's bodies as objects to give them pleasure, and many women view their bodies in the same way. They very much identify with their looks, and value themselves according to how attracting their bodies are.

When we instead put God in the center of our lives, and use our bodies to serve Him, we eat to live, instead of living to eat. We appreciate the food that the Almighty gives to sustain us. We eat, speak, work, have sex, and dress in ways that draw us close to our Creator and reveal His Presence to the world. We make our physical endeavors mindful and holy, and live in the loving embrace of our Heavenly Parent.

Since Sarah devoted her life and her actions to elevating the physical, Abraham had to go to great lengths to purchase the Cave of Machpelah in Hebron as her burial place.[416] Our mystical tradition tells us that a spiritual tunnel connects that cave with the afterlife. Every soul that leaves this world passes through that tunnel.[417]

In describing her death, the Torah says that Sarah was "one hundred years, and twenty years, and seven years (old)."[418] The *Midrash* explains this to mean that when Sarah was 100, she was as innocent of sin as she was at age 20.[419] This means that she was able to keep her body perfectly integrated with her soul all of the time. Once she achieved that level of spiritual and physical unity, it didn't waver over the years. The *Midrash* adds that when she was 20, she was as beautiful as she was at age 7. A biblical statement praising a woman's beauty does not mean that she was only physically beautiful. Her physical beauty emanated from her spiritual wholesomeness and was praised because she used it only as a tool by which she served the One Above.

## SARAH'S CONTRIBUTION TO US

Sarah's main contribution was her implanting in each of her female descendants a spark that motivates us to live and teach God's values.

There was once a national, central sanctuary where the Almighty's Presence rewarded people who spiritually lit up the world and served

Him enthusiastically. After the Israelites left Egypt, this special place was the Tabernacle that they built. Hundreds of years later, the holy Temples in Jerusalem served this purpose. Altogether, those were in use for more than 1,200 of the more than 3,300 years of Jewish history.

However, the Jewish home is where our Creator has, and still does, reveal Himself to us individually, regardless of whether or not we have a Temple. Sarah gave us the wherewithal to make our homes sanctuaries for the Divine Presence. She gave us the intuition to see what is truly meaningful and good, and the wisdom to know how to achieve that. She also modeled how we can develop the means to transmit this legacy to others.

For millennia, Jewish women have been inspiring our families and ourselves with lofty spiritual values that we live and teach in our homes. We use Sarah's model to turn our domestic lives into living laboratories where everything in the material world serves a higher purpose.

Sarah played many roles in her life, all of them unified by her desire to bring God's Presence into this world. Everything that she did, whether cooking for her family or guests, buying real estate, teaching the pagan women in her area about ethical monotheism, or raising her son, was her way of contributing something vital to the world. All of her actions left behind a legacy that link us with her, as our actions will link our children and subsequent generations with us.

# 16

# *Raising Jewish Children*

I is hard to imagine how modern Jewish parents can overcome all of the challenges in raising healthy, moral, well-adjusted children. Physical health problems abound, partly thanks to junk food, chemical additives, and lack of exercise, and partly due to unhealthy attitudes about food. Obesity is an epidemic, affecting 17% of American children ages 2-19. Eleven percent of American high school students have been diagnosed with an eating disorder, and another 15% of young females who have not been so diagnosed have disordered eating habits and attitudes.[420]

Alcohol abuse among children is also worrisome. In an ongoing study[421] of 50,000 American eighth-, tenth- and twelfth graders, 41% had used alcohol during the prior year. Twelve percent of the sample had had five or more drinks in a row (binge drinking) during the prior two weeks, and 19% of twelfth graders had done so. One in 17 twelfth-graders smokes marijuana daily or nearly every day. Eleven percent of tenth graders and 16% of twelfth-graders used illicit drugs besides marijuana in the prior year. As well, 14% of twelfth graders misused dangerous prescription drugs such as narcotics and amphetamines during the prior year.

Violence and bullying are in the news every day. Seven percent of high school students were threatened or injured with a weapon at least once on school property in the prior year, and 20% were bullied.[422]

Not only is sex rarely reserved for marriage, it often isn't even used as a means for constructive bonding. The average age at which Americans lose their virginity is seventeen.[423] By the time they finish college, two-thirds of the students have had sex in a "friends with benefits" relationship, citing the lack of commitment as the main advantage to doing so.[424]

Nor do most children have parents who can model how to have healthy relationships with the opposite sex. Divorce rates in the United States hover around 50%,[425] and in Israel around 35%.[426] The details of these statistics are quite daunting: The parents of half of all American children will get divorced, and nearly half of those children's parents will divorce a second time before the children are age 18.[427] One in ten American children whose parents get divorced will live through three or more parental marital breakups.[428] These children often suffer significant emotional scars and often physical and social fallout as a result.

Finally, there are challenges of living in a world of ubiquitous technology. A study of 1,000 college students in ten countries asked them to refrain from media use for 24 hours. A majority in every country reported that they simply could not go without their phones and internet for an entire day. Twenty-three percent of the American students said that they could not because they were addicted. Many who attempted to go without showed symptoms of withdrawal. A common reaction was that many felt as if their phone is literally an extension of themselves and they could not live without it. Many felt "dead" and/or paralyzed without being barraged by a constant stream of information from machines. Some felt they were going crazy. Others said, "I hope that I never, ever again have such a day in my life." As one student from the U.K. reported, "We feel the need to be plugged into the media all day long. Our lives basically revolve around it." Across the board, it was difficult for the majority of them to think of ways to fill their time without resorting to a device with a screen.[429]

## CREATE GOODNESS

Given the myriad challenges and dangers that surround our children, what can parents do? Is it possible for parents to instill meaningful Jewish values into their children where something else is always vying for their attention? Can we raise children with self-esteem and excitement about living a religious lifestyle that transcends feeling good in the here-and-now? How can we teach them to have healthy relationships and not settle for instinctual couplings that leave them feeling empty and detached?

It is important for parents to inculcate a feeling in their children that living a Torah lifestyle is emotionally, intellectually, and spiritually satisfying, but we can't do this in the abstract. The best way to start is for parents to build a solid foundation for our children by doing the work necessary to have a happy, fulfilling and functional marriage, and by being "good enough" parents to their children. Many parents today don't have the tools to accomplish these. It is advisable that they seek whatever professional help, parenting classes, or support groups that are necessary for them to be successful at these critical tasks.

Neither having a good marriage nor raising children is easy. Both require a great deal of mindfulness, skills and work. Many people who become observant (*baal teshuva*) think that becoming religious will solve their emotional problems. They likewise think that once they become observant, God will take care of raising their children. Someone who grew up in an emotionally unhealthy family is unlikely to have learned the practical skills to create a great marriage and be a good parent. They owe it to themselves and to their offspring to read books and take classes on how to be good parents, and to consult with an expert mental health counselor as necessary.

When we raise children in a loving home, with clear and reasonable boundaries, it protects them from a lot of the negative influences of the outside world. Many parents think that it is not politically correct to tell their children that some behaviors are not acceptable, and to say "no" when a child wants things that the parent has good reason to think are harmful. It is a parent's job to protect children who don't yet have the life experience or knowledge to know what is good or bad. The Torah models to us the importance of setting limits, at the same time telling us to refrain from certain behaviors while engaging in others. The Almighty did this in the context of taking us out of Egypt, then protecting, nurturing, and caring for us every day for more than 3,300 years. We only happily accept His telling us what to do if we know that He loves us.

This is also a model for parents. When children feel that their parents love each other, and them, it gives them a foundation of stability and protects them from many of the harmful influences in the world. Parents give their children a sense of self-worth by setting reasonable expectations that the children can achieve, and praising them when they do good things. When a child knows that a parent loves him or her, he or she can also appreciate that the limits that a parent sets are for their good. When there are open lines of communication, a child learns that his parents value him and his feelings, and that if he faces trouble his loving parents will be there to help him navigate through it.

Parental authority is resented when children do not feel that their parents love them just as Jewish restrictions are resented when they are not perceived to be coming from a loving God. One of a parent's tasks is to create a relationship with a child where he or she feels loved. Not only it is a foundation for an emotionally healthy life, it is also a foundation for a child to grow up and feel that God loves him or her. It is very difficult for children who don't feel that their parents love them to feel that God does.

A home is the most important school that children have. Unlike secular schools, which mostly teach factual knowledge, a Jewish home primarily teaches children how to live. The way that parents relate to one another and to their children models how to relate to the world at large and what to expect from it. For example, when parents speak in respectful and loving ways to each other and to their children, even when the parents are upset, children learn how to love others and expect others to treat them respectfully. When children are rewarded and praised for obeying the rules that parents give them, children learn to respect their parents and authority. When parents discipline with love, children learn to modify their innate egocentrism and desire for immediate gratification with making room for others' needs and wants. They also learn not to judge how to live by what feels good only in the moment. They internalize the ability to consider long- term consequences and take responsibility for their choices and actions.

Children who have poor relationships with their parents, or whose parents have a bad marriage, are especially prone to have a troubled childhood or adolescence. As they grow older, they may rebel and seek acceptance and love from people and experiences that are not wholesome. They are also more prone to turn to eating, alcohol and/or drugs to dull their emotional pain.

As well, if they have ADHD, intellectual limitations, learning disabilities, and/or do poorly in school, they may get shamed or belittled. Many such children are told that they are lazy or stupid, and are not helped to find positive ways that they can shine and get praise. Not infrequently, if they cannot conform to the rigors of a religious Jewish school, they are likely to drop out and/or rebel against the Judaism that they associate with their failings.

When children can choose to be in a religious environment where they feel that they are failures, versus going to a secular peer group that promises freedom and good feelings, guess what they will do?

Adolescents rarely get involved with sex, alcohol and drugs only because their friends are also involved. Just as people assimilate religiously to find a life that is more satisfying than the one they left behind, teens usually get involved with sex and drugs because they want to fill an inner void with happy feelings, or numb an inner pain. Children who are raised in an environment where they feel good about who they are, and whose parents help them internalize appreciation for living as observant Jews, are less likely to assimilate, use drugs or misuse alcohol.

When parents are never far from their phones or the internet, and they make those a center of their lives, why shouldn't their children? Parents need to teach children how to fill themselves with good feelings that are based in real and lasting sources—the satisfaction of helping another person, the joy of being a contributing member of a family and one's community, happy experiences such as singing around the Sabbath table, at a Passover *seder*, or lighting a Chanuka *menorah*, pride in acting like a good Jew, the pleasure of communicating with others in a way that everyone feels understood, and so on.

Jewish parents do not have the luxury of raising children who will automatically stay observant just because their parents go through the motions of keeping Jewish rituals. Parents have to teach and model to their children how it is emotionally and spiritually fulfilling to keep *mitzvot*, in ways that are meaningful to the children.

## IMPORTANCE OF QUESTIONING

Over time, parents should explain to children why the Jewish ways of seeing the world and doing things are good, the dangers inherent in certain activities, and why certain behaviors that might feel good are spiritually (and often practically) bad. When children get to be a certain age, parents can ask the children to tell what pros and cons they would find in various situations if they were parents!

When children ask questions about sensitive topics, religious or otherwise, parents need to answer according to the child's ability to understand. Sometimes parents feel challenged by their children's questioning of Jewish ideas. Instead of becoming impatient or angry with the child, a parent can say, "That is a great question and I don't have a good answer for you. Give me a few days and I'll ask my rabbi, then I'll tell you what he says." What a great message for a child to hear—that it is okay to question everything because that is how we learn and develop our understanding of things. At the same time, he learns that having questions does not mean that we have to stop believing in Judaism or stop keeping *mitzvot*. There may even be times when a parent will tell a child, "It's so funny you should ask that. I've been wondering about that myself for years. If I don't find that answer in this lifetime, I'll ask about it when I get Upstairs."

Jews don't have to be afraid of not having all of the answers. Telling a child that there are things that a parent doesn't know, and showing them that we take them seriously by asking experts their questions is a wonderful message for children. Sometimes a parent might even say, "You know what, that is an amazing question. I never thought of that. Let's look up the answer together." What an empowering feeling for a child! It can only enhance the mutual love and respect that a parent and child have for each other.

Imagine someone asking a physicist to explain everything about how the world works. A good physicist will get to a point where he says, "We still don't have any idea how that works." People are more real and credible when they don't "know it all."

Not infrequently, there will also be times when parents should broach topics and not wait until children ask them questions first. Otherwise, children may get information from their friends, the internet, or even strangers that parents don't consider credible or healthy.

The author has had many friends over the years who were not raised religious, who became so as teens or adults. One of them had a very bright four-year-old daughter. One Saturday, as they walked to synagogue, she asked her father, "How come those Jews are driving on Shabbat?"

He lied to her, "Those people aren't Jews." He didn't want his daughter to know that Jews desecrated the Sabbath. The author disagrees with this approach. We are supposed to distance ourselves from lying. Also, the girl's father will be discredited in her eyes as soon as the girl finds out that most of the Jews in their very Jewish neighborhood drive on the Sabbath.

The author's approach is to tell such children, "Most Jews today didn't have the benefit of a good Jewish education, and they never learned how precious Shabbat is. It is our job to invite them to our homes for Shabbat so that they can see how wonderful it is. We have an obligation to show and teach Jews in a loving way how beautiful Judaism is."

If parents are not secure in their own Judaism, if they don't find it emotionally, spiritually, and intellectually the best way to live, they will not be able to convey a sense of fulfillment with Judaism to their children. There is no reason to feel threatened by a child's questions, and the last thing that parents should do is quell their child's curiosity. Hopefully, a child's questions can motivate both the child and the parent to grow in their knowledge and wisdom.

It is possible for different Jews to appreciate very different aspects of

Judaism. It is a parent's job to help each of her children to identify and develop aspects of Judaism that excite him or her. One child may be inspired to excel in doing kind deeds, another may care a great deal about praying in a deep and musical way, yet another may find satisfaction with the intellectual rigors of learning Talmud for hours. One child will love to cook and bake for Shabbat and holiday meals, another child will get excited by preparing words of Torah to say at the meal. One child will do her best to show respect to her parents and grandparents, while another will do his best to make guests feel welcome in his home.

There is an expression, "The Torah has 70 facets." No one facet of Judaism excites everyone equally. In one sense, Judaism is a one-size-fits-all religion. The Torah was designed to have meaning for every Jew. On the other hand, it is only by recognizing that we each have our individual ways of learning and living Judaism that keeps it vital and relevant to millions of individuals. That is why in the book of Proverbs King Solomon, the wisest of men, wrote, "Educate the youngster according to the way that suits him. When he grows old, he will not depart from it."[430]

## INTERNET AND SOCIAL MEDIA

Today, almost everyone is connected to social media and the internet. Parents have to learn the real effects of both. For example, we know that many children use their phones and the internet in ways that have negative repercussions. These range from altering their brain functioning and attention spans, to opening up possibilities for addiction, to causing children to become sleep-deprived, to making them prey for online pedophiles. It is important for parents to set sensible limits on how and when children use phones and computers, and to screen out unsuitable content.

Even though it is important for parents to discuss potential problems and dangers of social media and the internet with their children, that alone is not enough. Parents also have the responsibility to limit how children access information, what information they can get, how many hours a day and what hours children use their devices. Children not only access internet and the like on their devices, but easily do so from their friends' devices as well.

While the internet has revolutionized the ways we get information and communicate, it is a very mixed bag. Ninety percent of all data that humans have ever produced has been generated in the past two years, thanks to the internet and social media.[431] On the other hand, much of that information is better left inaccessible. For example, fourteen percent of internet searches and four percent of websites are devoted to sex sites.[432]

Parents don't have the luxury of burying their heads in the sand and hoping that their children won't see information or graphics that they shouldn't, discover explicit pornography on the internet, or be tracked by pedophiles. Dangers to children abound, and parents have to teach their children about them and take appropriate precautions. For example, many parents have no idea how easy it is for pedophiles to read their child's personal information online and then befriend their child. Gaming platforms are also a popular venue for pedophiles to groom children. Pedophiles frequent places that children go, such as forums of popular teen singers or actors. Children whose parents don't educate them about the dangers of becoming "friends" with people online can get into serious trouble. Seventy percent of children become friends with total strangers on their social media page.[433]

Parents need to place safeguards on what their children can access on the internet, the details of which are beyond the scope of this book. They also need to teach their children how to use technology responsibly, and make sure that they have substantive and wholesome relationships and activities. It is challenging, yet necessary, for parents to spend quantity and quality time interacting with their children. Children need relationships with a caring parent and friends, where they learn to communicate meaningfully and constructively, and develop their minds, emotions and creativity.

Unfortunately, many parents think that all is well when children are quietly occupied while glued to the internet, social media, video players, or phones. These short-term "solutions" may turn out to be very problematic in the long-term.

For example, in 2015, children aged five to 16 spent an average of six-and-a-half hours a day in front of a TV, video game, phone, computer, or tablet screen. Teenagers averaged seven-and-a-half to eight hours per day. Five to 10-year-olds averaged four-and-a-half hours per day.[434] Children often use more than one device at the same time, for example, watching TV while surfing the internet.[435]

Some researchers believe that children's watching so much of these media is shortening their attention spans and making it hard for them to concentrate. For example, a study assessed the viewing habits of 1,323 children in third, fourth, and fifth grades over 13 months. It found that children who spent more than two hours a day in front of a screen, either playing video games or watching TV, were 1.6 to 2.1 times more likely to have attention problems. It also found that college students who watched a lot of "screen media" had attention problems. The researchers concluded, "This study contributes to a growing body of research that shows media may have an effect on attention."[436]

Dr. Dimitri Christakis spent a decade studying how entertainment affects children's mental processing. He believes that overstimulation from media may be a possible cause of some ADHD. In one of his research studies, children under age five who watched two hours of TV a day were 20 percent more likely than those who watched no TV to have attention problems at school age.[437]

The American Academy of Pediatrics recommends that children spend no more than one to two hours a day interacting with screen-based media, such as TV and video games, and that children under the age of two watch no TV at all.[438] Since the brain adapts to the way we use it, it makes sense that fast-paced video games, frequent What'sApp and text messages, and surfing the internet could adversely alter the way the brain reacts to stimuli.

Needless to say, children who spend much of their time as active participants in life can be more physically fit, develop better social skills, have more educational and real-life experiences, and engage in more pro-social activities than they can passively getting information.

## PARENTAL MODELING

Speaking of real-life experiences, parents convey what is essential about Judaism by how they live, what they teach their children, and how they answer their children's questions. If the topics of conversation in the home center on bad-mouthing others, gossip, politics, money, and the like, why shouldn't children think those are important as they grow up? If a child sees that her parents don't speak badly about other Jews, and no one in the family is interested in hearing gossipy stories, children will learn to speak about positive things instead. It is a skill for parents to always find positive topics to discuss, especially at meals, rather than the latest scandal, upset, or what the children did wrong. How much more valuable meal time is when someone talks about good things that happened to them, or about a challenge and how they overcame it, instead of focusing mostly on what went wrong with their day, or what is wrong with others.

Children learn what parents truly value by observing them much more than by what parents say they value. When parents' words and deeds don't match, their deeds are what will count. This is why is not enough for parents to send their children to school or to give them some information about how Judaism is practiced. Parents have to live the messages that underlie Jewish rituals and traditions or children will see both the rituals and the messages as hollow.

A story is told about a wealthy man who invited a well-known rabbi to his house for Shabbat dinner. The man was so proud that the rabbi agreed to eat at his house insofar as the rabbi got many other invitations from members of the synagogue. After escorting the rabbi to his home, the host asked his family to sit down for the meal. As the host got ready to say *Kiddush*, he yelled at his wife when he noticed that she had forgotten to cover the two *challah* loaves. The rabbi promptly noted to his arrogant host that the whole purpose of the *challah* cloth is to cover the bread so that it won't be "embarrassed" when we first make *Kiddush* over the wine, instead of giving the usual precedence to saying a blessing over the bread. The husband completely missed that message by humiliating his wife publicly over the very item that was supposed to remind him to be sensitive to other people's feelings!

The *mitzvot* between man and man are every bit as important as the *mitzvot* between man and his Creator. It is important for parents to show that they are kind to the members of their family and not only to outsiders, and vice versa.

Children need to see that parents are honest and have integrity. They should not promise children things, then not fulfill their promises. They should also not ask their children to lie for them, or make excuses for the parents' behavior, then expect their children to be honest and be held accountable for their actions.

Some unfortunate situations have to be mentioned in this age of immediate gratification and technology. First, even though children may get lectures in school about how dangerous smoking cigarettes, drinking alcohol, and using drugs are, all too many parents do these very things at home. If parents take pills every time they have an ache or pain, or have more than one or two drinks at Shabbat or holiday meals or when they want to unwind, it sets a terrible precedent for children to use substances. It would be far better if parents learn constructive ways to cope with stress and challenges and teach them to their children.

Parents should model to children by the food that they eat, how they eat, drinking alcohol in moderation, and using medications sparingly that the Almighty loaned us our bodies as gifts. We are not at liberty to damage them. The Torah specifically commands us to take good care of our bodies.[439] We will be held accountable for abusing ourselves. Rabbi

Shimshon Rafael Hirsch commented on this verse,

> You may not in any way weaken your health or shorten your life. Only if the body is healthy is it an efficient instrument for the spirit's activity... Therefore you should avoid everything that might possibly injure your health... And the law asks you to be even more circumspect in avoiding danger to life and limb than in the avoidance of other transgressions.

It is well-known that overeating and junk food damage our health (that's why it's called "junk" food). Maimonides instructed people to eat only until we are two-thirds full. Our overindulging on Shabbat and Jewish holidays sets a bad example to our children of the way we should treat our health. Plying children with sugary, chemical-filled "Shabbat treats" is not doing them any favors. We don't honor the image of God in us or others when we treat our bodies as if they are garbage cans, or do the same to our children.

Children should be raised to understand that what we do to our bodies and with our bodies is very consequential. If we train our children not to eat foods that can spiritually damage us, we want to reinforce that message by avoiding foods, drugs or alcohol that are physically damaging. If we train our children to thank the Almighty before and after every food that we eat, it reinforces the idea that we should not to ingest substances that destroy our Creator's handiwork.

The One Above gave us bodies to serve Him. We should do our best to model and teach our children that we must try to stay physically and mentally healthy, while making both enjoyable.

A mother once lamented that her three-year-old screamed in pain every week from the intestinal problems that eating a lot of "Shabbos treats" caused him. The author reminded the mother that she is the mother and is supposed to set limits on her son according to what she knows is good that he doesn't. She knew that the chocolate and candy was harming him. It was her job to tell him that he couldn't eat as much as he wanted and to offer him healthy substitutes. She refused because he would have temper tantrums if she didn't give him what he wanted. How well this three-year-old had trained his mother! If a mother doesn't have the resolve to protect her children and deal appropriately with tantrums, getting professional help or taking parenting classes is advised.

The way many parents use technology gives children the messages that phones and computers are sacrosanct. Parents often ignore their children while being glued to communication devices and computers, even using them as babysitters when parents are "too busy" to interact with their children. It is sad that instead of parents greeting their children when the children come home, many parents are either absent, are glued to their computers, or are in the middle of an "important" phone conversation. Children will not be terribly interested in learning Torah and doing *mitzvot* when they are preoccupied with getting parental love and attention. Even worse, some children learn that it is much easier to get attention by using their screen media than by trying to interact with their parents. It is terrible for children to feel that many things, including money and inanimate objects, are more important to their parents than they are.

Besides teaching about Jewish values, ethics, laws and rituals, parents also model to children what the Almighty is like. If parents are harsh and critical, children assume that God must also be that way. When such children become adults, few of them will realize that God doesn't have their parents' shortcomings, and their views of Judaism will consequently be very limited. If they stay observant, it may be only because they don't want an angry and authoritarian deity to punish them if they go astray. They will have difficulty appreciating the essence of Judaism as having a relationship with a loving deity.

When children are raised by loving parents, they simultaneously learn that having a relationship with their Creator is wonderful. Keeping the Torah can be delightful if it keeps them close to the Source of all love. When such parents tell their children not to do something because it is harmful, they extrapolate that God is a Heavenly Parent who only tells them to do that which is also in their best interests.

Since the Creator gave parents the awesome ability to be his stand-ins, they must exemplify how Jews should live Torah values. It is not enough to behaviorally go through ritualistic motions. Parents have to identify with divine values and rules, which includes loving their spouse and children, loving other Jews, doing kind deeds to people outside their families, and being honest in their dealings with people. If parents show that it is a great *mitzvah* to honor their own parents, their children are more likely to follow suit. If children learn that relating to a parent feels wonderful, they will also feel great serving God. They will want to be as beloved in the Almighty's sight as they are to their parents.

When some parents put their children to bed, they ask, "Who loves you?" Of course, the child usually says, "Mommy," or "Daddy," depending upon who is speaking to them. Some parents then say, "Who loves you the most?" The answer, of course, is "Hashem" (God).

## PARENTING—INFANCY UNTIL THREE

Parents know that their job begins even before a baby is born, yet they start molding the child's character at birth. The parents' main task raising infants is to make them feel loved, secure, cared for, and protected. This teaches children that parents are dependable caretakers. That forms the foundation for being able to trust that other people are dependable and worth relating to. When babies are hungry, they are fed; when they are cold, they are clothed; when they are wet, they get their diaper changed; when they are uncomfortable, they are soothed. Parents' unending acts of love set the stage for children to later trust people outside of their family, and God. By spending meaningful time with each child until he or she reaches maturity, parents teach their children how to become emotionally healthy, observant Jews.

It has been suggested that our Creator gave us parents whom we depend upon for so long because He wants us to have human models that let us to experience how He constantly takes care of us. Parents who are loving, giving, and trustworthy constantly show children how our Heavenly Parent takes care of them in similar ways. If parents are aloof, arbitrary, and/or punitive, children will assume that God has the same problems their parents do. By showering young children with love, by being dependable caretakers, and by protecting children from bad influences, parents set the stage for children to be psychologically healthy. That is also a prerequisite for having a healthy relationship with our Heavenly Parent.

A challenge for mothers at this stage is to stay spiritually connected when their days are full of changing diapers or toilet training, doing laundry, cooking, cleaning, and singing the same song over and over again (let's not forget including the hand motions). Sleep deprivation also interferes with feeling enthusiastic about being Jewish. It is often difficult for mothers of young children to go to inspiring Torah classes or to pray every day without being interrupted.

One mother of young children, Meira, had not been able to attend synagogue even on the holidays for a few years. She was so looking forward to finally attending one Yom Kippur. She brought her three-year-old daughter Penina with her. As soon as Meira got settled in her seat and opened her *machzor* (holiday prayer book), Penina became curious about how all of the pearls on her little necklace were connected. She pulled them apart, and the necklace broke, scattering little beads all over the floor of the women's section. Instead of praying for forgiveness with intense concentration, Meira spent the better part of the service trying to make sure that she collected every bead, lest someone slip on one. So much for her hope of having a spiritual Day of Atonement that year.

Even though mothering can be challenging, there is no part of life where God is inaccessible. It may, however, require extra preparation and changing our attitudes to feel His Presence. By internalizing certain perspectives, and preparing ourselves when unexpected situations arise, we can potentially sanctify every part of life, even the most mundane.

A rabbi once heard his toddler calling for help from his crib after the little boy woke up from his nap. The rabbi went over to the child's room and saw that the baby had opened up his dirty diaper and smeared the contents all over himself. The rabbi couldn't deal with the stench and the mess and called over his wife. When she came and took in the horrible sight, her reaction was to think about how beautiful her son would be when he was cleaned up. She saw the Divine Presence in this little boy underneath all of the filth. She took a breath outside the room and declared, "I hereby take upon myself the commandment to love my fellow Jew as I love myself." With that, she went into the room and cleaned up her child.

She is a wonderful model of how it is possible for Jewish women to find their holy calling, even in the most mundane tasks of motherhood.

We learn this lesson from the way the Jewish priests served God in ancient times. For more than 1,000 years, male priests (*cohanim*) who descended from Aaron, Moses' brother, served the Almighty in the Tabernacle and Temples. Some people considered them the most exalted of Jews, yet much of their special role ceased once the Second Temple was destroyed two millennia ago. Jewish women before and since have served God in their homes as the priests did in the Temple, and have made their homes into sanctuaries.

When we had a Temple, the first order of the day was for a priest to remove the ashes of the animal offerings that had burned overnight on the altar. This was considered such a prestigious task that the priests fought over who would have the honor, even though contemporary people think it is trivial and might even feel demeaned when they take out the garbage. This shows that such people have the wrong attitude.

A few decades ago, sanitation workers in New York City went on strike, and the piled up garbage nearly brought the city to a standstill! Both physically and spiritually, we have to clear away the garbage in our lives in order to function and serve God best.

A spiritual message that we learn from the Temple ritual of removing ashes is that we have to begin each day with a clean slate. Each morning, we have to remove the emotional and physical dross that sullies our minds, hearts and homes. If we yelled at our children yesterday, today is a new day. We should apologize, make amends, and do what it takes to be better today. Only then can we reach for the stars, be our best, and see ourselves as worthy and beloved in God's eyes.

## SECURITY AND AUTHORITY

It has been suggested that Jewish women are absolved from doing certain *mitzvot* because their primary mission is to help their children develop a sense of security, trust, and well-being. Children would not feel very secure if their mothers were abandoning them two or three times a day to run off to pray in the synagogue. Children would learn that there is always something more important than them if their mothers often left them to do specific time-bound *mitzvot*. Although we must all eventually learn that the universe doesn't revolve around us, young children need to feel that the world does exist only for their pleasure and gratification. This promotes their self-esteem and security in the first year and more of life.

As babies grow, parents set limits on them for their own welfare. Children can eat, but not foods or quantities that make them sick. They can leave the house, but not at all hours and not running into traffic. They can play with toys in the living room, but are forbidden to play games with the stove in the kitchen. Through these and other rules, children learn that real love is accompanied by limits that sometimes deprive them of what they think they must have. They need structure and boundaries. They learn at the same time that their actions have consequences, and they must develop self-control as they interact with the world around them.

Children only feel safe when they have boundaries. Rather than being overly restrictive, it gives children a feeling of security to know what they can and can't do. Children who can do whatever they want don't feel protected. When a toddler stands ten feet away from a mother, he is free, yet he may soon feel scared that he is totally on his own. When his mother wraps her loving arms around him, he is restricted, but feels totally safe.

This is analogous to what the Almighty does with us. He gives us many *mitzvot* that seem to restrict us. In reality, they protect us in His embrace so that we can't hurt ourselves.

## Mitzvot and Young Children

Until children are three years old, parents are not obligated to educate them about what Judaism requires them to do or not do. A mother's task during these first few years is to nurture her child without creating barriers that prevent the child from absorbing Jewish values. Even though parents are not required to train such young children to do certain *mitzvot*, it is good to expose them to positive experiences and values.[440] For instance, a child should see that his parents learn Torah, pray, and dress modestly.

Parents should try to ensure that their children, even infants, eat only kosher food.[441] "We are what we eat" applies to our spiritual health as well as to our physical health. Feeding children non-kosher food allows negative influences to affect their budding spiritual sensitivities and dulls their ability to properly absorb parental communication.

In addition to raising children in environments where they are exposed to a positive Jewish way of life, they should not be exposed to negative influences. The early years of life have a very powerful and lasting effect on children's sense of security and self-esteem. To this end, parents should do what it takes to have a healthy marriage, since it plays a vital role in raising emotionally and spiritually healthy children. When parents argue or hurt each other in front of, or within earshot of even very young children, it erodes their well-being. Children feel anxious, helpless, and unsafe when their parents don't get along with one another. Parents who fight also destroy children's trust and confidence in the parents' ability to protect them. This simultaneously interferes with the parents' ability to transmit religious values to them.

## EDUCATION–AGE THREE

By the time most children are three years old, they face the startling realization that the world does not exist only for them. They can feel very helpless when they realize that almost nothing belongs to them and how little power they really have. At this very sensitive time, Judaism gives them a new way to assert their ownership and power. They may not own the world, but they can do *mitzvot* that affect the world.

Formal Jewish education begins at age three. At this age, parents should formally teach their children according to each child's capacity to learn what they should and should not do. This is also the age when parents start to formally discipline a child for doing what is wrong.[442]

Among other things, parents should teach children of this age to say blessings before and after eating food, to ritually wash their hands when they wake up in the morning and before eating bread, to say the *Shema* prayer before they go to sleep at night, and to learn short verses from the Torah. Children can often retain these prayers and blessings best when they sing them.

At the very time that a boy might feel that nothing is his, his parents give him his own *yarmulke* (head covering).[443] If a boy is able to keep from soiling or wetting himself, he should wear *tzitzit* (a fringed, four-cornered undershirt) as well. When their fathers make *Kiddush* on the Sabbath and holidays, boys should be given their own *Kiddush* cup with grape juice (or wine), and make a blessing over it, just as their fathers do. This gives them *mitzvot* that adult men have, and they begin to identify with the male role.

In some circles, girls light Sabbath and holiday candles alongside their mothers. Just as a boy's self-image includes wearing a *yarmulke* and *tzitzit*, a girl's self-image should include dressing modestly.[444] This enables her to identify with her female role and do the same *mitzvot* that women do. Both boys and girls at this age can be encouraged to put a few coins into a charity box before the mother lights the Sabbath or holiday candles.

At this age, both sexes get a strong sense of importance and power from the many rituals they can now observe. In addition, each holiday gives children a chance to feel loved, important, and that they are contributing to the world. On Passover, they can help clean the house, rid it of any leavened products, and participate in the search for *chometz* (leavened products) on the eve of the holiday. They can also do small things that assist in preparing and serving the holiday meals. They play a central role in asking questions at the *seder* (special Passover meal) and finding the *afikoman* (*matzah* that was hidden) at the end of the meal.

On the holiday of *Succot* (Tabernacles), children can help build and decorate the *succah* (a temporary booth). They can carry the *lulav* (three species of plants held together) and *etrog* (citron) to the synagogue, and go *succah*-hopping with friends and family. On *Simchat Torah*, they can sing, dance, and get sweets in the synagogue as they celebrate the annual completion of reading the Torah. A special *aliyah* to the Torah is reserved on *Simchat Torah* for all of the children to come up together, as they are the future of the Jewish people.

Every Shabbat, children can help set the table and straighten up the house in honor of the day. The necessity for one or both parents to teach children about the day's rituals reinforces the child's sense of mastery and accomplishment doing these *mitzvot* with a bond of love from parent to child.

Parents should encourage positive behavior while putting limits on what children can do. For example, children should be given healthy food that is kosher, on which they say a blessing, and should be limited in the unhealthy food they eat. They should know in advance when their bedtime is and be given ample time to get ready for it, with a routine that they do to get ready. If they get ready in a timely way, it is a great reward to read children a bedtime story or play a quiet game with them. The last part of the day can be singing *Shema* together, followed by a hug and kiss.

Since children are very concrete at this age, parents should reward their good behavior with tangible and concrete rewards. For example, if they do a *mitzvah*, they can get a hug or kiss with praise ("What a great *mitzvah* girl you are!") as reinforcement. If they are not interested in doing *mitzvot* that are appropriate for their age, such as saying a blessing before eating food, it is better to reward them with a few raisins, craisins, dried apple, some orange juce or other treat than to punish them.

## LIMITS AND PUNISHMENT

When parents are loving and they set limits on children according to what is best for the child (as opposed to mostly setting limits for the parents' interest or convenience), children learn that parents, and by extension God, limit them for their own benefit. In the same way that children learn that eating too many sweets or fried foods make them sick, they internalize the idea that eating non-kosher food makes them spiritually sick. They learn not to cross the street without the parents' permission, which paves the way to learn that it is spiritually harmful to travel by car on the Sabbath and Jewish holidays. As children learn that their day-to-day observable behavior has consequences, they also learn that their religious behavior has spiritual consequences.

In time, parents teach and reward children for doing good deeds and show disapproval, give time-outs, or on rare occasions give punishments when children do what they were taught is forbidden. For instance, they cannot hit their siblings, break things in anger, or steal. As children internalize clear rules about preserving their and others' physical safety and welfare, they do the same with rules that affect their spiritual welfare.

As long as parents don't destroy their credibility by setting arbitrary or inconsistent rules, or discipline mostly to show their children who is the boss, children will automatically respect appropriate limit-setting done with love. God made children want to model, love, and respect their parents. It is important for parents to use this gift wisely.

Many parents think that children should automatically know what is expected of them, or do everything that parents tell them to do as soon as they are told. That isn't realistic, and parents need to bear that in mind. The Almighty grants parents authority over their children only for the children's benefit. For example, children must be trained to do household chores so that they will learn to be decent, responsible, and helpful adults when they grow up. Parents should not ask their children to do chores only because the parents don't feel like doing them. All parental orders and rules must be geared toward what is needed for a child's growth, rather than forcing a child to accommodate to his or her parents' needs.

Sometimes parents convince themselves that a child must do something for the child's welfare, when in reality, their motivation is to show the child who is in charge, or to vent their anger. Children are very sensitive not only to what parents say, but also to their motivations. It is easy for many children to see through their parents' orders or explanations when they are not genuine, and to discern when parents are lying or being hypocritical.

Some of the most important qualities that parents need to develop are patience, the ability to listen to and understand their children, and ways to communicate that they love and like each child. It is a wonderful nightly ritual to tell each child a story that is suitable for him or her, ask about his or her day if they have not yet talked about it, say *Shema* together, and tell the child that you and God love them.

Parents should not give children unnecessary rules and limits. Parents should also emphasize what children *can* do, not only what they shouldn't or can't do. When the author's daughter was young, she often took her to the supermarket. Inside, the first thing they did was to find a few shelves stocked with heavy, unbreakable cans or packages. The author then told her two-year-old, "You can touch everything here. Enjoy!" The little girl would excitedly run along one side of the aisle touching cans, and get out of her system the desire to touch things that could be fragile or fall off the shelves. A few minutes later, there would be an aisle where she could bring a light item or two that was on the shopping list. She would feel so important placing them in the cart. By the time this was repeated a few times, she behaved nicely until we got to the checkout counter, and she had no interest in grabbing any of the gum and candy that were placed to entice children before leaving the store.

There is an idea that for every non-kosher food, there is a kosher food with a similar taste. This can be applied to children's behavior. When possible, we shouldn't tell our children only what they can't have, but also what substitutes are available. If parents make certain choices off-limits to their children, parents should also help children find alternatives, if possible.

When parents mostly criticize or notice what is wrong or forbidden, it may not take long before children rebel against their authority. Parents must encourage children's individuality, independence and creativity. It often happens that God gives a very conservative parent who is concerned with what everyone else thinks a child who wants to think and act "outside of the box." Just because other people don't do things a certain way is not a reason to dissuade a child from doing things differently. When children are prevented from asserting themselves in a way that is healthy for them, albeit unconventional, their focus will shift to how they can get their needs met in unhealthy ways. Or, they might just shut down emotionally.

Children need to accept parental authority so that they can accept societal rules and function in society. When children feel that rules benefit them in their personal world, they will also feel that way about societal and Jewish rules. To this end, parents need to behave in ways that a child will want to respect them. If parents need to demand respect from young children, they probably need to learn better ways of parenting that automatically make the child respect them.

It is also crucial that children accept parental authority because it is the basis for accepting God's authority. If a parent destroys his or her credibility, or a child believes that the parent is not fair or wise, they will not believe that the One Above is fair or wise, either. This does not mean that parents need to act as if they know everything, or that they can never make a mistake. To the contrary—it can be a wonderful model to children to do our best to behave wisely and properly, yet apologize when we make mistakes. That teaches children the importance of taking responsibility for their behavior, and that there is no shame in admitting when we are wrong.

Susan made a play date for a Shabbat afternoon with a boy named Jonny for her six-year-old son Tommy. When it was time to leave, Susan asked Tommy to put on his shoes so that they could go to Jonny's house.

"But Mommy," Tommy pleaded, "I don't like Jonny anymore. He isn't one of my friends now."

Susan looked into Tommy's eyes and responded, "I'm so sorry, I should have asked you. I made a mistake. How about if you go today so that he won't be embarrassed? I promise that next time I'll make sure to ask you first."

Tommy accepted his mother's request, went to his friend's house, and even had a nice time.

Even the best of children tend to ignore rules and requests more often than not. Instead of shaming or punishing them for not immediately doing as they are told, parents need to be realistic about how children behave. Sometimes a parent also needs to make the request more palatable to help the children comply.

For example, it is unlikely that a child who is in the middle of watching a show or playing a game will stop if someone tells him then to do a chore or get ready for bed. It is advisable for parents to give children plenty of advance notice. For instance, if Mark is playing with his sister, a parent can tell him that when they each have taken three more turns, they will have to put the game away until tomorrow. If they get ready for bed quickly, and there is time left over before bedtime, they can finish the game the same night.

Children who don't concentrate well, or whose memory span is short, should not be given a long list of things they need to do before going to bed. They will also need reminders along the way of what to do next. When children have regular routines every day, it is much easier for them to get ready for bed at night and for school in the morning.

Punishment should be used sparingly, and reserved for times when other avenues of education aren't appropriate. The purpose of punishment is to educate children how to behave better in the future, not to express parents' frustration and anger. Although children need to learn that certain actions have negative consequences, punishment should be appropriate for the misdeed, and not geared to showing children who is the boss.[445] When children do certain inappropriate things, parents can tell them, "That kind of behavior is beneath you." Shaming children in front of others is not a good punishment and is forbidden by the Torah.

The way that parents punish their children teaches children how the Almighty punishes us for disobeying Him. If children learn that punishments are meted out in order to help them mature and prosper, they will view God's punishments the same way. If punishment is a tool that insecure and angry parents use to wield power over, and control their children, children will view their Heavenly Father as similarly malevolent and nasty.

Parents can erode their children's natural desire to imitate them by being punitive, aloof, or repeatedly frustrating. In order not to undermine children's self-esteem or respect for parents, parents should discipline by emphasizing children's positive points and then note a shortcoming.

When criticism is necessary, it should address a specific behavior and give one or two suggestions about how to improve it the next time. This approach does not erode children's self-esteem and maintains parents as loving yet concerned caregivers.

## MORAL AND SOCIAL DEVELOPMENT

As children grow, parents teach them moral and social values. Children learn to share their toys with others, to play nicely with their peers, and to be concerned about others' feelings. In general, children learn as much, if not more, from what their parents do, not only from what they say. For example, parents should teach children that giving 10% of what they earn to charity is very important. It is even more important that children see their parents do it, and get pleasure from so doing. When children are old enough to earn money, it is good to discuss with them a few choices of where they can give their charity. It is a wonderful learning experience to visit such organizations at work so that children can get pleasure from what their giving will accomplish.

Besides modeling social behavior, parents also model attitudes about two crucial aspects of Jewish living: learning Torah and not gossiping (speaking or listening to *lashon hara*—bad speech about other Jews). When parents don't listen to or share gossip, slander, or say negative things about others gratuitously even when it is true,[446] children learn how important it is to control their speech. When parents don't indulge in the tempting pastime of slandering people, they set a powerful example of self-control and love of one's fellow Jew to their children. Likewise, when children see their parents learning Torah, they appreciate its fundamental importance. When parents live the cardinal values that these two *mitzvot* exemplify, and don't only give them lip service, children can internalize these messages.

### Gratitude and Respect

When parents show respect for their children's feelings, express gratitude to God and to others, and regularly compliment children, children learn how to do the same.

A rabbi taught his children that they must knock before entering his study or bedroom. One day, the rabbi entered his four-year-old son's room, and his son asked him why he didn't knock. From then on, the rabbi always knocked on his children's doors as a sign of respect.

Gratitude is central to being a Jew. The word for Jew, *Yehudi*, means someone who is thankful. We must train ourselves to appreciate what we have and what others do for us, rather than feeling entitled and noticing mostly what we don't have. When parents say blessings and pray, they show children what it means to thank God. If parents don't appreciate what their Heavenly Parent is constantly doing for them, why should children appreciate what their earthly parents do?

Another attitude that is important to show children is the pleasure that we get from giving to, and doing for, others. If parents make it seem that extending themselves to others is a chore, children won't want to do kind deeds for others. Instead, if children see their parents helping family and strangers, offering hospitality to those in need, visiting the sick, and comforting mourners, doing such acts will become part of children's consciousness. It is not enough for parents to speak about the beauty of doing kind deeds; it makes an indelible imprint on children to see words put into practice. Mothers should show at least as much excitement about doing good to others as they do about going out to a restaurant or getting a new item of clothing.

Parents need to ask themselves from time to time—what do I really get excited about? Am I as excited about doing a *mitzvah* as I am about shopping? Do I talk as much to my children about how good it feels to share or help others as I do about the newest furniture, shoes or dress that I bought, or the latest kosher restaurant that opened nearby? When children see that their parents really value doing *mitzvot*, each time a child obeys a parent, is nice to another child, or helps a sibling, the intrinsic value and parental compliments add to the child's self-image.

When chores need to be done, a parent can ask, "Who wants to do a *mitzvah*?" A child is more likely to be interested in that kind of approach than when he or she is ordered to take out the garbage or clean up the kitchen.

## SCHOOL AGE

By the time children are six years old, they have learned that they become powerful by identifying with and imitating the same sex parent. To a child, a parent is almost as powerful as God. By attaching themselves in this way to their powerful parents, a child enjoys the process of growing up.

In the Garden of Eden, the Almighty told Eve after she sinned that she will "give birth to children in sorrow."[447] One interpretation of this verse is that when parents see their children imitating the parents' bad character traits, the parents find that terribly painful. Sometimes, though, that is the only way to get parents to change important things that they do. If they didn't see the bad effect their character defects have on their children, they would deny that they are so negative.

Five-year-old Jay was running around the house one morning spewing out a series of curse words. When his mother heard him, she wanted to punish him, but she first asked, "Where did you hear those words, Jay?"

Without batting an eyelash, he replied, "From Daddy. He cut himself slicing bread this morning and I'm repeating what I heard him say."

Needless to say, Jay's mother educated him about the impropriety of using such words and asked her husband to use more appropriate words when upset.

Even though many parents think that they can turn over their children's education to schools once children start first grade, the fundamental responsibility for raising children always rests with the parents. Judaism has always viewed the home as the backbone of Jewish survival. Jewish schools only started around two thousand years ago because fathers, whom the Torah obligates to teach their sons how to be proper Jews, no longer knew how to do so.

Judaism is a system whose myriad rituals, traditions and ethical guidelines are meant to be modeled and reinforced by the love bonds between parents and children. Even though home schooling children about Judaism is not an option for most parents today, schools cannot compensate for parents who lack adequate parenting skills, and/or who don't live consistent and meaningful Jewish values at home.

Parents who don't take primary responsibility for showing their children how to live as Jews cannot blame the school for their inadequacies. Teachers are not surrogate parents; rather they are mentors who can reinforce and augment what children learn at home.

Parents model how children should feel about being Jewish. If parents do Jewish rituals and pray by rote, or put their Jewishness on a back burner, why shouldn't their children do likewise? If parents practice their religion out of habit, many children will seek new experiences and lifestyles that are more fulfilling once they leave home.

## Imposing Judaism

Unfortunately, many non-observant Jewish parents say that they don't want to "impose" Judaism on their children. They give their children minimal or no Jewish education, then let the children decide when they go to college if they want to learn about a religion that they had nothing to do with, and which seemed meaningless to their parents. These same parents don't mind "imposing" twelve years of English, math, social studies, physical education, sports, and sometimes dance, music and/ or art on their children. And of course, they want their children to learn about other cultures and religions. Judaism has changed the world for the better more than anything else in history. It is sad that so many parents don't know what it has to offer, and therefore assume that it can only be a burden to their children.

In order not to have children who first learn about Judaism in college, or who never learn about it at all, parents should educate themselves so that they can raise their children with some Judaism in the home. They should include children from the age of three to participate in *mitzvot* in ways that are attractive and appropriate for the child. Parents shouldn't think that children should be shielded from the "burden" of doing *mitzvot* any more than they would shield a child from playing sports or going to summer camp. Parents should show the same desire and enthusiasm for sharing *mitzvot* with their children that they would show for intellectual achievements or for monetary prizes. The more children are "protected" from doing *mitzvot*, and the less enthusiastic parents are about them, the more they disenfranchise children from living a meaningful Jewish life.

Parents can include children in doing *mitzvot*, according to their interests and abilities, in preparing for the Sabbath, welcoming guests, praying, going to the synagogue, building and decorating a *succah*, putting coins for charity (*tzedaka*) in a special box before lighting the Sabbath and holiday candles, helping take care of younger children, making food and braided bread (*challah*) for the Sabbath, and so on. A three-year-old's *mitzvot* might include putting two *challahs* on the dinner table before Shabbat and making a blessing over grape juice when the father makes *Kiddush*. A ten-year-old might bake a batch of chocolate chip cookies in honor of the Sabbath, call an elderly person and wish her a good Shabbat, make up a bedroom for a guest, or help her two-year-old brother get bathed and dressed for Shabbat. All of these are part of the *mitzvah* to love other Jews as one loves oneself.

When a father wears *tzitzit* and a *yarmulke*, goes to synagogue, and makes *Kiddush* at Shabbat meals, his son will want to do the same. When a mother cooks and serves meals for the Sabbath and holidays, lights candles, and sings prayers, her daughters will want to do likewise. All of this creates walls of protection that shield children from negative outside influences and fills their psyches and hearts with meaningful memories and feelings.

Every Friday night and Jewish holiday, mothers say special prayers for their children when they light candles. Before the meal, parents customarily bless their children, then the entire family sits down and shares a leisurely evening together. This is real quality time, when children can share words of Torah that they learned during the week in school, and parents can share interesting Torah or other appropriate thoughts. Many families enjoy singing Shabbat or Passover songs together, especially in harmony! Those beautiful memories can last a lifetime.

Shabbat guarantees that families will sit down to at least two meals together every week where they talk to one another instead of watching a screen. Family meals have become increasingly rare in the 21st century. A 2003 Gallup Poll showed only 28% of adults with children under the age of 18 ate dinner together at home every night. Almost half of families ate together between four and six times a week, yet another quarter only ate together three or fewer nights a week.[448]

How families eat dinner is the best predictor of how children will fare in adolescence. The more often children eat dinner with their families, the better they do in school, and the less likely they are to get involved with drugs or alcohol, suffer depression, consider suicide, or become sexually active during high school.[449]

Why? Children learn how to communicate and connect to others when this is modeled at the dinner table, and it tends to create a more cohesive family. That can be a tremendous support system. It is also likely that parents who structure their lives so that they eat dinner with their families also supervise and spend time with their children more than other parents do. Perhaps such parents are more aware of where their children are and what they are doing. They may notice and offer help when they are struggling with school or homework, or praise them more when they are excelling. We also know that children thrive with structure and a feeling of belonging, and daily meals provide both.

The home rituals of Judaism provide emotional and spiritual building blocks for children's self-esteem, give meaning and the feeling that they are connected to something bigger than themselves. Every time children do a *mitzvah*, they experience having a unique and irreplaceable contribution to make to the world. Jewish rituals and family cohesiveness give children a framework of stability, clarity, and direction. As well, when life is challenging, they have a family and God to fall back on. This total package will later protect children when they become young adults from the negative temptations and inner emptiness that is so much a part of the technological age.

*Jealousy*

When parents show children that they are secure with what God gave them, including their looks, their money, their family, and so on, it helps children to internalize the idea that the Almighty gives each of us what we need. Sometimes we need to pray or work hard to get what we need to fulfill our mission in this world. Feeling jealous of others is not going to help us.

Sibling rivalry is very common, and is often fueled by parents playing favorites with one of their children. Even if parents like one child more than another (and most parents do, even if they don't admit it), they have to remember that the Almighty hand-picked each of their children for them to raise. To that end, they should not treat each child the same, but rather try their best to give each child what he or she needs.

The job of parents is not to make their children happy all of the time, nor to give children everything that they want. Parents need to differentiate between giving what is needed for a child to become who he or she was meant to be, versus giving what the child wants even if it won't help the child to prosper and grow.

When two sisters were young, one would sometimes cry to the mother, "She got more than I got!"

The wise mother would retort, "Don't tell me what your sister got. Tell me what you need. If you really need it and I have it to give, I will do it. What anyone else has is not relevant to you."

These girls learned to focus on what they had or lacked, and became the best of friends. Even as adults, they are not jealous of what the other has because that has nothing to do with what each needs to thrive.

*Peer Influences*

Until children are of school age, they mostly learn from the models their parents (and siblings) set. When they start school, teachers, and later peers become important role models for children.

Once peers become important to children, they should have friends who will be positive influences on them and not accentuate their negative traits. For example, close friends should eat kosher food, observe the Jewish holidays and Sabbath, and wear similar clothes (a *yarmulka* and *tzitzit* for boys, modest clothing for girls). They should be compassionate, honest, sharing, and so forth. It is not good if peers tolerate or reinforce a child's aggressiveness, dishonesty, or passivity. Ideally, peers should bring these issues to the attention of an adult who will know how to help that child.

## ENCOURAGEMENT, NOT PUNISHMENT

Children should be encouraged to do *mitzvot* that are appropriate for their ages, and not be punished or shamed when they don't want to. It is much more effective to reward children for doing *mitzvot* than to teach them to associate not doing *mitzvot* with punishment. We want children to have good associations to keeping the Torah. Similarly, when a child is not interested in learning Torah, parents and teachers should try to make it more interesting or enjoyable rather than berating or punishing the child for not learning.

The intellectual challenges of reading Hebrew and Aramaic (language of the Talmud) are very daunting for many children, especially those with learning disabilities. Encouraging such children's creativity and using their strengths (such as math, construction, art or music) to relate to Torah (or Talmud, for older children), and making it more experiential than simply reading, can sometimes make learning exciting for them.

When children are young, it is the parents' job to help them to love and feel loved by God, and later to fear Him. Children who are raised by loving parents will care when their parents disapprove of their behavior, and parents can instill the same feelings in their children regarding their Heavenly Father. For example, a parent's disapproval when a child does something wrong that he should have known not to do can give the child a powerful message. Just to know that a parent or God is not proud of a child's behavior can be the most appropriate punishment.

When parents unreasonably limit, insult, or humiliate their children, they discredit themselves as transmitters of the divine will. In addition, such bad parenting may eventually cause children to stop caring what their earthly and heavenly parents think. Parents need to set expectations their child can meet, learn how to understand their child, and not punish when it is not warranted or necessary.

Children have many limitations due to their lack of physical maturity and experience with certain things. We would expect them to stumble over words or read slowly when they learn how to pray and read Torah. They may do tasks slowly and clumsily. Some get restless and seem to be in perpetual motion, and are not geared to sitting for long periods of time. Many children can study better if they attend classes after a half-hour of exercise, and they can stand and move around during class.

Parents should notice their children's good behaviors and successes and reward them. It is useful to identify what a child's strong points are in order to help him build self-esteem around that, as well as to guide him to do things better.

God judges our efforts, not the outcome of what we try to do. Parents should likewise reward children's good efforts, even when the outcome doesn't reach the desired goal. It is good to teach children that failure is sometimes the first step toward success, as our Bible says, "A righteous person falls seven times and gets up."[450] Failure is not the absence of reaching a goal, it is not trying. The only people who never fail are those who never try.

It would be wonderful if every married person took a practical course in developing patience and staying calm in stressful circumstances before becoming parents. Parents' anger can erode a child's self-esteem and sense of security, make children feel unloved, and cause other long-term emotional problems. Parents who want their children to follow their wishes and who try to control them might sometimes get their children to comply, but when the children get older, they will rebel, or look for love in all the wrong places.

Parents who are mostly concerned with the details of how to be observant and who don't let their children be children may present an unappealing picture to children of what Judaism is all about. For example, some parents portray Shabbat to their children by stressing the many things that we can't do, plus some boring things that we must do. Parents should bear in mind what it feels like to a child to have to forfeit playing, sit through extra- long meals and synagogue services, and having to wear special Shabbat clothes that they can't keep clean. As well, some parents give boring Torah explanations and/or mostly talk to adults during the meals and ignore their children. Parents need to design Shabbat (and the Jewish holidays) in a way that they are enjoyable and meaningful for their children. This usually means arranging time for children to play with friends, going to a youth group, singing, asking the child what she learned in school, and so on. On Pesach, we have a *seder* to fulfill the *mitzvah* of "you should tell your son on that day" about how God took the Jews out of Egypt. That means keeping the *seder* short enough to engage the children's interest and enthusiasm until they have sung the songs at the end. Save the long-winded and advanced explanations of the *Hagada* for after the *seder* is over or once the children have gone to bed.

## BUILDING SELF-CONFIDENCE

Many people think that life has no objective meaning. They think that this world is all there is, and the purpose of life is just to get as much pleasure and satisfaction as we can in the here-and-now. Some people only feel good about themselves when life goes their way. When it doesn't, they sink into depression, feel worthless and don't get much out of life.

Judaism instills self-esteem in us by telling us that we are each indispensable to the divine plan for the world. Parents teach their children that the Almighty custom-designed each of our strengths and challenges because He needs us to be us, not someone else. If we are here, it is His vote of confidence that we can be the person that He wants us to be. Whether or not our lives are easy, or life is going the way that we would like, there is purpose and meaning to every moment.

The world is not complete without our being here. The fact that each of us has a slightly different role to play only underscores how essential each of our contributions is to the world. That the Master of the World rewards us for our good deeds and punishes us for our bad ones emphasizes that each of our behaviors is consequential. It is hard to feel unimportant when our religion teaches that each of our actions, thoughts, and words can have eternal ramifications. Parents can convey these validating messages to their offspring from early childhood.

Parents are supposed to help their children find goals that are worth striving for, and give them the encouragement and guidance that will help them to achieve them. Setting goals, making efforts, and accomplishing them throughout childhood give children a sense of purpose and emotional well-being. When they become young adults, they hopefully will have the self-confidence to know that they can, and should, separate from their parents and make their unique contributions to the world.

One of the earliest memories that Jewish children have is of their mothers greeting them every morning and reciting a prayer with them, "I thank You, Living and Existing God, that You returned my soul to me with compassion. You have great faith in me." As children grow older, they understand that they must be very important for the Master of the Universe to give them their souls anew every morning. Children begin each day affirming that they have something unique to accomplish and that their Creator has faith in them that they can do it. Over time, children internalize this message.

## BAR AND BAT MITZVAH

By the time children who are raised in observant Jewish homes reach ages 12 (for girls) or 13 (for boys), they have learned the basics of how to be Jewish women or men. The rites of *bat* and *bar mitzvah* teach adolescents that they are mature enough to make adult choices and to be held accountable for the consequences of their actions. At the very time when children start wanting to assert their independence from their parents, Judaism gives them a framework within which they can do so without harming themselves or those around them. The Jewish rites of passage reinforce to budding adolescents that their emotions should not run their lives. They must take into account how their behavior will affect not themselves and the world in the short- and long-term. This is especially important once their newfound sexual and rebellious feelings can easily drive them to do destructive things and not think about the long-term consequences of their actions.

Unfortunately, the original meaning of these rites of passage is often overshadowed by lavish parties and celebratory meals. Or as some have quipped, "They have the *bar* without the *mitzvah*." The real significance of a girl becoming 12 years and a day, or a boy becoming 13 and a day, is that they are now obligated to observe the Torah. For centuries in Europe, these events were commemorated by modest meals, usually at home.

In the United States, *bar* and *bat mitzvah* parties are often gala celebrations with minimal religious significance. Instead of lavishing so much money on the parties and meals, parents should reconsider the true meaning of these life cycle events as a transition into responsible Jewish adulthood. Boys should acknowledge this by starting to put on *tefillin* (boxes with Torah portions inside that are strapped onto the head and arm) and by being called up to the Torah. Girls can acknowledge this by preparing a talk about a specific area of Jewish observance that they would like to pursue in earnest. Or, they might prefer to study some aspect of Judaism that they haven't learned in school, or commit to doing some kind deeds for others. For example, some young women visit patients in a local hospital or nursing home every week, or help new mothers when they return home from the hospital. Others start saying Psalms on a regular basis, or start to pray more intensively. Some mothers and daughters study that week's Torah portion together, or do a *mitzvah* such as baking and taking *challah* together. Some families celebrate the *bat mitzvah* with a trip to Israel, where the family visits a charity such as Leket, Yad Eliezer, or a soup kitchen where everyone physically participates in helping those in need. Many *bar mitzvah* boys and *bat mitzvah* girls donate at least 10% of their gift money to charities as well. The possibilities are endless.

Regardless of how a *bat mitzvah* is celebrated, it should be a commitment to a life ahead that includes Torah study, doing *mitzvot*, and serving God in daily life. Just as no devoted parents would be satisfied with their children getting a secular education but a few hours a week until they become teens, or getting minimal job training, parents should not be satisfied with their children (or themselves) only learning about or practicing Judaism superficially. Sending children to Jewish day school, Hebrew or Sunday school, or for religious instruction only until *bar* or *bat mitzvah* is simply inadequate to teach them how to live as Jewish adults.

## LIFELONG JEWISH EDUCATION

Children need more than an elementary school education in morality and ethics. Both boys and girls have to be taught what about being Jewish makes us unique and how we are different from the rest of the world. Otherwise, simply instilling "good" values in our children without anything more is setting them up to intermarry and assimilate with other people who seem nice. Moreover, children who had a very weak or nonexistent Jewish education will be unable to transmit anything meaningful about Judaism to their children.

Parents who want their children to get graduate and professional degrees should also want them to develop their Judaism in a way that is commensurate with their intellectual and vocational aspirations.

Years ago, mothers would educate their daughters about Judaism at home, at least until the daughters got married, and often thereafter as well. Jewish education consisted of full-time learning the details of how to run a Jewish home, how to help in the community, Torah stories, Jewish laws and customs, prayer, Jewish history, how to raise a family, and often how to make a living according to Jewish law. Judaism was taught in a living laboratory, with mothers supplementing their teaching through a wealth of relationship factors with their children. Multigenerational families provided a tangible link to family traditions and previous generations. People knew where they had come from, and had a vision of where they were going spiritually.

Parents need to be secure in their own Judaism if they want to convey the richness and beauty of Judaism to their children. Parents who are not secure should learn more, and sometimes with their children. Joint educational, social, and ritual programs include model *seders*, where parents and children participate; family Shabbatons, where families can meet others like themselves and experience the warmth and beauty of Shabbat together; musical events where Jewish songs are taught and sung; art projects such as making *mezuzah* covers or charity boxes that include explanations of those *mitzvahs*; *challah* baking; and classes in Judaism.

## CONFRONTING CHALLENGES

The Torah doesn't tell us to deal with the challenges of the secular world by sequestering ourselves away from anyone who doesn't live the way we do. A Torah way of life is rich enough to enable us to live in many kinds of environments. At the same time, Jews should not live where there are unnecessary temptations and hazards. For example, we are told to stay far away from evil neighbors and not befriend the wicked.[451] Presumably, there are many situations where we think that we won't fall prey to a negative environment. We must be careful not to overestimate ourselves or underestimate the insidious influences around us.

It used to be easier to say that the temptations of the outside world were not appealing to children whose Jewish world was emotionally and spiritually rich, secure, and nurturing. While that is often still the case, the world and people can be very complex and sometimes threatening. Parents can sometimes use what goes on in the secular world to illustrate to children what we don't believe, and why. This can sometimes inoculate our children against going down the wrong paths.

For example, a child may be walking outside with a parent when she smells a delicious aroma coming from a non-kosher restaurant. She tells her mother, "I would love to eat that bacon. It smells so yummy."

Her mother can say, "Yes, it smells delicious and probably tastes delicious, but *Hashem* (God) has told us not to eat it. Non-kosher food is bad for our *neshama* (soul) and hurts our relationship with *Hashem*. There are many things in this world that feel good, but only *Hashem* knows if they are really good for us. If something seems good but really isn't, *Hashem* has given us a great gift by telling us to stay away from it."

Torah-observant children will inevitably confront people whose behavior and beliefs differ from theirs. These situations present excellent opportunities for parents to explain to a child why he or she has been taught to live as the Torah tells us, and why other lifestyles lack the spiritual, emotional, and sometimes physical benefits of the way we live. It is also important to teach children not to disparage Jews who don't live according to Torah. Usually nonobservant Jews have not been pɪɪ៴˳ ˳ to have had a meaningful Jewish education or upbringing.

Parents can help children resolve conflicts between the secular and Jewish ways of living and viewing the world, and to make sense of the discrepancies between what they were taught and what they see others doing. Parents' credibility in these matters is enhanced when they live as emotionally healthy, committed Jews.

An example of this comes up every December for many Jewish parents who raise their children outside of Israel. People in the Diaspora are bombarded by non-Jewish music and light displays everywhere for a month before, and for a few weeks after Xmas. Many Jewish children enjoy the beautiful lights and displays. They ask their parents why they can't have a tree in their home and get many gifts for Xmas just like the non-Jews in their neighborhood.

The author does not believe that Jewish parents should try to compete with what the non-Jews are offering their children. Parents have little to fear if they create a home with warmth, love, delicious and happy Shabbat meals every week, and meaningful observance of Shabbat and the Jewish holidays. Such parents can tell their children, "It is true that the non-Jews have one holiday every year with beautiful lights and music. The trees that they decorate have a nice smell and the glitter and lights that they put on them look beautiful. The decorations in their yards do look pretty, but we have so much more. We have Shabbat every week. We have Rosh Hashana with its special rituals. Succot is our week-long holiday when we decorate with beautiful lights and tree branches. We decorate our synagogues with flowers on Shavuot. We have wonderful rituals and foods on Pesach, and you children get gifts when you find the *afikoman* (half a matza that is hidden during the *seder*). We sing our special songs on Shabbat, Succot and Chanuka, and light our special Jewish lights on Chanuka. Isn't it fair that the non-Jews should have one holiday when they have their music and lights?"

It is no small feat to deal with the challenges posed by the secular world in making females into objects, yet it also can be done when our way of life is satisfying. The author spent a Shabbat at her rabbi's house many years ago. After hearing *havdala* (the ceremony with a braided candle, spices and wine that marks the end of the Sabbath), his ten-year-old daughter brought in the mail that had been delivered that morning. One letter was addressed to her. It was an invitation to enter the Junior Miss Beauty Pageant. She asked her father what a beauty pageant was.

He answered, "It's when a lot of girls or young women get dressed up in bathing suits and fancy gowns and then judges decide who is the most beautiful."

His daughter reacted, "Oh, you mean like the party that Vashti went to in King Achaverosh's court?" (The king summoned his queen Vashti to appear naked at a banquet where many men were feasting, in order to show off her beauty. He had her beheaded for refusing to attend, then held a beauty contest to replace her.)

The rabbi smiled, "Yes, it is something like that." As the girl continued to turn the pages of the invitation, her father asked, "Do you think you would like to enter a contest like that?"

"No," his daughter replied. "I'd rather be Jewish."

When children live a beautiful and fulfilling Jewish way of life, the allure of superficial alternatives is lessened.

## Sex

If we live holy lives in homes that are filled with love of God, love of our family members, and love of other Jews, we build walls of protection against many of the dangers in the outside world. When a child lives in a home that is emotionally toxic, he or she becomes very vulnerable to the influences of the outside world.

When parents live with the healthy self-restraint that is part of Judaism, their children feel loved, and the family spends meaningful time together, children are less likely to have premarital physical relationships. When adolescents feel insecure and unloved, males sometimes try to prove their adequacy by having sex, or they use females in other ways. Girls who feel unloved, especially by their fathers, look for love with males who can't give them what they truly seek. Many females today have meaningless sex because their parents have a bad marriage, and they have no model that it is possible to have a fulfilling relationship with real intimacy.

When children's parents are divorced, the parents often have sex with and/or live with other partners without getting married. If parents won't wait until after marriage to have sex, or they don't know how to have a successful marriage, why should their children?

For the most part, both parents making their children feel loved is one of the best protections there is against children having uncommitted sex. Teaching respect for one's body, the sanctity of sex, and the beauty of waiting until one is married to the right person have a greater impact when the parents have a happy home.

Some parents hope that if they don't discuss sex or drugs with their children that the children won't get involved with either. Research has shown that teens often name their parents as the biggest influence on their decisions about sex.[452] When parents discuss sex with their teens, children delay having sex and have fewer partners than when parents don't talk to them about it.[453] Parents can't trust that children will get accurate or helpful information about sex from the child's peers, teachers, or the internet.

It is important that children feel that there are open lines of communication with parents, and that they can talk to their parents about anything. Parents should show children that there are no topics that their children can't discuss with them in a way that is sensitive, empathic, and not judgmental of the child.

If parents combine good communication with emotional and spiritual storehouses at home, children will be less tempted to look for cheap substitutes elsewhere.

# 17

# *Being All We Can Be*

From time immemorial, Jewish women have been the backbone of Jewish survival. They have raised children and supported husbands through the best and worst of times. They have built homes whose hallmarks were charity and hospitality and created social networks to help those in bad socioeconomic and emotional straits. Their selfless giving and abiding faith in God have been cohesive forces that have helped our people to thrive throughout the generations.

Our biblical foremothers courageously risked social ostracism and death to do what was morally right. They put others' welfare and survival of future generations above their personal comfort. Each recognized that she, and only she, could accomplish her particular mission in life, and that every day she could make choices that would change the course of Jewish history forever.

The main task of our foremothers was to ensure the spiritual welfare of the Jewish people. Each strove to do this in a different way. Sarah understood that she would have to raise her son Isaac in an environment that was devoid of bad influences so that he could carry on the mission of the Jewish people. Mothers today often have this same challenge.

Rebekah helped her son Jacob understand that he had to learn how to integrate the spiritual and material worlds. It was not enough for him to simply learn Judaism in an ivory tower; he also had to live it in a world with immoral and unethical people. His mother insisted that he leave an easy, comfortable environment and deal with a deceitful uncle and murderous and jealous twin brother. Along the way, he also learned to deal with immoral neighbors, and wives and children who did not get along with one another.

Rachel's role was to unify all of Jacob's diverse children so that each could complement, love, and respect the others. Her job was to create a harmonious nation who loved God and one another. Unfortunately, she was taken from this world at a young age, and this task still remains for today's Jewish women to facilitate.

Leah's main task was to encourage each of Jacob's children's individuality. She appreciated that each needed to make his or her unique contribution as founders of the Jewish people. Outliving her sister by a few years, Leah was able to accomplish much of her mission as a mother to half of the twelve tribes.

In the Book of Esther, which we read on the holiday of Purim, Esther's uncle Mordechai was one of the Jewish leaders who sat in the Sanhedrin (Jewish Supreme Court).[454]  Esther was forced to marry a non-Jewish Persian King around 2,400 years ago. After the evil viceroy Haman got permission from the king to murder all of the Jews in the empire, Mordechai told Queen Esther that she must go to the king and try to convince him to protect her people. Esther balked because it meant risking her life. She hoped that the Almighty would save the Jews using some other means. Mordechai convinced her, "Perhaps it is solely for the purpose of saving the Jews that you became queen. If you don't act on their behalf, don't think that you and your family will be spared. You will be destroyed and the rest of the Jews will be saved through some other means."[455]

Esther could have thought that she didn't have any special qualities that would convince the king to spare the Jews. She could have decided to save her own skin and hide out in the protection of the palace where no one knew she was Jewish. She could have delegated the potentially suicidal mission to someone else. Instead, she heeded Mordechai's advice and risked death with the hope that she could save her people. Although she was but a single individual, she prayed that God would make a miracle and enable her to save the Jews. He did.

After saving the Jews from annihilation, Esther gave birth to the king's heir. When he became king, he allowed the Jews who had been exiled from Israel to return to their homeland and build the Second Temple. The consequences of Esther's single act remind us that we can never know the ultimate effects of even the most seemingly small deed that we do.

Each of these women reminds us never to trivialize the effect that our seemingly small acts can have for eternity.

## DOING FOR OTHERS

The Torah tells us that the Almighty put Adam into the Garden of Eden "to work it and to guard it."[456] From the time humanity was created, we were asked to contribute to the upkeep of the world. The Creator shows us by example that each day offers a new opportunity to renew the world physically and elevate what is here spiritually.

Each day, God makes the sun rise, causes rain to fall in the appropriate places and in the proper amounts, and makes crops, fruits, vegetables, trees, flowers, and grass grow. He continually creates new animal and human lives and sustains them. He "forever renews with His goodness every day, the act of Creation." [457] We are supposed to imitate Him. One of the many ways we do so is by using our talents to give thanks and pay forward some of the goodness that He gives us.

Unfortunately, there are many people who feel that they have no need to give to anyone beyond themselves or their families. They feel that they are primarily here to be served or to be left in their personal comfort zone.

We say in the first prayer in the *Shemoneh Esrai* that God is "great, mighty, and awesome, and above all worlds, who does deeds of loving kindness." If the Creator is above all worlds, yet lovingly takes care of us, we should realize that no matter how important the things we do are, we still need to help other Jews.

Once we say to our fellow Jew in distress, "I don't have to help you; your needs don't concern me," we are no longer acting as if we are part of the Jewish people. Women cannot fully use their potentials when they say, "You do your thing and I'll do mine. Find someone else to help you in your hour of need. I have my life to live."

## LIVING UP TO OUR POTENTIALS

A story is told about a righteous man named Reb Zusha. As he lay on his deathbed, his students surrounded him and were dismayed to see him sobbing.

"What is the matter, Rebbe?" they asked.

Reb Zusha replied, "I'm terrified of meeting my Maker in a few minutes when my soul leaves this world. I don't know what to tell Him when He asks me what I've done with my life."

His students hastened to reassure him that he had indeed lived a very pious life, but Zusha would not be consoled. He explained, "When the Almighty asks me, 'Zusha, why weren't you as kind as your forefather Abraham?' I'll know what to say. 'I wasn't Abraham.' And when He asks me, 'Zusha, why weren't you as great a Torah teacher as Moses was?' I'll respond, 'I wasn't Moses.' But when the Master of the Universe asks me, 'Zusha, why weren't you Zusha?' for that, I have no answer."

At various points in our lives we should ask ourselves, "Why was I put here? What should I be accomplishing with the unique gifts that the Almighty gave me? Am I living up to my potentials?" Whatever our particular answers are, we should know that like Esther, we were each put here at this point in time, with our unique circumstances, to make our special contribution to the world. As Esther did initially, we can think that we have done enough, or that we aren't special enough to do more. We can rationalize that it is up to others who are more gifted or who have more time or more inclination to help spiritually fix the world. However, one of the lessons of Purim is that if we are Jewish, we all share in the fate and destiny of the entire Jewish people. If we shirk our responsibilities to give of ourselves, then we have no right to share in our people's accomplishments and ultimate redemption. We also risk being spiritually obliterated in the process.

Perhaps the Almighty put us here to give to others and to encourage others to do the same. Every day is a new chance for us to add building blocks to our people's ultimate redemption. If we don't contribute to the world's spiritual upkeep, we are not entitled to take from it, either.

## THE IMPORTANCE OF GIVING

An aftermath of the "Me" generation was that people became more afraid than ever of giving. They worried that if they gave away their emotions, time, or money, they would end up being deprived. Of the world's nearly 2,100 billionaires, only 6.5% have pledged to give away at least half of their wealth to charity.[458] People often think that giving to charity will diminish their wealth. Some also worry that if they give of themselves, maybe it will deplete them instead of making them feel nourished and fulfilled.

People always have excuses to not give a tenth of their after-tax income to charity. However, even the poorest Jewish pauper who relies on public donations is required to give something to other poor people because everyone needs to be a giver.

In a famous public lecture, Rabbi Moshe Feinstein, *z"tl,* pointed out that we must tithe our time as well as our money. Most people who insist that they don't have enough time to help others usually find time to pursue their own interests. Conversely, when a woman wants to give, she will find a way to do so. When she doesn't want to give, she will never have enough time or money to share.

When people feel that the Almighty has blessed them, they feel happy and want to share what they have. Ironically, Americans are now the wealthiest people in the history of the world, yet two-thirds of them say they are unhappy.[459] It seems that the rabbis were right when they said in the *Chapters of the Fathers,* "Who is rich? The person who is happy with what he has."[460]

Our sages also say in the *Chapters of the Fathers* that there are four types of people:[461]

The first type says, "What is mine is mine and what is yours is yours." This person is termed average, but there are those who say, "This is the attribute of the people of Sodom."

The second type says, "What is mine is yours and what is yours is mine." This person is termed an ignoramus.

The third type says, "What is mine is yours and what is yours is yours." This is a pious person whose deeds are characterized by loving kindness.

The fourth type says, "What is mine is mine and what is yours is mine." This person is termed wicked.

It is easy to understand why the rabbis characterized the four types as they did. It is perplexing, though, that someone who says, "What's mine is mine and what's yours is yours" is considered to be as wicked as the Sodomites, whom God destroyed.

Perhaps the reason for this is that Jews who think that they do not have to share what they have are living only in order to serve themselves, not to fulfill their divine mission. Our job here includes giving to others. We are supposed to see ourselves as comptrollers of whatever material and other gifts the Almighty gives us. They are not here solely for our use and pleasure.

Once a Jew says, "I don't have to help others," she severs herself from the Jewish people and from our national purpose. Grabbing what they could and turning a deaf ear to the needy were hallmarks of the Sodomites. They believed that it was fine to take what they wanted and not concern themselves with anyone else's needs.

When women choose their life paths, they should ask how they can use their careers, family situations, money, and the like to contribute to the world. People are unified by mutual giving and are divided by taking. There is a finite amount of material things, jobs, and people in this world. That means if you take the job, husband, or things that I want, they won't be there for me. If instead, we all focus on what we can contribute, there is more than enough to go around.

## BEING MERCIFUL AND COMPASSIONATE

The Talmud says that the hallmarks of a Jew are that we are compassionate, modest, and do deeds of loving kindness."[462] We are termed "compassionate people who are children of compassionate people." If there is one quality that sets us apart from the rest of the world, it is our desire to imitate our Creator's endless kindness.

How do we do this? Just as the Almighty is merciful, we are supposed to be merciful. Just as He is compassionate, we should be compassionate. Just as He is a Giver, we are supposed to be givers.[463] He gave us our good fortunes, talents, and life situations so that we would use them to make the world a more spiritual, better place, a place where He feels welcome dwelling among us. If we have no places in our hearts for our fellow Jew, if we don't give our share of charity, offer hospitality to strangers, and help with communal needs, God says that there is no place for Him among us.

Every morning, we say a Talmudic selection in our morning prayers:

These are the things that one eats the fruits of in this world, but the capital remains to enjoy in the World-to-Come. They are: Honoring parents, doing kind deeds, going to the synagogue morning and evening, being hospitable to guests, visiting the sick, making weddings for poor brides, burying the dead, praying intensively, and bringing peace between a man and his friend, and between a man and his wife....[464]

There are many ways that we can, and should, do these things in our personal and professional lives. When Torah-observant women choose careers, or are mothers and housewives, we can ask, "How can I best use my talents and interests to serve my Creator and help the Jewish people?" It is not enough to ask, "What do I want to do with my life?" then try to fit in God and being Jewish in our spare time.

Here are a few traditional ways that women do kind deeds for others: hosting guests, especially Jews who don't know much about Judaism for Shabbat and Jewish holiday meals; inviting singles, college students, widows, and divorced people to the Passover *seder*; making, delivering or ordering in food to new mothers or to mourners; visiting patients in nursing homes and hospitals; introducing singles who want to get married to one another; comforting the bereaved; hosting parlor meetings for worthy Jewish charities; publicizing and organizing charitable events and Torah classes in one's community.

No matter what age we are, imitating our Creator is part of our life's work.

## MAKING LIFE MEANINGFUL

One of the most remarkable things about Judaism is that it touches on every facet of our lives, from the most mundane to the most sublime and esoteric. There is no part of life about which Judaism has nothing to say. Every action we do and each word we speak, even those about which we might not give a second thought, can have moral and metaphysical effects.

Our physical existence doesn't usually last more than a century, if that. We weren't here 100 years ago and probably won't be here in another hundred. We seem to be existentially insignificant in the context of the history of the world and the vastness of the universe. We could easily feel that we are mere drops in a cosmic bucket. Yet, our Creator has deemed it necessary for us to be here.

Judaism tells us how to invest life with infinite meaning, how to take our basest instincts and make them holy and pure, and how to take the seemingly trivial and make it Godly. Our every act, thought, and word can elevate our soul and connect us to our Infinite Source.

Torah teaches us that although our bodies are mortal, finite, and time-limited, we are greater than our physical vessels. We each have not only a body, but a soul, which has some essence of the divine. It enables us to transcend our animalistic and sensual desires, our emotional needs, and the limits of our intellects. We can become great by elevating our physical and emotional drives to serve our Creator.

No aspect of our lives needs to be mundane or meaningless. How we dress, speak, eat, and even how we are intimate with our spouse can be made holy, connect us to the Infinite, and draw down the Divine Presence. When we follow His will, we become His partners in fulfilling the purpose for His having created the world. We can invest our every action with holiness and cosmic significance, and thereby elevate ourselves and the soul of the entire Jewish people. Or, we can defy the divine will and thereby damage the entire world. The more we recognize His involvement in our daily lives, the closer we bring the universe to redemption.

## THE MESSIANIC ERA

At some point, either Jews will live the way God has asked of us or we will have failed to do so. At that time, the world will reach its final stage of existence and the Messiah (*Mashiach*, meaning "the anointed one") will come. When that happens, all humanity will clearly see God's Presence in their lives.

Every Jew has an individual soul, but the entire Jewish people shares a common soul as well. Just as damaging an arm, a leg, or any other limb affects our entire body, so it is with the Jewish people. It is impossible for us to do any spiritually positive or negative actions that don't affect the collective soul and destiny of the entire Jewish nation. This is why our every deed affects the entire realization (or hampering) of the divine plan for the world.

## BEING ALL WE CAN BE

Living fully as a Jew is not always easy. The *Chapters of the Fathers* says, "The task is a difficult task, and the day is short....You are not obliged to finish the work, but neither are you free to desist from trying."[465]

It may make the job easier to know that whatever we do to develop our spirituality will not be eradicated when we die. It prepares us for a beautiful spiritual afterlife where we are rewarded by the closeness to God that we developed during our time on earth.

Our tradition tells us that in every generation, there are righteous women in whose merit the entire Jewish people are worthy of being redeemed. May we have the intellectual honesty and emotional strength to take on the challenges of becoming Torah-observant Jews and bringing the divine plan for the world to fruition.

# ABOUT THE AUTHOR

Lisa Aiken received her Ph.D. in clinical psychology from Loyola University of Chicago. In the 1980s, she was the Chief Psychologist of Lenox Hill Hospital in New York City, a clinical assistant professor at New York Medical College and St. John's University, and a clinical associate professor at Long Island University.

For nearly 40 years, Dr. Aiken has been a psychotherapist for individuals and couples. She has authored and co-authored 11 books, and has lectured to diverse Jewish audiences in more than 250 cities on six continents. She is also a licensed Israeli tour guide.

She is listed in thirteen *Who's Who* books, and has appeared on television and radio.

Dr. Aiken can be contacted at lisaaiken@ymail.com.

## *ALSO BY LISA AIKEN*

Lisa Aiken, *The Family Guide to Touring Israel.* Createspace, 2010.

Lisa Aiken, *Why Me, God? A Jewish Guide to Coping with Challenges.* Createspace, 2012.

Lisa Aiken, *The Hidden Beauty of the Shema.* Judaica Press, NY, 2004.

Lisa Aiken, *Guide for the Romantically Perplexed.* Jerusalem, 2003.

Lisa Aiken, *The Baal Teshuva Survival Guide.* Rossi Publications, Los Angeles, CA, 2009.

Yitzchok Kirzner with Lisa Aiken, *The Art of Jewish Prayer.* Judaica Press, NY, 2003.

Lisa Aiken and Ira Michaels, *Genesis: The Untold Story.* Rossi Publications, Los Angeles, CA, 2007.

# Notes

1.  Exodus 6:6-7.
2.  Genesis 1:27; 2:7; 2:15-25.
3.  Genesis 1:27.
4.  *Eruvin* 18a.
5.  *Berachot* 61a.
6.  Genesis 2:7.
7.  Genesis 2:15-17.
8.  Radak on Genesis 1:26; *Pirkei d'Rabbi Eliezer* 12.
9.  Samson Raphael Hirsch on Genesis 1:26.
10. Hirsch on Genesis 1:26.
11. Sforno on Genesis 2:18.
12. Genesis 2:18.
13. *Torah Temimah* on Genesis 2:18.
14. Genesis 2:19-20.
15. Raavad on Genesis 2:19.
16. Sforno on Genesis 2:19.
17. Malbim on Genesis 2:18; Rashi on Genesis 2:20.
18. Genesis 2:21.
19. Sforno on Genesis 2:20.
20. Genesis 2:22.
21. *Niddah* 45b.
22. Genesis 2:23-24.
23. Genesis *Rabbah* 17.
24. S. R. Hirsch on Genesis 2:24.
25. Rashi on Genesis 2:24.
26. *Pirkei d'Rabbi Eliezer* 34.
27. S. R. Hirsch on Genesis 2:22.
28. See *Yevamot* 63a.
29. Genesis *Rabbah* 8:10; *Pirkei d'Rabbi Eliezer* 12.

30. Psalms 8:5.
31. For example, God is deemed a helper in Genesis 49:25. Woman is referred to as a helper in Genesis 2:20.
32. *Pirkei d'Rabbi Eliezer* on Genesis 2:23.
33. Unlike regular snakes, this serpent had arms and legs and could speak.
34. Genesis 3:1.
35. Rashi on Genesis 3:1.
36. Genesis 3:4.
37. Genesis *Rabbah* 19.
38. *Ha-emek Davar* on Genesis 3:4.
39. Genesis 3:5.
40. Genesis *Rabbah* 19.
41. S. R. Hirsch on Genesis 3:4.
42. Genesis 3:6.
43. Rashi on Genesis 3:6.
44. Genesis *Rabbah* 14:4.
45. Genesis *Rabbah* 20:8.
46. Rabbi Dessler on Genesis 3.
47. Rashi on *Sanhedrin* 70b.
48. Genesis *Rabbah* 15:7.
49. Genesis *Rabbah* 15:7.
50. *Shabbat* 55b.
51. Sforno on Genesis 3:6.
52. Genesis *Rabbah* 20.
53. Rashi on Genesis 4:1.
54. Rashi on Genesis 4:1.
55. Genesis 3:16.
56. *Eruvin* 100b
57. Nachmanides on Genesis 3:16.
58. Rashi on Genesis 3:16.
59. *Me'am Loez* on Genesis 3:17-19.
60. Rabbi Dovid Cohen on Genesis 3:16.
61. *Ha-Emek Davar* on Genesis 3:20.
62. Malbim on Genesis 3:20.
63. Rabbi Dovid Cohen on Genesis 3:20.
64. Genesis *Rabbah* on Genesis 3:20.
65. Isaiah 34:14.
66. *Eruvin* 100b; *Niddah* 24b; *Bava Batra* 73b; *Shabbat* 151b.
67. S. R. Hirsch on Genesis 1:24.
68. See Genesis *Rabbah* 17 and 18:2.

69. Rashi on *Kiddushin* 35a.
70. Psalms 34:15.
71. *Mishnah Kiddushin* 29a.
72. Genesis 2:22.
73. *Niddah* 45b.
74. Exodus 31:3.
75. Some of the 613 biblical commandments that apply to most modern women who live in the Diaspora: [For a fuller listing and explanation, see *The Concise Book of Mitzvot*, Chafetz Chaim (New York: Feldheim, 1990).] To believe that there is one God; to love and fear Him; to sanctify His Name and do nothing to desecrate it; to walk in His ways; to pray to Him; not to make, own, benefit from, or worship idols; to say grace after meals; to rise before an old person; to honor Jewish priests and Torah scholars; to observe the Sabbath and Jewish holidays by not doing forbidden creative activities; not to eat or possess leavened foods on Passover; to eat only kosher food; to fast on the Day of Atonement; and to love every Jew, and especially Jewish converts, as oneself.
76. *A Hedge of Roses* (Jerusalem: Feldheim, 1977), p. 76.
77. Due to the Women's Movement, the percentage of American women working outside the home rose from 53% in 1970 to 71% in 2012. The Working Mothers Research Institute surveyed more than 1,000 working parents in 2015 and found that 79% of working mothers were responsible for doing the laundry and most other household chores, and twice as many mothers as fathers cooked for the family. Working mothers also did most of the child care. "Working Moms Still Take on Bulk of Household Chores." www.cnbc.com/2015/04/28/me-is-like-leave-it-to-beaver.
78. Avudraham.
79. Maharal *Drush al Hatorah.*
80. These are collectively known by the acronym *Tanach.*
81. Chofetz Chaim in *Chomat Ha-dat.*
82. Literally, 18 (blessings). However, nearly 2,000 years ago one blessing was added, making a total of 19 blessings.
83. *Midrash Tanchuma* 2.
84. Using at least 3.7 pounds of wheat, rye, oats, spelt or barley flour.
85. Based on Numbers 15:17-21.
86. *Shulchan Aruch*, Chapter 242; *Mishnah Brurah, Se'ef Katan* 6.
87. Ezekiel 44:30.
88. The first chapter of the book of Genesis says about each day of Creation, "And it was evening, and it was morning..." The Jewish "day" begins with sunset the prior evening and ends at sunset or nightfall the same day. Thus, the Sabbath begins at sunset Friday and ends at nightfall Saturday evening.

89. If a man lives alone or in a dormitory, he lights candles prior to the Sabbath in his domicile. If he is unmarried and living with a family, the woman of the house lights candles for everyone in her home.

90. Kosher foods are those permitted by Jewish dietary laws. Prohibited foods include pork and shellfish; beef, chicken and sheep that were not ritually slaughtered and had the blood removed through a process of salting and soaking the meat; foods that contain both meat and dairy; and foods that were cooked in ovens or utensils that were used to cook non-kosher food.

91. Many people erroneously think that Christianity initiated the idea of a Messiah who will usher in a utopian era. In fact, Christianity took and distorted the Jewish idea. Judaism posits that a man, descended from King David, will unite the Jewish people and get them all to keep the Torah. Then the nations of the world will stop worshipping their false gods and will observe the seven Noahide principles of morality incumbent on all non-Jews. There will then be universal peace. It is pointless for a Messiah to come to a world that is not ready for him. Christianity dispensed with the Jewish notion of personal responsibility for living according to Torah, then changed the Jewish idea of the Messiah to suit their theology.

92. According to the Midrash, Adam transmitted God's command to her. In the Process, he added that she should not touch the tree, either.

93. *Mei Shiloach*.

94. *Aleinu* prayer.

95. For a detailed discussion of this topic, see Lisa Aiken, *Why Me, God? A Jewish Guide to Coping with Challenges*. Createspace, 2012.

96. Paraphrased from Genesis 21:9-12.

97. Rashi on Genesis 21:12.

98. The story appears in Genesis 27:1-19.

99. Genesis 29:18-27.

100. *Megillah* 13b.

101. Genesis 29:31-30:15.

102. Genesis *Rabbah* 72; see Rashi on Genesis 30:24. This took place hundreds of years after Jacob's death.

103. *Yoma* 9b.

104. Introduction to *Midrash Rabbah* on Lamentations, paragraph 24.

105. Mount Moriah is where the Temple Mount in Jerusalem is today. The first and second Temples were built where Abraham offered Isaac to God. Islam began some 2,400 years later. Seventy years later, Moslems came to Jerusalem and built the Dome of the Rock on the holiest place in the world for Jews to show that Islam had superseded Judaism.

106. The story of Abraham obeying God's command to offer his son on Mount Moriah is called the binding of Isaac, or *Akeidat Yitzchak* in Hebrew (Genesis 22:1-19).

107. Jacob's name was changed to Israel after he left Lavan's house and he returned to the land of Canaan. Thus, his descendants are called Israelites, and his sons are known as the 12 tribes of Israel.
108. *Berachot* 60a.
109. Genesis 34:1-2.
110. Genesis *Rabbah* 76.
111. Genesis 38:12-30.
112. Some generations later, King David descended from Judah. Subsequently, all Jewish kings were to come only from his dynasty. Historically, Judah and his descendants were leaders of the Jewish people. Most Jews today descended from him, which is why we are called "Jews."
113. For example, Rashi wrote that the Egyptians had at least 1,000 deities. Incest was common in Egypt, and some of the pharaohs (like King Tut) married their sisters.
114. *Iggerot Moshe*, vol. 7, p. 168.
115. After God gave the Israelites the Ten Commandments at Mt. Sinai, He taught Moses the Oral Law for 40 days. The Oral Law explains how to observe the Torah. At the end of Moses' absence, some men built a Golden Calf. When the Israelite men asked their wives to donate their gold jewelry to the cause, the women refused (based on Exodus 32:3 that says the men broke off the gold earrings from their wives' ears.) The men got so little gold that the entire amount was only enough to make a calf. When God asked the Jews to build him a Tabernacle, the women gladly gave what they had. They donated so much gold that Moses had to tell them to stop bringing it.
116. Rashi on Exodus 38:8.
117. *Sotah* 11b.
118. Exodus 1:15-19.
119. Exodus 2:2-10.
120. *Shemot Rabbah* 28:2.
121. The Written Law is called the Torah, Five Books of Moses, or *Chumash* in Hebrew. Since no code of law can be applied without case examples and further explanation, God taught Moses the Oral Law that elaborated on and explained the *Chumash*. Moses then taught the Oral Law to the Jewish leaders, who taught it to the rest of the Jews. This oral transmission continued in each generation until Roman persecutions made it necessary to preserve the Oral Law by writing it down as the Mishnah around the year 200 CE. Over the next 200-300 years, the Mishnah was elaborated upon in the Palestinian and Babylonian Talmuds, respectively.
122. *Pirkei d'Rabbi Eliezer*, Chapter 44.
123. *Shulchan Aruch* 419:1.
124. These two men were Caleb the son of Yefuneh and Joshua the son of Nun. Joshua became Moses' successor and led the next generation of Israelites into the land.

125. Leviticus 22:32.
126. Except for Miriam, Moses' sister, who died shortly before the second generation of Israelites entered the land.
127. Judges Chapter 4.
128. *Megillah* 14a.
129. *Yalkut Shimoni.*
130. She was a non-Jewish descendant of Yitro, Moses' father-in-law.
131. *Nazir* 23b.
132. *Sanhedrin* 7a.
133. Judges 5:24.
134. Judges 5:7.
135. *Me'am Loez* on Judges 5:7.
136. Abarbanel on Judges 5:7.
137. *Metzudat David* on Judges 5:7.
138. Rashi on I Kings 2:19.
139. *Mishnah Avot* 1:2.
140. http://www.livescience.com/24102-50-facts-sex.html. The study appeared in the July 6, 2012 journal *Sex Roles*.
141. Paul P. *Pornified*. New York, NY: Times Books, 2007.
142. http://www.nytimes.com/2011/12/15/health/nearly-1-in-5-women-in-us-survey-report-sexual-assault.html?_r=0. This 2010-11 study used a representative sample of more than 16,500 adults. However, most mental health studies estimate that one out of four females has been raped, many of them as children.
143. *Shabbat* 10a.
144. Rutchick, A. *Social Psychological and Personality Science*, August 2015, vol. 6 no. 6, pp. 661-668.
145. *Ibid.*
146. Hajo, A. and Galinsky, A. *Journal of Experimental Social Psychology*. Vol, 48 (4), July, 2012, pp. 918-925.
147. Genesis 3:7-11.
148. Micah 6:8.
149. *Shulchan Aruch*, vol. 1, 3:1.
150. See *Avodah Zarah* 47b and *Berachot* 62a.
151. See commandment #22 in the list of constant commandments in the Preface to the Book of Psalms.
152. Exodus 25:8.
153. Proverbs 11:2.
154. Genesis *Rabbah* 17 and 18.
155. *Niddah* 45b.
156. *Shulchan Aruch, Even Ha'Ezer* 21:1; *Mishnah Berurah* 75:7.

157. *Shulchan Aruch, Orach Chaim* 75:1; *Mishnah Berurah* there.
158. *Mishnah Berurah* 75:2.
159. *Ketubot* 72a; Bet Shmuel, *Even Ha-Ezer* 21:5.
160. Y. Fuchs, *Hilchos Bas Yisrael*. Oak Park, MI; Targum Press, 1985, p.72.
161. *Minchat Yitzchak*, vol. 2, no. 108.
162. *Shulchan Aruch, Even Ha-Ezer* 21:1, based on *Berachot* 24a.
163. Nevertheless, many Sefardic rabbis do not permit married women to cover their hair using a wig.
164. *Shabbat* 127a.
165. Genesis 2:7.
166. See Yitzchok Kirzner and Lisa Aiken, *The Art of Jewish Prayer* (Judaica Press, Brooklyn, NY, 2003) for an excellent introduction to Jewish prayer in general, and explanation of the main Jewish prayer, *Shemoneh Esrai*.
167. I Kings 8:39.
168. Rashi on I Kings 8:43.
169. Such as Jacob's beloved wife Rachel dying in childbirth.
170. Such as the Roman destruction of Jerusalem, the Second Temple, and the murder of 580,000 Jews during the Bar Kochba Revolt.
171. *Berachot* 29b.
172. Chaim Volozhin, *Nefesh Hachaim*, Gate 1.
173. Rashi on Deuteronomy 33:18; Rashi on *Zevachim* 2a; *Sotah* 21a.
174. Based on Genesis 49:10.
175. II Chronicles 26:16-22; *Sanhedrin* 48b. The Hebrew term *tzaraat* is usually mistranslated "leprosy." It was a skin ailment similar to psoriasis, caused by one of several spiritual deficiencies, including slandering other Jews. The Greek word probably came from the Hebrew.
176. E.g., Rashi on *Pesachim* 46a and on *Chullin* 122b.
177. Nachmanides, *Milchamot Hashem* to *Megilla* 5a.
178. *Mishnah Sanhedrin* 4:5.
179. Rabbi Mordecai Tendler on Tractate *Betzah*.
180. Unless the demanded deed involves idolatry, murder, or adultery/incest. A Jew must forfeit his or her life rather than do one of these cardinal sins.
181. See *Sefer Ha-chinuch*, *Mitzvah* 296, and *Minchat Chinuch* there.
182. It is unclear if Chana invented her way of praying or simply modeled a pre-existing mode.
183. I Samuel 1.
184. Leviticus 9:1-10:3.
185. *Shulchan Aruch* 106:1.
186. *Magen Avraham* on *Shulchan Aruch* 106:1.
187. See Maimonides, *Hilchot Tefillah* 1:1-3.

188. *Mishnah Brurah to Orach Chaim* 106:1.
189. *Orach Chaim* 70:1.
190. *Tanna D'vai Eliyahu Zuta* 17.
191. *Bava Metzia* 38a.
192. Genesis 3:1.
193. Genesis 3:4.
194. Genesis 3:5.
195. Genesis 3:5.
196. Rashi on Genesis 3:5.
197. *Eiruvin* 13b.
198. *Galatians* 3:28.
199. Some readers may wonder how Judaism allowed Jews to own or to be slaves. Jewish slavery in the Torah is not what it seems at face value. For example, a male Jew could only become a slave to another Jew if he stole something and did not have the money to pay back the value of what he stole plus a penalty, or if he sold himself into slavery because he was impoverished. In the first instance, the slave owner rehabilitated the slave and took care of his entire family until the Sabbatical year, when the slave was freed. During his term of "slavery," the man learned how to be a refined, productive person with self-respect by living with a good family. If the owner had only one pillow, the slave got it. If there was only one expensive piece of meat and one simple dish for dinner, the slave ate the meat. The slave could only be asked to do work that he was used to, and nothing demeaning. When the slave was release, the master furnished him with whatever food and clothing the slave needed to start a new life. Thus, the rabbis said that whoever acquired a slave got himself a master!
200. The Divine Presence hovered over Sarah's tent while she was alive. It returned when her son Isaac married Rebekah and they lived in Sarah's tent. (Rashi on Genesis 24:67.)
201. *Bava Batra* 4a.
202. Josephus, in *The Jewish War*, chapter 6, claims that 1,100,000 Jews were trapped in Jerusalem when the Romans besieged the city because so many had come to celebrate Passover.
203. The prescriptions of how the Tabernacle and its furnishings were to be made and used, how the priests and Levites were to serve there, and the various laws governing offerings there constitute many of the 613 *mitzvot*.
204. The earliest known synagogues date to the 3rd or 4th century BCE.
205. A dedication stone from a 2,000-year-old synagogue that stood near the Second Temple says that the building was used for studying Torah and hosting travelers (who ate and slept on the premises). Synagogues then apparently had multiple functions.

206. Deuteronomy 11:13.
207. *Taanit* 2a.
208. Leviticus *Rabbah* 24:6.
209. Leviticus 19:30.
210. *Megillah* 29a.
211. The Ark of the Covenant was hidden toward the end of the First Temple era. The Holy of Holies in the Second Temple was therefore empty.
212. *Mishnah Avot* 5:5.
213. *Sukkah* 51b.
214. *Sukkah* 51b.
215. I Chronicles 28:10-12, 19.
216. Zechariah 12:12.
217. Jerusalem Talmud, *Succah* 5, law 2.
218. *Mishnah Torah, Hilchot Bet Ha-bechirah*, Chapter 5, law 9.
219. Commentary on *Mishnah Succah*, Chapter 5, *Mishnah* 2.
220. *Iggerot Moshe, Orach Chaim*, vols. 39 and 42.
221. J. B. Soloveitchik, "On Seating and Sanctification." In *The Sanctity of the Synagogue*, ed. B. Litvin (New York, Ktav, 1987), pp. 115-116.
222. Samuel S. Cohen, "Reform Judaism," in *Jewish Life in America*, ed. Freedman and Gordis, p. 86.
223. Said in the *Alenu* prayer three times every day.
224. *Yevamot* 62b.
225. *Yevamot* 63b.
226. For practical ways to have a successful marriage using Jewish and psychological wisdom, see Lisa Aiken, *Guide for the Romantically Perplexed*, Jerusalem, 2007.
227. Aramaic was the vernacular of Jews in Israel and many other Jewish communities when the Sanhedrin required 2,000 years ago that *ketubot* be written documents.
228. Jewish law requires them to be two Torah-observant adult males who are not related to one another nor to the bride or groom.
229. S. R. Hirsch on Exodus 22:16.
230. S. R. Hirsch on Exodus 22:15; *Kallah Rabbati* 3; Rashi, *Midrash HaGadol* on Genesis 49:9.
231. This was done in the time of Shimon ben Shetach, the brother of Queen Salome.
232. Tosefta, *Ketubot* 12:1.
233. *Ketubot* 7a; *Shulchan Aruch, Even Ha-Ezer* 66:1.
234. Rabbi Meir, *Ketubot* 57a.
235. *Ketubot* 10a.
236. For example, a man would have to think twice before divorcing the woman who had taken care of him for many years, given birth to, and raised his children, and leaving her for a beautiful woman half his age.

237. Comments in parentheses are the author's and not part of Maimonides' text.
238. Maimonides stipulates that it must have a toilet outside the house!
239. Rashi, *Yevamot* 66a.
240. *Iggerot Moshe, Even Ha-Ezer*, vol. 4, Chapter 91.
241. Many of these laws seem predicated on the assumption that the father and daughter had a good relationship, and that he would do what was in his daughter's best interests.
242. *Ketubot* 64b. It means "additional amount."
243. *Hachalat Shiva* 21:49:3.
244. Current estimates of its monetary value are between $15,000-125,000, depending on the value of silver at any given time.
245. Rema, *Even Ha-Ezer* 61:1.
246. *Yerushalmi, Bikkurim* 3:3.
247. He lived during the first and second centuries. The Romans publicly tortured him to death around the year 135 for teaching Torah.
248. *Yadayim* 3:5.
249. *Sotah* 17a.
250. I *Corinthians* 7:9.
251. *Iggeret HaKodesh* chapter 3.
252. As in Genesis 4:1, 4:17 and 4:25.
253. *Tosfot Rid* on *Yevamot* 12a.
254. Based on Deuteronomy (24:15): "He must remain free for his home for one year and gladden the wife that he took."
255. *Gittin* 90a.
256. *Iggeret HaKodesh*, quoted by Maimonides, ed. Chavel, 2:336.
257. Leviticus 18:19.
258. Leviticus 15:19.
259. The Torah obligated different amounts of time that a woman had to wait before she could immerse, depending upon what day in her cycle she got her period and how long it lasted. Eventually, women were afraid that they would make mistakes and they asked the sages to require all women to wait a week after bleeding ceased before they could immerse. As a result, certain rare situations (such as certain marital problems or specific forms of infertility) might allow a rabbi to give a leniency allowing a woman to count fewer days than usual before immersing.
260. These included, but were not limited to, a man having a seminal emission; a person having a certain venereal discharge; someone having *tzaraat*; touching certain dead reptiles; childbirth; and contact with a dead body.
261. For example, the Torah's prohibitions against non-marital sex made venereal diseases rare among Jews. Rabbinic requirements to bathe in honor of the Sabbath and to wash hands multiple times daily made Jews less susceptible to bubonic

plague during the Middle Ages.

262. Usually mistranslated as "leprosy."

263. *Shabbat* 112b; *Eruvin* 53a; *Yerushalmi, Shekalim* 13b.

264. *Kiddushin* 30b.

265. Some kinds of uterine bleeding do not make a woman *niddah*.

266. One can buy special "*bedikah*" ("examination") cloths for this purpose at *mikvahs* and some stores.

267. The protocol for immersing on Shabbat or a Jewish holiday is slightly different.

268. From *Chupat Chatanim*.

269. For modesty reasons, a husband who wants to meet his wife immediately after she leaves the *mikvah* building must do so at a distance if he might see other women coming from, or going to, their immersion.

270. According to Torah law, a woman's period often rendered her a *niddah* for a total of one week, after which she immersed. However, uterine bleeding could cause other statuses that shortened or lengthened that time. Today, *niddah* is a generic term for a woman who has had hormonely-induced uterine bleeding and not yet immersed in a *mikvah*.

271. *Niddah* 31b.

272. Leviticus 19:2.

273. Rashi on Leviticus 19:2.

274. Even if a couple is unable to conceive, the laws of family purity still apply. This specific aspect, however, is irrelevant.

275. This is but one example of how Jewish women have had a say in some Jewish laws that apply to them.

276. Genesis 2:10-14.

277. Aryeh Kaplan, *Waters of Eden*. (New York: Union of Orthodox Congregations of America, 1982), p. 13.

278. Genesis 1:28.

279. Genesis 9:7. See Rashi on *Ketubot* 5a.

280. Abarbanel on Genesis 1:28.

281. *Sefer Ha-Chinuch, mitzvah* #1.

282. *Yevamot* 63b.

283. *Yevamot* 6:6.

284. Genesis 1:27.

285. *Yevamot* 62a.

286. Isaiah 45:18.

287. Ecclesiastes 11:6.

288. *Yevamot* 62b.

289. *Mishnah Torah, Hilchut Ishut* 15, 16.

290. Tosefta on *Yevamot* 8:2.

291. *Isurei Biah* 21:26.

292. *Yevamot* 65b.

293. *Meshech Chochmah* on Genesis 9:1. Although dying in childbirth is now rare in the Western world, one-third of Jewish women in Jerusalem died in childbirth or of its complications as recently as the late 1800s. Historically, estimates are that women had a 1-2% chance of dying with each birth.

294. *Chidushei HaRan* on *Kiddushin* 41a.

295. *Aruch Ha-Shulchan, Yoreh Deah* 246.

296. *Bava Batra* 9a.

297. *Yevamot* 62a.

298. This presupposes that a couple does not have at least one halachic justification not to have more children.

299. Isaiah 38:1.

300. *Berachot* 10a.

301. According to tradition, he married Isaiah's daughter, and they had a son who was very wicked. Even so, the Almighty wanted Hezekiah to father children.

302. Currently, approximately one-quarter of American Jewish women will never marry. Those who do marry tend to do so at a later age than non-Jews, with a corresponding decline in fertility.

303. http://www.scientificamerican.com/article/american-consumption-habits/, 2015.

304. Sierra Club's "Sustainable Consumption," www.sierraclub.org/sustainable_consumption; National Geographic Society's Greendex, www.nationalgeographic.com/greendex.

305. There is a hierarchy to giving charity. Our first priority is to give to needy Jews and to support schools that teach Torah.

306. *Rosh Hashana* 1:5, *Yevamot* 62b-63b; cf. Rashi ad locum.

307. *Shulchan Aruch, Even Ha-Ezer* 1, 3, and 8; Maimonides, *Hilchot Deot* 5:11.

308. Shlomo Aviner, "Family Planning and Contraception," in *Assia* (Jerusalem: Rubin Mass), vol. 4, 1983, pp. 167-181.

309. Weisz, *Responsa Minchat Yitzchak*: vol. 1, #100:3 and 115, vol. 3, #25:5 and 261-263; vol. 4, #120; vol. 5, #100-103; vol. 6, #144. *Iggerot Moshe, Even Ha-Ezer*, vol. 1, Chapter 63; vol. 2, Chapter 12. Waldenberg, *Responsa Tzitz Eliezer*, vol. 10, sec. 25, part 10.

310. Immanuel. Jakobovits, "Medicine and Judaism—An Overview," in *Assia* (Jerusalem: Reuben Mass), 1983, pp.289-310.

311. Based on Exodus 21:10.

312. *Pesachim* 72b.

313. Rabbi Chaim Sofer, *Responsa Mahaneh Chaim* (Pressburg, 1862), #53.

314. Genesis 2:24.

315. *Yevamot* 12b.
316. Psalms 116:6.
317. Immanuel Jakobovits, *Jewish Medical Ethics*, 2ⁿᵈ ed. (New York: Bloch, 1975), p. 389.
318. Luria, *Yam Shel Shlomo, Yevamot* 1:8.
319. Sofer, *Responsa*, #53.
320. *Ketuvot* 39a.
321. Song of Songs 8:6.
322. *Iggerot Moshe, Even Ha-Ezer*, vol. 1, Chapters 62 and 65.
323. *Iggerot Moshe, Even Ha-Ezer*, #63.
324. David Feldman, *Marital Relations, Birth Control and Abortion in Jewish Law*. (New York, Schocken Books, 1989), p.128.
325. Uziel, *Responsa Mishpitei Uziel*, vol. 3, *Choshen Mishpat* #51.
326. Waldenberg, *Responsa Tzitz Eliezer*, vol.9, #51:2-3.
327. David Feldman, *Marital Relations, Birth Control and Abortion in Jewish Law*. (New York, Schocken Books, 1989), p. 231.
328. Moshe Feinstein, "Women in Whom Pregnancy is Dangerous to Life," in *Halachah U'refuah*, ed. M. Hershler (Jerusalem: Regensberg Institute, 1980), vol. 1, pp. 328-331.
329. Leviticus 22:24.
330. Tosefta on *Yevamot*, Chapter 8.
331. *Responsa Chatam Sofer, Even Ha-Ezer*, #20.
332. Maimonides, *Mishneh Torah, Hilchot Isurei Biyah* 21:18; *Teshuvot Ha-Rosh* 33:3; Karo, *Shulchan Aruch, Even Ha-Ezer* 2:5.
333. *Iggerot Moshe, Even Ha-Ezer*, loc. cit., p. 162.
334. Exodus 21:10.
335. *Iggerot Moshe, Even Ha-Ezer*, #102.
336. There are 24 pregnancies per 100 women who use such methods. http://www.livescience.com/24102-50-facts-sex.html.
337. *Shabbat* 110b, based on Leviticus 22:24.
338. *Mishnah Sanhedrin*, Chapter 4, *mishnah* 5.
339. Genesis 9:6.
340. These are known as the seven Noahide laws. Violating any one is a capital crime for a non-Jew.
341. *Sanhedrin* 57b.
342. *Responsa Koach Shorr*, vol. 1, #20, 1755; *Responsa Maharit*, #97 and 99.
343. Exodus 21:22-23.
344. *Mechilta*, Exodus 21:12; *Sanhedrin* 84a.
345. *Sanhedrin* 84b.
346. *Iggerot Moshe, Choshen Mishpat*, vol. 2, Chapters 69 and 70.

347. B. T. Frankel, *Responsa Ateret Chachamim, Even Ha-Ezer*, #1; Emden, *She'elat Yaavetz*, pt. 1, #43.

348. J. Rosen, *Responsa Tzafnat Paneach*, pt. 1, #49.

349. Mizrachi on Exodus 21:12.

350. These require that the medical benefit is greater than the risk (S. Drimmer, *Responsa Bet Shlomo, Choshen Mishpat*, #132) and that wounding (such as curettage) benefits the mother (J. Trani, *Responsa Maharit*, pt.1, #99; Zweig, in *Noam*, vol. 7 (1964): 36-56).

351. On *Shemot* 3b.

352. http://www.abort73.com/abortion_facts/us_abortion_statistics/. The statistics are mostly from the Alan Guttmacher Institute and the Center for Disease Control.

353. Ibid.

354. http://www.timesofisrael.com/israels-abortion-rate-continues-to-fall-report-says/

355. Ibid. US statistics are from the Center for Disease Control.

356. http://www.abort73.com/abortion_facts/us_abortion_statistics/.

357. Ibid.

358. Ibid., based on data from the National Abortion Federation's 2009 teaching text.

359. http://www.timesofisrael.com/israels-abortion-rate-continues-to-fall-report-says/.

360. *Arachin* 7a.

361. *Yevamot* 69b. This status is derived from technical laws that discuss how long after widowhood from an Israelite a priest's daughter who might be pregnant had to wait before she could eat sanctified food (*terumah*). Western doctors count duration of pregnancy as if it started with the last menstrual period, not from conception. Thus, a fetus who is 40 days old according to Jewish reckoning is approximately 54 days old according to obstetricians.

362. *Keritot* 1:3-6.

363. A. Lifschutz, *Responsa Aryeh Debei Ilay, Yoreh Deah*, #19; E. Deutsch, *Responsa Pri Ha-Sadeh*, pt. 4, #50. There are some pregnant women whose lives are threatened by intractable vomiting, where the doctors' only solution is abortion.

364. Yosef Chaim ben Eliyahu, *Responsa Rav Paalim, Even Ha-Ezer*, #4.

365. B. Z. Uziel, *Responsa Mishpetet Uziel, Choshen Mishpat*, pt. 3, #46.

366. I. M. Mizrachi, *Pri Ha-Aretz, Yoreh Deah*, #21.

367. N. Z. Friedman, *Responsa Netzer Metaat*, pt. 1, #8; *Iggerot Moshe, Orach Chaim*, pt. 4, #88.

368. Yaakov Emden, *Responsa She'elat Yaavetz*, pt. 1, #43; *Iggerot Moshe, Choshen Mishpat*, vol. 2, Chapters 69 and 70.

369. M. Y. Kaufmann, *Kuntres Acharon*, #19, p.58b.

370. Yaakov Emden, *Responsa She'elat Yaavetz*, pt. 1, #30; B. Z. Uziel, *Mishpatei Uziel, Choshen Mishpat*, pt. 3, #46.

371. http://americanpregnancy.org/infertility/fertility-faq/. Statistics are from the Center for Disease Control.

372. http://adoption.com/wiki/Jewish_Adoption.

373. http://adoption.com/wiki/How_to_Adopt_from_Israel.

374. http://www.efrat.org.il/english/about/.

375. Moshe Feinstein, *Ha-Pardes*, Nissan 5738.

376. Waldenberg, *Tzitz Eliezer*, pt. 9, p. 237.

377. Unterman, *Noam*, vol. 6, pp. 1-11.

378. M. Y. Zweig, *Noam*, vol. 7, pp. 36-56.

379. Immanuel Jakobovitz, *Journal of a Rabbi*, (New York: Living Books, 1966), pp. 262-266.

380. R. J. Rosen, *Tzafnat Paneach*, #59. This is 40 days post-conception, not from the time of the last menstrual period. Obstetricians use the latter to date a pregnancy.

381. *Gittin* 90b.

382. Malachi 2:13-14.

383. *Kiddushin* 2b.

384. Moshe Meiselman, *Jewish Woman in Jewish Law* (New York: Ktav, 1978), pp. 98-99.

385. Deuteronomy 24:1-2.

386. *Shulchan Aruch, Even Ha-Ezer* 154.

387. Due to this historical precedent, Rabbi Moshe Feinstein wrote similar conditional divorces for Jewish servicemen to give their wives prior to going away during World War II.

388. Maimonides' beloved brother David died this way, going down at sea with the family fortune. This forced the great rabbi to become a physician in order to support himself.

389. Once the Torah was given, Jewish men were forbidden to marry two sisters. According to some commentators, the reason that Rachel died shortly after Jacob returned with his family to the land of Israel was because the holiness of the land required that Jacob not live there married to two sisters.

390. Rashi on Genesis 11:29.

391. Rashi on Genesis 21:12.

392. *Seder Eliyahu Rabbah* 9.

393. *Seder Olam*, Chapter 21.

394. Genesis 11:2.

395. Exodus 15:20.

396. Judges 4:4.

397. 2 Kings 22:14.

398. I Samuel 1.

399. I Samuel 25.

400. *Megillat Esther*.

401. Genesis 12:14-20.

402. Genesis 21:10, 12.

403. *Midrash Tanchuma* on *Chayei Sarah*.

404. Proverbs 31:10-31.

405. Genesis *Rabbah* 60.

406. Abraham was not lying when he asked Sarah to say that she was his sister. First, she was his half-sister. Second, archaeologists discovered that husbands who lived near the place Abraham and Sarah originated from made their wives into legal sisters. In their culture, wives could not inherit a husband but sisters could.

407. Genesis 21:9-12, and Rashi there.

408. After Abraham showed his total willingness to sacrifice his son at the Almighty's request, he was told that the Almighty wants us to serve Him, not kill our children for Him. Child sacrifice was commonly practiced by the Canaanites.

409. Genesis *Rabbah* 60.

410. Quoted by Rashi on Genesis 24:16.

411. Rashi on Deuteronomy 11:13.

412. Genesis *Rabbah* 60.

413. The story of the Binding of Isaac is told in Genesis 22.

414. Rashi on Genesis 23:2.

415. Genesis 23.

416. Genesis 23:4-20.

417. That may be why people who have near-death experiences commonly see their soul passing through a tunnel before it emerges in a realm full of light where they experience God.

418. Genesis 23:1.

419. Genesis *Rabbah* 58.

420. https://www.ndsu.edu/fileadmin/counseling/Eating_Disorder_Statistics.pdf. Anorexia is the third most common chronic illness among US adolescents.

421. http://www.monitoringthefuture.org/pressreleases/14drugpr.pdf. Data are from 2014.

422. http://www.cdc.gov/ViolencePrevention/youthviolence/schoolviolence/ index. html. Data is from 2013.

423. http://www.livescience.com/24102-50-facts-sex.html. Average age for boys is 6.9 and for girls is 17.4.

424. http://www.nbcnews.com/id/37853719/ns/health-sexual_health/t/surprising-sex-statistics/#.Vm7IaMtulMs.

425. http://www.therichest.com/rich-list/world/worlds-10-most-divorced-nations/?view=all. This article gives US divorce rates as 53%, France 55%, Luxembourg 60%, and Belgium a whopping 71%!

426. http://www.timesofisrael.com/israels-divorce-rate-up-5-in-2012/. Data is from

2012.

427. http://www.marriage-success-secrets.com/statistics-about-children-and- divorce. html.

428. Ibid.

429. https://theworldunplugged.wordpress.com/.

430. Proverbs 22:6.

431. http://www.bbc.com/news/technology-23030090. Data is from Scandinavian Research Center Sintef's 2013 estimate.

432. http://www.bbc.com/news/technology-23030090. Statistics from Dr. Ogi Ogas, co-author of the 2010 study, "A Billion Wicked Thoughts."

433. More about how pedophiles operate can be found at https://www.fbi.gov/news/ stories/ 2011/may/predators_051711/predators_051711.

434. http://www.bbc.com/news/technology-32067158. Results of annual studies by Childwise of 2000 British children ages 5-16.

435. http://www.bbc.com/news/technology-32067158.

436. http://www.everydayhealth.com/adhd-awareness/does-technology-cause-adhd. aspx. Published in *Pediatrics*, August 2015.

437. Ibid.

438. Ibid.

439. Deuteronomy 4:15.

440. *Sofrim* 10:6.

441. Rema on *Yoreh Deah* 81:7.

442. *Magen Avraham* 3433:1; *Kaf Ha-Chaim* 225:14.

443. *Shulchan Aruch, Orach Chaim* 91:3.

444. *Biur Halachah* 75.

445. The *Love and Logic* books are excellent parenting guides. See Jim Fay and Charles Fay, *Love and Logic Magic for Early Childhood: Practical Parenting from Birth to Six Years*. Love and Logic Institute, Inc., Golden, CO, 2000.

446. These restrictions don't apply if there is an immediate, constructive purpose to be served by saying negative things, such as preventing someone from investing in a financial scam, or warning someone not to date an individual who has a criminal history. Laws of *lashon hara* are detailed in the Chafetz Chaim's book *Guard Your Tongue*.

447. Genesis 3:16.

448. http://www.gallup.com/poll/10336/Empty-Seats-Fewer-Families-Eat-Together. aspx.

449. http://www.ahaparenting.com/parenting-tools/family-life/dinner-connected-family.

450. Proverbs 24:16.

451. *Mishnah Avot* 1:7.

452. https://www.plannedparenthood.org/parents/talking-to-kids-about-sex-and-sexuality.

453. Ibid.

454. Esther 2:7 and 2:15 describe Esther as Mordechai's first cousin. *Targum Sheni* says that Mordechai's father and Esther's father were brothers. *Megillah* 13a states that Mordechai eventually married Esther.

455. Esther 4:13-14.

456. Genesis 3:15.

457. Morning prayers.

458. http://money.cnn.com/2015/06/02/news/companies/giving-pledge-billionaires-buffett-gates. As of mid-2015, 137 billionaires had pledged to give away at least half of their wealth to charity. In February, 2015, there were 2,089 billionaires in the world. http://www/independent.co.uk/news/world/there-are-now-2089-billionaires-in-the-world-this-is-who-they-are-where-they-live-and-how-they-made-10026128.html.

459. In 2013, a Harris poll of US adults showed two-thirds were unhappy! http://www.dailymail.co.uk/news/article-2334471/Two-thirds-Americans-say-theyre-unhappy--Hispanics-college-grads-disabled-discontented-survey-says.html..

460. *Mishnah Avot* 4:1.

461. *Mishnah Avot* 5:13.

462. *Yevamot* 79a.

463. Judaism tells us how to be merciful, kind, and compassionate. There is a hierarchy of how to give charity—first giving a job or loan to help a Jew become self-sufficient rather than giving money. We first help a needy relative, then needy Jews in our city or in the land of Israel. There are times when we may not be merciful, such as executing certain criminals and preemptively killing those who want to kill us. Otherwise, "a person who is kind to the cruel will end up being cruel to the kind" (*Kohelet Rabbah* 7:16).

464. *Shabbat* 127a.

465. *Mishnah Avot* 2:21.

Printed in Great Britain
by Amazon